# Reader Con

GW00835890

"Reading *New Money for a New World* is like having a veil lifted from the mystery of money. As a cabinet member in several administrations and as an adviser to the Congress for many years, I thought I knew a lot about this vexing subject. After reading this wonderful book, it is now clear to me why the world, and the United States in particular, is having such a difficult economic time. No matter how well meaning our monetary leaders are, they simply do not have adequate tools to deal with the situation today.

We should all be grateful to Bernard Lietaer and Stephen Belgin for a masterful job in exposing the flaws of the current system and of offering workable complementary solutions that will better serve society in the future. Everyone who cares about the financial future of the world should read *New Money for a New World*. No matter who wins the next election, every senior government official should be *required* to read this truly important book.

~Hon. David M. Lindahl
former Assistant U.S. Secretary of Energy

"This book is truly essential for our survival. I was surprised how much I learned, (and how much I didn't know) about money. The writing style is as enjoyable as it is instructive."

~Margaret Wheatley
Author of *Management and the New Physics*

"Here is a life-serving vision gifted to us all with the history, social psychology, inspiration and how-to's needed to make it happen. I believe it is an immensely potent lever for moving civilization-in-upheaval through a healthy transformation."

~Tom Atlee
Founder of the Co-Intelligence Institute
Author of *The Tao of Democracy* and *Reflections on Evolutionary Activism*

"These are the smartest people thinking - and rethinking - about money today. If you are among the sad majority who still think money is that green paper in your pocket, think again. The kinds of money available to us are varied as goals we have for our economy. In a world where there is more than enough stuff to go around, we deserve a money capable of reflecting rather than undermining the abundance we have achieved. This book proves the point and points the way."

~Douglas Rushkoff
Author of *Life Inc.,* and *Program or Be Programmed*

"Exciting, challenging and profound; a unique and essential contribution to our understanding of money."

~Dr. Peter Russell
Author of *The Global Brain* and *Waking Up in Time*

"Something extraordinary and largely unreported is happening to money. This book looks set to be the herald of the future money revolution."

~David Boyle
New Economics Foundation, London

"National currency is cold and selfish by itself. So let's create community currencies with which we can warm up our communities as *New Money for a New World* recommends."

~Tsutomu Hotta
Former Japanese Minister of Justice and Supreme Court Judge
Founder of the Japanese "Fureai Kippu" currencies

"This is a wise and incisive analysis of the nature of money in our society; the remarkable and pragmatic solutions it offers demand of us that we think about money in entirely new ways."

~Professor Jacob Needleman
Philosopher; author of *Money and the Meaning of Life*

"In our present finance dominated world of tragic inequities, the authors' brilliant analysis of what money is and how it can be put into the service of all humanity is a vital key to truly democratic globalization--the next evolutionary leap for our species!"

~Elisabet Sahtouris, Ph.D.
Evolution biologist; author of *A Walk Through Time: From Stardust to Us* and *EarthDance: Living Systems in Evolution*

"Bernard Lietaer and Stephen Belgin compel us to rethink our assumptions about money, economics, and commerce today. Their analyses and historical insights are incisive and provoke thought about what's gone wrong with economies all over the world. But more importantly, they provide tangible solutions—illustrated in real-world examples—to challenges we face with building more just, prosperous and sustainable global societies."

~Martin N. Davidson, Ph.D.,
Associate Professor at Darden Graduate School of Business
Author of *The End of Diversity as We Know It*

"This book gives the recipe on how we in the future can create a social economy which is more responsible, more friendly towards the environment, and less filled with conflict."

~Professor Jesper Jespersen
Churchill College, Cambridge University, and University of Roskilde

"Every so often, something comes along that changes our perceptions, turning our world upside-down and inside-out. *New Money for a New World* will shatter the views of anyone who uses money, and show how we can make money work for us, creating greater prosperity and possibility, while bringing balance to our greatest social and environmental problems."

~Nitin Gadia
Videographer of *Creating Our Own Money*
Facilitator of the Central Iowa Currency Initiative

"*New Money for a New World* makes a simple and profound proposition: Unless we can balance the current social and monetary structures, whose remedies are well described here, our shared desire for a just, sustainable, and peaceful planet is simply not possible. ALL the good works that many of us are involved in, admirable, even 'successful' as they may be, are mere band-aids, fingers in the dike. I challenge any serious reader of this book to arrive at a different conclusion. That's the bad news. The good news is WE CAN MAKE IT! *New Money for a New World* offers unique effective tools by which to resolve our core issues and co-create a better, vibrant future."

~John Steiner
Global Citizen

"The medium is the message. As the authors point out, the money system is not neutral. One way or another, our behavior is heavily influenced by it. Can we change the way it works? This question concerns us all. The answer will help to decide the future of humanity and life on earth. The authors' authoritative practical experience of money and finance, underpinned by their awareness of the worldwide shift of consciousness now taking place, results in many thought-provoking insights...It is not necessary to agree with every detailed proposal in this informative and stimulating book, in order to welcome it as an outstanding contribution to a vital question - the future of money in the Information Age. I wholeheartedly recommend it."

~James Robertson
Author of *The New Economics of Sustainable Development*
Co-author of *Creating New Money*

"This book really opened my eyes as to what money is about, and what its future is - and is not."

~Stephen Denning
Program Director, Knowledge Management, World Bank

"Others have shared Bernard Lietaer's concern about a sustainable economy, but have not been able to provide a realistic solution. In *New Money for a New World*, he and Stephen Belgin show us such a solution in a bold and fresh manner, and it is in this sense that this is an epoch-making book."

~Toshiharu Kato
Director Services Department,
Ministry of International Trade and Industry (MITI), Japan

*"New Money for a New World* is one of those rarest of rare books that can truly help change the course of humanity—in just the way so many of us sense but don't know how to get there. With disarming simplicity and amazing clarity, authors Bernard Lietaer and Stephen Belgin reveal the secret liberating variable to empower rapid and profound societal and consciousness transformation and environmental healing—monetary redesign. Read this book to see how you can participate in accelerating our arrival at a regenerative and fulfilling new world."

~Richard Ruster, Ph.D.,
Founder of the Center for the Human Dream
Co-Creator, the Hummingbird Community
Author of *The Homing Process: A Unifying Theory of Evolving Systems*

"I have read three books which I consider to be truly uplifting and transformative: *A Course in Miracles, The Power of Now*, and most recently, *New Money for a New World*. This work offers a clear roadmap by which to resolve many of humanity's seemingly insurmountable crises without the need for international treaties, more taxation, or the redistribution of wealth, all the while respecting and potentially expanding our spiritual underpinnings. *New Money for a New World* is a gift to humanity, to be read by everyone who dares to dream of a world gone sane. Bernard Lietaer and Stephen Belgin have created a masterpiece."

~Dr. Frank Baylin
President, CEO - Baylin Publications

Additional comments available online at:
http://www.newmoneyforanewworld.com

# New Money for a New World

## By

## Bernard Lietaer & Stephen Belgin

*New Money for a New World*
A Qiterra Press softcover original
6" x 9" / 388 pages
Category: Non-fiction
ISBN 978-0-9832274-0-3

This edition is published by Qiterra Press, LLC
1905 15th Street
Box 565
Boulder, CO, 80302-9998
United States of America

Design and Cover Design: Stephen Belgin and Chad Morgan
Currencies featured on cover: U.S. dollar, Croatian dinar, Greenback
(Telluride, Colorado), LETS (Australia), and Rubi (Brazil).

*The illustrations in this book are, unless otherwise stated, original drawings by Moreno
Tomasetig and Brian Hutchinson. The publishers are making all reasonable efforts to
contact copyright and license holders for permissions for both pictures and cartoons, and
apologize for any omissions or errors in the credits given.*

**ISBN #**
978-0-9832274-0-3

*This book is dedicated to the beloved memory*
*of two extraordinary women and mothers,*
*Agnes Lietaer-Catry (1914-2011)*
*and*
*Edith Dernis-Belgin (1923-2011).*

# Acknowledgements

The authors would like to thank Dr. Sally Goerner and Dr. Robert Ulanowicz for their groundbreaking work in systems physics and theoretical ecology, which provided the scientific basis in Chapters Twelve and Thirteen.

We would like to acknowledge and thank our editors Jonathan Kolber and Daniel Drasin, Jennifer Dunne for her many vital professional and personal contributions, Jillian Reitsma for her valued assistance with graphic design, Stephen DeMeulenaere for his research and input regarding Balinese complementary currency systems, and Margrit Kennedy for her work regarding demurrage. We wish to express our sincere gratitude to Michael Spolum and family, Tesa Silvestre, Eric Karlson, Sean Karlson, Derek Garcia, Rebecca and Rob Gordon, the Lipman Family, Lisa Spiro Price, Lisa Stone, Rachel Bagby, Ruby Begay, Susan Belchamber, Evan Reeves, Ben Romsdahl, Molly Stranahan, Edward Ciaccio, William Donohoe, Mark Finser, Lion Albaugh, David Uhl, the Hummingbird Community, the Triskeles Foundation, Chris Tucker, Phyllis Karlson, Evelyn Resnick, Bertha Paul, Phontip Honu, Alexander Belgin, and many others too numerous to mention here for their generous support. We wish to also thank Jacqui Dunne, Deb Shapiro, and Ed Shapiro for their assistance with a previous version of this book.

Finally, we are very grateful to the many pioneers and communities, past and present, whose insights and efforts have contributed to a greater understanding of money.

BAL; SMB

# TABLE OF CONTENTS

# INTRODUCTION

*Everything is possible when everything is at stake.*

~NORMAN COUSINS

Humanity is at a critical juncture, faced with two very real yet vastly different prospects. The unparalleled achievements over the course of recent decades in one domain after another offer hope of a vast renewal and golden age for society. In direct opposition to this is the persistence of a constellation of seemingly insurmountable global issues that threaten us as never before. What is required is as straightforward as it is profound. Our global civilization needs a new operating system, and fast.

Our seemingly paradoxical situation is explained by the fact that the very same ways of thinking that brought about the Industrial Age and made possible so many of our advancements, have also fueled the myriad crises that are now converging upon us. In particular, many of the socioeconomic rules under which we currently operate were actually put in place centuries ago, and were heavily influenced by a worldview that failed to recognize that our planet is a living system and that every form of life has its unique and valuable place and purpose in sustaining the larger web of life. In ignoring the conditions that are necessary to the health of our ecosystems and communities, we have inadvertently fouled our nest.

As a direct consequence of our centuries-old ways of being and doing, we are now faced with: great financial instability, growing disparities of wealth, resource wars, the breakdown of community, alarming rates of species extinction and ecosystem depletion, and accelerating symptoms of climate change. As our food, energy, health, education, economies, and financial systems show increasing signs of failing us, we are being collectively called to harness our creativity and resources to take a major evolutionary leap.

*Transitioning from self-destructive ways to life-affirming understandings, lifestyles, and systems is indeed the great work of our times.*

The looming question is, how can we reverse the downward spiral in which much of our world has been caught?

One of the many blessings of our time is that there is a fast-growing global movement afoot, consisting of many communities, businesses, not-for-profits, and governments hard at work on this very question. Their innovative efforts are already providing many success stories and inspiring new models to point to. Neither creativity nor good intentions are lacking.

What *has* been sorely missing is an understanding of the important systemic causes of the challenges we face, and a clearer sense of how fragmented efforts and experiments might evolve into comprehensive solutions. The widespread deterioration of conditions that has occurred over the course of the last several decades is bound to continue until and unless we can identify and effectively address the source of our many concerns. To this end, there is at last some significant news.

A far more effective and resilient way to harness and direct our creativity and energy is now possible and directly available to us. What is required of us is to start paying careful attention to a piece of the puzzle that has been under the radar of the official and public debate: our monetary system.

Over the course of the past several decades, a quiet but significant transformation has been taking place within the monetary realm. Thousands of initiatives from around the world—run by villagers, non-governmental organizations, small and medium-sized enterprises, multinationals, and governments—have each been rethinking money. They have made use of *complementary currencies*—monetary initiatives that do not replace but rather supplement the national currency system—to match unmet needs with unused resources.

Among the almost inexhaustible range of vital concerns being addressed by new monetary initiatives let us mention: social and ecological issues such as improved education, disease intervention, juvenile delinquency, healthcare for the elderly, environmental cleanup, and city restoration; and commercial applications such as job creation, loyalty mechanisms, stabilization of the business cycle, and more.

These new initiatives burden no one and offer benefits to the whole of society. These innovations do not require raising taxes, the redistribution of wealth, bonds, charity, or loans from lending institutions or government. Given what is at stake and what has already been achieved, it is encumbent upon us to at least carefully consider what is now possible.

*New Money for a New World* is dedicated to pragmatic improvements in conditions through a greater understanding of money, and by means of monetary tools and initiatives that better serve the diverse and sometimes divergent needs of each member of our global society and the living systems of this planet.

## An Overview of New Money for a New World

The goal of each of the four parts of this book is to report on insights and options that are now available to us by rethinking money.

In Part I—Our Money, Our World—we examine key features of today's monetary and banking paradigms. The topics explored include:

- o  how one city managed to address many urban concerns without having to raise taxes, redistribute wealth, or seek outside assistance (Chapter One—A Tale of Two Cities);
- o  the mismatch between our money and our age (Chapter Two—Welcome to Moneyville);
- o  key issues facing our world and the monetary questions they pose (Chapter Three—Megatrends and Money);
- o  long-held mysteries and key agreements related to our money (Chapter Four—A Money Primer);
- o  the impact of seemingly innocuous properties of our monetary system upon society (Chapter Five—Money is Not Value-Neutral);
- o  a little-known, historical golden age and its unusual monetary paradigm (Chapter Six—Back to the Future);
- o  how our money replicates beliefs, perceptions, and objectives of a former age (Chapter Seven—A Change of View);
- o  traditional theories and assumptions about how economies work and the measurements used to gauge their supposed health (Chapter Eight—Economic Myopia);
- o  the lessons of several communities that not only met their needs but were able to prosper during the depths of the Great Depression (Chapter Nine—Lessons from a Depression);
- o  how limited understandings regarding money impact economic notions and policies (Chapter Ten—The Blind Spot).

In Part II—New Money—we examine some of the many monetary tools and new economic insights available to us. The topics explored include:

- o the unparalleled shift now taking place in society (Chapter Eleven—Great Change);
- o new economic insights derived from natural ecosystems and flow systems (Chapter Twelve—Efficiency, Resilience, and Money);
- o an analysis of economic vitality and economic growth (Chapter Thirteen—Sustainable Development);
- o two of the most ubiquitous complementary currencies in use today (Chapter Fourteen—LETS and Time Dollars);
- o currency designs to help address specific social concerns (Chapter Fifteen—Social-Purpose Currencies);
- o currency designs to meet the needs of small and medium-sized enterprises (Chapter Sixteen—Commercial-Purpose Currencies);
- o a reference currency to tackle limitations in the global economy (Chapter Seventeen—The Terra, a Trade Reference Currency);
- o the likely consequences of trying to address our many concerns by the limited use of today's national currency model (Chapter Eighteen—Two Worlds).

In Part III—The Mystery of Money—we examine the relationship between money and the human psyche. The topics explored include:

- o patterns of emotions and actions that can be observed across time and cultures (Chapter Nineteen—Archetypes);
- o a fundamental archetype and its deep-rooted relationship to money (Chapter Twenty—The Missing Archetype and Money);
- o the long and systematic repression of this missing archetype (Chapter Twenty One—Repression of an Archetype);
- o the manner in which repressed psychic energies manifest (Chapter Twenty Two—Shadows);
- o the link between collective psychology, Taoism, and monetary systems (Chapter Twenty Three—Money and the Tao);
- o the impact of the current monetary paradigm on society (Chapter Twenty Four—Consequences of Repression).

In Part IV—Money, Archetypes, and Past Ages—we examine the monetary systems, archetypal constellations, and general conditions of several notable civilizations. The topics explored include:

- o  medieval Western Europe viewed from an archetypal perspective (Chapter Twenty Five—Central Middle Ages Revisited);

- o  one civilization whose unusual prosperity spanned two millenia (Chapter Twenty Six—Dynastic Egypt);

- o  Dynastic Egypt examined from an archetypal perspective (Chapter Twenty Seven—Dynastic Egypt Revisited);

- o  the particular monetary and archetypal features of one society that has endured more than a millenium (Chapter Twenty Eight—The Balinese Exception);

- o  a review of the key findings of this work (Chapter Twenty Nine—Invitation to a New World).

- o  the vital role of money in the process of societal maturation (Chapter Thirty—The Dynamics of Transformation and Money). This bonus chapter and additional supporting materials, including a bibliography, are available online at our companions websites:

http://www.newmoneyforanewworld.com

and

http://www.lietaer.com

A number of chapters contain inserts that, while not essential to the argument at hand, offer supplementary information that may be of interest to the reader. Each of the inserts is clearly indicated.

## PART I

# OUR MONEY, OUR WORLD

*Economics is about money, and that's why it is good.*

*~WOODY ALLEN*

*And money is about...what ?*

# CHAPTER ONE

# A Tale of Two Cities

*If the only tool you have is a hammer,*

*you tend to see every problem as a nail.*

~ABRAHAM MASLOW

Garbage was a major problem in Curitiba, the capital of the southeastern state of Paraná, Brazil.[1] Its urban population had mushroomed from 120,000 in 1942 to 2.3 million in 1997. Many of the inhabitants lived in *favelas,* shantytowns made of cardboard and corrugated metal. Garbage collection trucks could not enter these favelas as the streets were not wide enough. The garbage thus piled up and disease broke out.

Jaime Lerner, who became mayor of Curitiba in 1971, did not have funds to apply customary solutions, such as bulldozing the area or building new streets. Bond measures, further taxation, or federal assistance were simply not options. Another way had to be found.

What Curitiba did have was an abundance of food, owing to the fertile lands and tropical climate of the region. It also had a municipal bus system that was underutilized, with many favela residents unable to afford public transportation. Mayor Lerner made use of these local resources to resolve urban issues and transform Curitiba.

Large metallic bins were placed at the edge of the favelas. Anyone who deposited a bag full of presorted garbage received a bus token. Those who collected paper and cartons were given plastic chits, exchangeable for parcels of seasonal fresh fruits and vegetables. The bus tokens were soon accepted at local markets in exchange for food. A school-based garbage collection program was started as well and supplied poorer students with notebooks. Tens of thousands of children responded by picking the neighborhoods clean.

In one three-year period, more than 100 schools traded 200 tons of garbage for 1.9 million notebooks. The paper-recycling component alone saved the equivalent of 1,200 trees each day! The 62 poorer neighborhoods of Curitiba exchanged 11,000 tons of garbage for nearly a million bus tokens and 1,200 tons of food. Parents made use of the tokens to travel downtown, oftentimes to find jobs. Other programs were created to finance the restoration of historical buildings, create green areas, and provide housing, all by methods that placed little or no financial burden on the municipality. Eventually, more than 70 percent of Curitiban households became involved in these programs.

The many initiatives—environmental cleanup, city restoration, job creation, improved education, disease intervention, hunger prevention—were each tackled without having to raise taxes, redistribute wealth, issue bonds, rely on charity, or obtain loans from the federal government or organizations such as the World Bank and the International Monetary Fund (IMF). The improvements burdened no one. Everyone benefited.

The results in purely economic terms are worth noting. From 1975 to 1995, the Gross Domestic Product (GDP) of Curitiba increased an average of 75 percent more than its parent state of Paraná, and 48 percent more than the GDP of Brazil as a whole. The average Curitibano earned more than three times the country's minimum wage. If nontraditional monetary gains such as the exchange of garbage for provisions are taken into consideration, the real total income for residents was at least 30 percent higher still. The results in human terms—in the renewal of dignity and hope for a better future—can only be imagined.

Curitiba discovered a means by which to match unmet needs with unused resources. They did so by making use of *complementary currencies*—monetary initiatives that do not replace but rather supplement the national currency system. This innovative approach provided much needed improvements to the local economy. It enabled a developing and formerly impoverished city to empower itself and vastly improve its conditions in the remarkable span of a single generation.

*In 1990, Curitiba was honored with the highest award granted by the United Nations Environment Program.*

Growing numbers of concerned citizens and public officials find it increasingly doubtful that the problems facing our communities, nations, and planet can be successfully addressed. The results achieved by complementary monetary initiatives in Curitiba, however, as well as many other places around the world suggest something quite different.

Our current difficulties persist not because they are insurmountable, but rather because we have focused on the *symptoms* rather than the *systemic causes* of our many concerns. Most importantly, we have failed to more fully understand and make greater use of one of the most powerful of all human creations—money.

To help illustrate what is taking place in our world, we offer a fictional absurdity, an allegorical place called Hammerville.[2]

## HAMMERVILLE

Hammerville derived its name from a peculiar oddity that distinguished it from other communities of its time. For practically every application imaginable—construction, plumbing, painting, demolition, harvesting, and more—the hardworking people of Hammerville made almost exclusive use of one tool: a hammer. It was the principal object used in popular sports such as the hammer throw and hammer bowl, a common fixture in all cultural celebrations, and the iconic symbol of civic pride.

Over time, the hammer also became the most important mark of individual wealth. Although a small number of hammer-dexterous individuals had the ability to use several hammers simultaneously, there was no intrinsic need to own more than a few of them. Nonetheless, it somehow came to pass that the more hammers in one's possession, the higher one's standing in society became.

For a while, no one questioned the inherent limitations of their world. With rare exceptions, if something could not be built, fixed, or measured with a hammer, it was simply left undone. Screwdrivers, ploughs, wrenches, and paintbrushes were nonexistent. Even the general concept of "tool" was not a part of people's reality. A hammer was a hammer and that was basically it. No other means existed to even imagine, much less implement, options commonly available elsewhere.

Over time, Hammervilleans found themselves unable to cope. Their population grew, but no means could be found to keep up with demands for sufficient housing, education, employment, healthcare, and a host of other requirements. Conditions deteriorated, but no one could quite understand why. People increasingly pointed the hammer of blame at one another. Some of the privileged hammer-rich questioned the abilities of those less fortunate, and were, in turn, the subject of mounting resentment by growing numbers of the hammer-less.

No one ever stopped to look at the limitations of the hammer itself. It was unthinkable that the most important and almost exclusive object of so much good was simply not designed to address all of the needs of this community. Nor could the citizenry grasp the powerful link between their collective ignorance regarding tools, the hammercentric ways in which they perceived themselves and their world, and what they believed to be possible or not. The good people of Hammerville were both defined and fated by the limitations of their hammer-monopolized world, a world that despite all good intentions found itself in peril.

Of course, the absurdities and collective lack of awareness of Hammervilleans could not possibly occur in our world.

Or could they?

## TWO WORLDS AND MONEY

This book recounts the story of two worlds, two paradigms. It offers a brief analysis of current conditions and the logical outcome of attempting to solve existing problems using the same thinking that created many of our concerns in the first place. The main body of this work, however, considers another prospect for society and the systematic means by which it can be pragmatically realized.

This other world is one in which the long-term interests of humanity and the sustainability of our planet balance the short-term interests of business and industry; where there is meaningful work for all and time for ourselves, our families, and our communities; where the upbringing and education of our children and quality care for our elders are realized and compensated for in equal measure to other forms of employment so vital to society. This other world holds dear the diversity and sanctity of all life and the life-affirming aspects of what it is to be fully human, and consequently, more humane.

The potential for just such a prospect is not only possible but is achievable within the span of *a single generation*. Many of the elements required for these improvements already exist. Additionally, a wide assortment of monetary tools similar to those used in Curitiba is readily available to us quickly, safely, and inexpensively by way of a greater understanding of money.

The current monetary paradigm and its relationship to the critical issues of our day are examined in the chapters that follow. We shall see that intentionally designed complementary currencies can match many of the world's unmet needs by using the underutilized resources already at our disposal.

## CLOSING THOUGHTS

Curitiba represents an important 25-year-old practical case study. It offers testimony that a "dual-currency" approach—one that uses both traditional national currencies and well-designed complementary currencies—can successfully address a broad range of seemingly intractable issues promptly and effectively by means that are non-punitive and of benefit to all. Other important case studies presented later in this work show the broad range of applications made possible by use of these monetary innovations.

The lack of awareness that defined and ultimately undermined Hammerville need not apply to us. But we need to better understand money—our hammer—and how it is interwoven into every element of modern society.

## CHAPTER TWO

# Welcome to Moneyville

*Our Age of Anxiety is, in great part, the result of*

*trying to do today's jobs with yesterday's tools.*

~MARSHALL McLUHAN

W e begin with this two-part, multitrillion-dollar question: How did a smart age like ours get into the mess it now finds itself in, and what do we do to move forward? Consider the following.

Our achievements over the last century are without parallel. We have gone from the most rudimentary understandings of genetics to mapping the entire human genome, from Morse code to binary code, from horse and buggy to space exploration. We now have near-instant access to one another and more information than all the universities and libraries down through the ages, combined!

Yet, while we can probe distant planets, we are threatened by a pollution mess on our own planet. Life expectancy is greater than ever before, but retirement is increasingly problematic. We produce more than enough food to feed the world, but too many go without. There is no end to the work that needs to be done, with legions of willing, able people to do it. Nevertheless, we are plagued by a chronic scarcity of gainful opportunities, made more dramatic still by financial crashes and chronic economic instability.

Though our many triumphs speak to a vast human potential, we find ourselves beset by vital concerns that have thus far eluded the many attempts aimed at their resolution. In fact, despite some breakthroughs and many valiant efforts in the public and private sectors, these challenges have escalated in scope and severity with each passing decade.

Why is this so?

The short answer is that it has something to do with money. Our plight is not, however, simply a matter of the lack of money or the allocation of ever greater amounts of it. Countless billions of dollars have been spent on one issue after another, but have not, and cannot by themselves, stem the tide of the continued deterioration of our environs, or prevent the next downturn of the so-called business cycle. Our failed efforts are instead linked to a collective lack of understanding regarding money and the use of a limited set of monetary tools.

Sound vaguely similar to another place?

As absurd is it may at first seem, our current dilemma bears some similarity to the plight of Hammerville. We too are confronted by issues that threaten us as never before. We too are baffled trying to understand what is going on and what to do. We are engaged in short-term practices that persist despite mounting evidence of the dangers they pose to us all. In addition, we limit most of our exhanges to the use of one tool that has become as important and ubiquitous in our monetized world as hammers were in Hammerville.

We invite you to take an initial look at our accomplished yet troubled moment in time; a place that we have come to think of as Moneyville.

## THE MONEY OF MONEYVILLE

"Fish are not aware of water." This proverb speaks to the fact that some elements of our lives are ever-present but simply taken for granted. Such is the case with our world and money. Certainly, we pay attention to how much money we have, how much more we need, and ways by which to try and obtain and invest it. Rarely, however, do we stop to question the nature of money itself or the system by which it functions. Money is simply, well…money. And we are all deeply immersed in its currents.

Money plays nearly as influential a role in Moneyville as hammers did in Hammerville, in more ways than we might care to believe. It is at once one of the oldest, most pervasive, and influential of all human-made creations. Yet, despite its enduring, prominent place in our world, money remains a mystery to experts and laypeople alike.

No one, for example, can pinpoint for certain when money came into being. What is known is that money predates the written word and recorded history. One of the most celebrated economists of the 20th century, John Maynard Keynes, pointed out:

> Money, like certain other elements in civilizations, is a far more ancient institution than we were taught to believe. Its origins are lost in the mists when the ice was melting, and may well stretch into the intervals in human history of the inter-glacial periods, when the weather was delightful and the mind free to be fertile with new ideas—in the islands of the Hesperides or Atlantis or some Eden of Central Asia.[1]

What is well established is that money's influence has grown steadily over the centuries. Richard Wagner, former president of the Institute of Certified Financial Planners, notes that, "money is the most powerful secular force within our world today."[2] French monetary theorist, Jacques Rueff, goes a step further, declaring that, "money will decide the fate of mankind."[3] Money is the principal means by which we conduct business and interact with one another through countless daily exchanges of billions of dollars, euros, and other national currencies. Today's global economy, the affairs of state, and our individual survival all depend on money.

Yet, what do we actually know about this curious human creation? Where does it come from? Who makes the rules? Why is it so hard to come by? Despite its role in our lives, most of us are simply baffled by money. A deep collective blindness is at work that not only contributed to the demise of once mighty Wall Street giants such as Lehman Brothers, but which threatens the fabric of modern society as never before.

Consider, for instance, the gulf that divides our age and the type of money that is in use.

**The Mismatch**

For some obscure reason, few of the good citizens of Moneyville were made aware of a particular disparity regarding our age and money. We are attempting to manage a host of 21st-century issues, while the majority of the components that define our existing banking and monetary systems date back to another era.

The money that is in use today was actually designed in the 17th and 18th centuries, a mostly preindustrial epoch untroubled by pollution, greenhouse effects, and overpopulation. The vast majority of the world's estimated 700 million people back then were farmers living in rural settings, who rarely ventured far from their homes or villages, and whose economic activity consisted mostly of local barter exchanges. Money was in limited use, especially in rural England, the country in which much of the world's current monetary paradigm originated.

But historical changes were beginning to take root. It was the dawn of the Industrial Revolution and modern-day nation states. Both domestic and international commerce were on the rise, as were the monetized transactions through which such commerce was facilitated. Whether by design or happenstance, the monetary and banking systems that came into being back then reflected a new Modernist worldview, and would become the most persuasive instruments of that age's key objectives: growth, competition, nationalism, and industrialization.

Over the course of the next three centuries, virtually every nation would come to adopt the same foundational tools that were built into those centuries-old systems. By performing their intended functions, the banking and monetary systems facilitated the most extraordinary technological and industrial achievements in all of history.

But today's dynamic, interdependent, 24/7, global village is vastly different from even a generation ago, let alone centuries past. Many of the needs of society and our beleaguered natural environs are quite different from any other known period of history. The finite set of tools that served so ably the ethos of another age are far too limited in range and are simply not designed to address the requirements and concerns of today's many diverse cultures, and the fusion of agrarian, industrial, and postindustrial economies that together constitute our complex, interwoven, socioeconomic reality.

Yet, notwithstanding the great divide that sets our current world apart from centuries past, we continue to employ almost exclusively the most persistent driver of the Industrial Age's values—its monetary system. This mismatch between our age and the ongoing monopoly of centuries-old money is at the core of so many of our most important issues.

The following account helps illustrate what is now taking place today with regard to society and money.

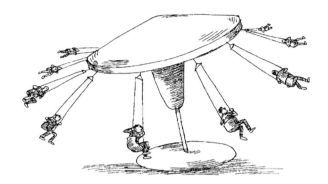

## THE MONEY GO-ROUND

A group of prominent citizens from a small town in Germany, which included the mayor, the head judge, and a number of leading businessmen all dined together at a local restaurant. There was plenty of wine with the meal, followed by after-dinner schnapps. It was well past midnight when the entourage finally got up to leave, with everyone by then quite tipsy. But the festivities were not yet over.

The plaza just outside the restaurant was empty at that late hour, with a seasonal carnival then shut down for the night. Nonetheless, one member of the inebriated group thought it would be good fun to take a spin on the carnival's merry-go-round. He turned on the motor and leapt onto a chair. The others followed suit.

The initial laughter soon ended, however, as one by one, each member of the group came to realize their situation. The merry-go-round's control button was now well out of reach, and no one could dismount the ride without incurring serious injury.

*The machine had been started easily, but the capacity to manage it was lost once it was in full swing.*

Given the hour, the group's ongoing cries for help went unheard. It was not until after six o'clock the following morning that the local police and fire department were notified and the ordeal finally brought to an end. But by then, one member of the group had died of a heart attack and three others were unconscious. Following the incident, one of the survivors joined an obscure religious sect, while others suffered psychological scars that lasted years.

The absurdity of this tale is amplified by the fact that it is a true story.[4] For our purposes, it serves as a metaphor for the state of the world's current monetary system.

We are riding on a huge planetary machine that is on autopilot and accelerating out of control. Money functions mostly without our awareness and in opposition to many of our current needs, placing each of us and life on this planet increasingly at risk. Our collective unconsciousness with regard to money impedes our ability to reach the stop button of this gigantic money-go-round, and has obscured our ability to identify and address the root causes of some of our most serious concerns.

As noted, our troubles persist not because they are insurmountable, but rather because we are treating symptoms instead of systemic causes and confining our efforts to the almost exclusive use of one type of monetary tool—national currencies. Such currencies act as the monetary equivalent of a hammer, and their virtual monopoly results in the persistence and escalation of the issues of our day.

Fortunately, there is another, more encouraging dimension to the tale of Moneyville. Many new monetary tools are available to us today, made possible in large part by thousands of communities around the world that are currently rethinking money. Like Curitiba, they are finding innovative ways to match unmet needs with unused resources. In the process, they are helping the rest of us to gain a greater understanding of money and its potential.

But before exploring what is possible in greater depth, we first need to better understand the relationship between the issues of our time and the existing monetary paradigm.

## CLOSING THOUGHTS

Today's monetary system, in the form of a monoculture of national currencies, has not changed essentially in centuries. This industrial-age paradigm continues to influence and dominate every important aspect of our lives and the many personal and collective choices we make—whether we are aware of it or not, whether we like it or not. Economists, financial experts, and laypeople alike have simply accepted the de facto monopoly of this one type of money as if it were an immutable fact of life.

## CHAPTER THREE

# Megatrends and Money

*The modern crises are, in fact, man-made and differ from many of their predecessors in that they can be dealt with.*

~REPORT TO THE CLUB OF ROME

There are a host of increasingly critical issues in Moneyville that require our attention. In ways that are both obvious and obscure, each concern is related to money. We know, for example, that many commercial practices, such as the clear-cutting of forests and unregulated pollution, are linked to long-term ecological consequences. We understand as well that issues such as unemployment, poverty, and the challenges of eldercare are each linked to a chronic insufficiency of money.

Far less evident, however, is the connection between our vital concerns and the particular *type* of monetary system in operation.

Examined in following are five large-scale shifts in conditions of vital concern to society, hereafter referred to as *megatrends*. These megatrends include: the age wave, the ecological credit crunch, the financial divide, the job crisis, and economic instability. Each megatrend is followed by a money-related question intended to encourage critical thought about the link between such matters and money.

In the examination of the following megatrends, we ask that the reader put on a special kind of lens that allows for a "journey less travelled." Certainly, the megatrends are of serious concern and if not dealt with effectively, have the potential to cause irreversible damage. In this context, it is quite common to view these matters as the enemy, intent on doing us harm. And like the chick below, we might prefer to run for shelter.

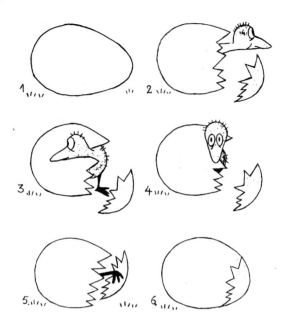

These very same concerns, however, present us with a unique opportunity. Like taskmasters, they guide us to places we would rather not explore. Though seemingly ominous, these megatrends oblige us to face deeper insights and truths about ourselves and the kind of society we operate in. They also invite us to explore new options in moving forward.

From this framework, the real enemies are not necessarily the problems, per se, but paradoxically our very reluctance to face up to our challenges and embrace the opportunity to transcend and grow. Such inquiry has led to profound insights and understandings about the influence of systems—the monetary system in particular—with the realistic potential to bring about a saner, more sustainable world.

The megatrends examined herein are not intended as a comprehensive list of concerns, but are among the most critical. Additionally, the data points cited were last verified in early 2012. They do not reflect the most current conditions but instead serve as markers to help indicate the general direction and extent of change taking place in our time.

We start with the Age Wave, the slowest of these megatrends, but the one that is most inexorably certain.

## THE AGE WAVE

When Baron Otto von Bismarck set up Germany's first social insurance system in the 1870s, the retirement age was established at 65. The catch was that the average life expectancy at that time was only 48 years. A mere two percent of the population would be left alive to enjoy their "golden years."[1] It was likely inconceivable back then that such a social security plan could ever pose a burden to the state.

For 99 percent of humanity's existence, life expectancy has averaged about 18 years.[2] This is clearly no longer the case. One remarkable result of improved medicine and living conditions over the last century is that two-thirds of all people who have ever reached the age of 65 are alive today.[3] Within the 30 developed member nations of the Organisation for Economic Co-operation and Development (OECD), one out of every 11 people in the 1960s was 65 or older.[4] Today, that number has increased to one out of every seven people. By 2030, the proportion of elders living in OECD nations is expected to swell to one out of every four.[5]

While one can hope that this global greying trend will transform the incoming Information Age into an Age of Wisdom, sobering economic issues must first be addressed.

One such issue is unfunded liabilities—benefits earned by today's workers but for which no reserves exist. Funds that were supposed to be secure for future retirement repayments by the U.S. Social Security system and other pension plans have been paid out to those already in retirement and may not be fully recovered. Unfunded liabilities have already accumulated to more than $35 trillion in OECD countries alone. Adding healthcare to these costs could easily double that figure.[6]

Meanwhile, healthcare is becoming increasingly expensive. In 2008, as the global recession deepened, the cost of total national health expenditures was expected to rise 6.9 percent—twice the rate of inflation.[7] At current rates, it is estimated that retiring couples in the United States will need at least $250,000 in savings just to pay for the most basic medical coverage.[8] As the availability of funds continues to decline, the pressure on retirees and on society to assist them becomes ever more difficult.

There are no historical precedents that we can draw from to handle the issues raised by this Age Wave.

The following hard "money question" synthesizes the dilemma that this Age Wave presents: *How will society provide the elderly with the money and resources needed to match their longevity?*

## THE ECOLOGICAL CREDIT CRUNCH

The Earth's natural systems provide many products and processes vital to our economies and lives. Increasingly however, the resources that enable these critical life-support functions are being consumed faster than they can be replenished. Human demand on the planet's living resources—our *ecological footprint*—now exceeds nature's regenerative capacity by nearly 30 percent.[9]

The World Wildlife Fund (WWF) reports that, "just as reckless spending is causing a recession, so reckless consumption is depleting the world's natural capital to a point where we are endangering our future prosperity."[10]

Over the past 150 million years, the rate of speciation—the creation of new species—is estimated to have either equalled or exceeded the rate of extinction. Humanity's impact over the past two centuries, particularly recent decades, has turned that upside down. Up to 150 species are now becoming extinct every day.[11]

Human encroachment is also shrinking the world's rainforests. According to the Food and Agriculture Organization of the United Nations (FAO), "deforestation continues at an alarming rate of about 13 million hectares a year,"[12] an area roughly equivalent to half the size of Great Britain. By way of an escalating feedback mechanism, tree loss contributes to and is exacerbated by other ecological concerns, including biodiversity loss, soil erosion, and rising temperatures. The UN Climate Change Conference in Bali 2007 warned that, "if we lose the forests, we lose the fight against climate change."[13]

Regarding climate change, global surface temperatures are rising. According to NASA's Goddard Institute for Space Studies, the decade from 2000 through 2010 was the hottest on record.[14]

The financial costs of climate change are staggering. Some 40 percent of world trade is based on biological products and processes.[15] A report commissioned by the British government estimates that by 2050 climate change will account for a yearly loss of at least five percent in global growth ($2.2 trillion at current values). If the environmental, health-related, and known subsidiary effects of rising temperatures are taken into account, the losses could amount to as much as 20 percent of annual global GDP ($9 trillion).[16] Even after tallying the total insurance losses from September 11, 2001, the world's largest reinsurance company, Munich Re, stated that its deepest concern for the future was not terrorism but rather climate change.[17]

Paul Volcker, formerly chairman of the Federal Reserve and head of President Obama's Economic Recovery Advisory Board, warned:

> If you don't take action, you can be sure that the economy will go down the drain in the next 30 years. What may happen to the dollar and what may happen to growth in China or whatever, pale into insignificance compared with the question of what happens to this planet over the next 30 or 40 years if no action is taken [on climate change].[18]

The UN Intergovernmental Panel on Climate Change (IPCC) has concluded that most temperature increases since the mid-20th century are very likely due to the increase in human-generated greenhouse gases.[19] Though some debate still continues, the IPCC's findings are supported by the national academies of science of every major industrialized nation.[20] Most other ecological damage is probably linked to human activity as well.

As is well documented, whenever serious financial interests are involved, calls for reform hit the proverbial brick wall. Financial markets focus on the next quarter's results, and even if a particular CEO were to advocate longer-term priorities at the expense of immediate results, he or she would be admonished or removed from office. Only when we have resolved the next "money question" is there any real chance to address the ecological credit crunch in a timely and systematic manner.

Our bottom-line money question here is: *How can we resolve the conflict between short-term financial interests and long-term sustainability?*

## THE FINANCIAL DIVIDE

The divide between the haves and the have-nots is growing worldwide. This disparity is now greater than at any time since the beginning of the

20th century. A 2005 UN report estimated that the 50 richest people in the world were earning more than the 416 million poorest.[21]

In the United States, most of the tremendous wealth generated in the past several decades has gone to a very small percentage of the very rich. "Of the surplus of over a trillion dollars generated between 1979 and 1999, 95 percent went to a mere five percent of Americans."[22] The financial wealth of the top one percent of U.S. households now exceeds that of the lower 95 percent combined.[23] The pay gap between top executives and average employees in the 365 largest U.S. companies soared from 42:1 in 1980 to 531:1 in 2000.[24] And while the average income has increased by 9 percent for those in the top fifth of the pay scale, it has instead decreased by 2.4 percent for those in the bottom fifth.[25]

Families are increasingly hard hit. After 50 years of work, the average American family manages to amass savings of just $2,300.[26] This is despite the fact that the average American worked two weeks more in 2000 than a decade earlier. Increasingly, both parents must now be employed. In 1968, only 38 percent of married mothers worked for pay, while today's figure is more than 70 percent.[27] Though such data reflects societal changes and improved opportunities for women, it also indicates the added demands on families.

Wealth concentration is not isolated to America. Indonesia's 15 richest families hold 61.7 percent of all stock market holdings. The comparable figure for the Philippines is 55.1 percent, and for Thailand, 53.3 percent.[28] Meanwhile, 80 countries have lower per capita incomes than a decade ago.

The outcome of this inequality is tangible: "Of the world's total population, 65 percent have never made a phone call; 40 percent have no access to electricity. Americans spend more on cosmetics, and Europeans more on ice cream than it would cost to provide schooling and sanitation for the two billion people who currently go without."[29] Three billion people presently live on $2 or less per day, and 1.3 billion of those get by on $1 or less.[30] Approximately 1.2 billion do not have enough food or protein, and between 2 and 3.5 billion do not get enough vitamins or minerals to remain healthy.[31]

The money question here is: *How will we address economic inequality globally when even industrialized nations are finding it increasingly difficult to provide for their own citizens?*

## THE JOB CRISIS

The world economy has been dramatically affected by the recent economic downturn, with the loss of jobs an especially destabilizing factor. In January 2009, U.S. employers slashed 598,000 jobs, the biggest monthly loss in 34 years.[32] In Japan, unemployment jumped from 3.9 to 4.4 percent in November 2008—the biggest monthly increase in almost 42 years.[33] In China, 20 million workers lost their jobs in 2008.[34] The UN International Labour Organization (ILO) estimated that up to 51 million jobs would be shed and push an additional 200 million workers into extreme poverty in 2009, mostly in developing economies.[35]

The global struggle for jobs is, however, not new. Former UN Secretary General Kofi Annan reported in 2006 that at least 576 million able and willing people worldwide were out of work or chronically underemployed, and were unable to escape extreme poverty.[36] According to former Wall Street Journal associate editor Paul Craig Roberts, Americans had already lost more jobs in the years *preceding* the subprime mortgage debacle than at any time since the Great Depression.[37] Citing the U.S. Bureau of Labor Statistics, the New York Times reported that, "the American economy has added virtually no jobs in the private sector over a 10-year period from July 1999 to July 2009."[38]

The competition for jobs in the United States is expressed as a gradual degradation of employment conditions. U.S. labor productivity, for instance, was up 1.8 percent in 2007, yet inflation-adjusted wages were down 0.8 percent in that same year.[39] According to the ILO, the average American worked 1,978 hours in 2000, up from 1,942 hours in 1990. This represents almost a week of extra work annually.[40] Workaholism has become for many a tacit requirement for keeping one's job.[41]

One telling sign of the U.S. job crisis is the growing burdens that workers are expected to bear. Corporations are scaling back on benefits such as health coverage and pensions. The average household income is now barely higher than it was in 1973, while the volatility of earnings and financial risks have soared. Unlike Europe, where job losses show up in raw unemployment numbers, U.S. indicators manifest through what Yale political scientist Jacob Hacker calls "the great risk shift,"[42] whereby new levels of jeopardy and compromise are being placed onto workers without commensurate increases in income. Even those families in which both parents are working are often one serious incident—a medical bill or factory closure—away from disaster.[43]

The future looms uncertain. Though the Information Revolution offers much promise, it has not yet shown any indication of leading to a postindustrial global economy that will provide sufficient job opportunities for the 7.5 billion forecast by 2020, much less the current population.[44]

Jobless growth—increased overall earnings without a proportionate expansion of employment—is not merely a forecast for major corporations, but has become an established fact and in many instances a desired goal. Political and economic columnist William Greider observes that, "the world's 500 largest corporations have managed to increase their production and sales by 700 percent over the past 20 years, while at the same time reducing their total workforce."[45]

Economists will correctly argue that improvements in productivity, which then lead to job losses in one sector, tend to create jobs in other areas. In the long run, therefore, technological change does not much matter to overall employment. These new technologies, however, are coming upon us faster and faster and necessitate fundamentally new sets of skills and a massive displacement of jobs. If the change is rapid enough, these job dislocations can be just as disruptive as permanent job losses.

Nobel laureate Wassily Leontieff has summarized the overall process as follows: "The role of humans as the most important factor of production is bound to diminish in the same way that the role of horses in agricultural production was first diminished and then eliminated by the introduction of tractors."[46] While we could let the horses die out peacefully, what will we do with people?

The money question here is: *How can we provide a living to additional billions of people when tens of millions are out of work and our technologies make jobless growth a clear possibility?*

## THE BANKING/MONETARY CRISIS

Our banking and monetary systems are in a state of great instability. Though the economic crisis of 2008–2009 was the most severe disruption in decades, it was certainly not the only one. In just one 25-year period (1971–1996), the World Bank identified 169 monetary crises and 93 banking crises, which hit 130 different countries.[47] These figures do not include more recent and serious troubles, such as the Asian crisis (1997), the Russian crisis (1998), the Argentinian crisis (2001), and the banking crisis of 2007-2008. In 2003, Nobel Laureate Joseph Stiglitz stated that, "something is wrong with the global financial system. International financial crises or near-crises have become regular events...The question is not whether there will be another crisis, but where it will be."[48]

One systemic cause for this fragility is the global casino of unprecedented proportions that currently determines our money's value. Daily turnover in foreign exchange in 2010 was $4 trillion.[49] This amount is more than triple that of 2001 and excludes the large amount of derivative trading.[50] Nearly 96 percent of these transactions are purely speculative— they do not relate to the "real" economy or reflect the global movements or exchanges of actual goods and services.[51] Functioning primarily as a speculative market, currency exchange is driven not only by tangible economic news but also by mere rumor and conjecture.

The economic pinch is being felt worldwide and by all sectors of the economy. Russian President Dmitry Medvedev noted correctly that, "failure by the biggest financial firms in the world to adequately take risk into account, coupled with the aggressive financial policies of the biggest economy in the world, have led not only to corporate losses. Most people on the planet have become poorer."[52]

According to the U.S. Federal Reserve, 2008 saw a decline of $11.2 trillion in U.S. households' net worth (the difference between assets and liabilities). It was the sixth straight quarterly decline since the peak in the second quarter of 2007 at $64.4 trillion.[53] Meanwhile, home equity fell to 46.2 percent of market value, the lowest level on record.[54]

The net effect of ongoing financial crises is the rapid shrinkage of the middle class. A few very rich individuals are left at the top of the economic heap, with most others nearing or already in poverty. This was the case with the Asian, Russian, and Argentinean crises, and could also occur in the United States and elsewhere.

A more in-depth analysis related to the financial crisis is presented later in this work. Suffice it to say here that given the key role of money in our world, disturbances to the banking and monetary sector adversely impact the whole of society and exacerbate the megatrends. Downturns affect jobs, health coverage, pension plans, and our ability to address a host of socioeconomic and environmental concerns.

*"Something is definitely going on. We're back to eating dog food."*

The last money question is straightforward: *How can we better prepare for or actually prevent future economic and monetary crises?*

To help illustrate why our megatrends have thus far resisted efforts aimed at their resolution, we offer the following parallel from the pages of medical history.

## A MEDICAL ANALOGY

The emergence of our monetary paradigm occurred at a time when the medical treatment of choice for the prevention and treatment of illness and disease was bloodletting—the removal of often-copious amounts of blood from patients. Though actually harmful to patients in the majority of cases, bloodletting remained the most common medical practice from antiquity up until the late 19<sup>th</sup> century. When, for example, George Washington came down with a throat infection, nearly four pounds of his blood were removed. It was far more likely the treatment and not the illness that contributed most to his demise.

The practice of bloodletting and the many notions that justified it, as well as the explanations that were offered time and again for a patient's inevitable decline, went unchallenged by one generation after another for the better part of 2000 years. Notwithstanding the brilliance of the theories in support of this practice and the physicians that espoused them, both theory and practitioner were profoundly mistaken. But in the absence of bacteriology, immunology, and other common understandings available today, this flawed medical procedure had the *appearance of certitude* and managed to endure for millennia.

A similar scenario exists today with regard to money. As mentioned, our megatrends persist not because they are not intractable, but rather because we are using a very limited, centuries-old set of monetary tools that are simply not designed to cope with today's myriad concerns.

## CLOSING THOUGHTS

Our ineffectiveness in the face of global challenges is not an expression of the intractability of climate change, job losses, or other pressing megatrends. The persistence of such issues is instead related to our continued inability, thus far, to identify and address their root causes, and in particular, to more fully grasp the link between so many vital concerns and money.

No matter how sincere the desire or how determined the effort, we simply cannot expect our difficulties to disappear until and unless we understand the functional dynamics and limitations of the current monetary system.

## CHAPTER FOUR

# A Money Primer

*Money is like an iron ring we put through our nose.*

*It is now leading us wherever it wants.*

*We just forgot that we are the ones who designed it.*

~MARK KINNEY

If you find yourself confused about money, take considerable comfort in the fact that you are not alone. John Maynard Keynes once quipped: "I know of only three people who really understand money: a professor at another university, one of my students, and a rather junior clerk at the Bank of England."[1] A prudent man, he didn't name them.

If the Great Recession has assured us of anything, it is the extent to which Keynes' assessment still runs true. Most of us, from leading economists and financial wizards to the average layperson, have never been properly introduced to money. Given what is at stake today, it is high time and to the benefit of all to put an end to this perennial mystery.

The following primer provides an overview of the basics of our monetary system.

## THE MYSTERY OF MONEY

Every modern society, regardless of its cultural or political background, has accepted the current monetary system. When the French and Russian revolutions overthrew the established order in their countries (in 1786 and 1917, respectively), they changed just about everything, save for their currency. Each society completely rebuilt its legal system. The French overhauled their entire classification of measurements by creating the metric system, and even tried to change the calendar. The Russians threw out the very concept of private ownership and nationalized all their banks and corporations. Nonetheless, the monetary system remained exactly as before, with only one cosmetic difference—the bills were now adorned with new mottoes and heroes. When Mao's communist takeover occurred in China, and when more than 100 colonial countries gained their independence over the past half century, the same phenomenon occurred, that is, each simply copied the now-standardized national currency system.

Little understood to this day is that virtually all national currencies operational in our world—regardless of their country of issuance; their designation as dollars, euros, or pesos; or their material composition, shape and particular motifs—are each the same *type* of money.

## Money and Magic

Money often appears to possess magical properties. The U.S. executive director to the IMF in the Clinton administration, Karin Lissakers, offered this revealing definition: "Money is magic. Central bankers are magicians. Like all magicians, they don't like to show their tricks."[2] Was she referring to real magic or simple parlor tricks? The answer is both.

Consider, for instance, that no self-respecting magician's routine is complete without a decent disappearing act, a feat that money performs in a rather spectacular fashion, especially of late! Once upon a time, when money was mostly gold and silver coins, banks started issuing pieces of paper. These papers were simply receipts indicating how much of the precious metal was being stored, and where. The disappearing act has since become increasingly more sophisticated as paper money rapidly dematerializes into binary bits in the computers of bankers, brokers, and financial institutions. There is now serious talk that it could all soon disappear into the virtual world. Perhaps when the last dollar, euro, or yen has evaporated into the electronic ethers, the nonmaterial nature of money will be understood.

Events in recent decades have made further evident the nonmaterial nature of money. In 1971, the United States ceased to define the value of the dollar in relation to the value of gold. Since then, the dollar has represented a promise from the U.S. government to redeem the dollar—but with what? Another dollar! At least when the dollar was backed with gold, it could more easily be assumed to have some material value.

Magic and mystery have surrounded money throughout its long evolution. For millennia, the magic was religious in nature. Now high priests of business, wielding impenetrable scientific equations, perform the magic using an intentionally cryptic language. William Greider, in his aptly named book on the Federal Reserve, *Secrets of the Temple*, wrote that, "like the temple, the Fed did not answer to the people, it spoke for them. Its decrees were cast in a mysterious language people could not understand, but its voice, they knew, was powerful and important."[3]

A congressional hearing with former chairman of the U.S. Federal Reserve Alan Greenspan, for instance, had as much ritual and ambiguity as did the oracles of Delphi in ancient Greece, as reflected in this typical Greenspan witticism: "If I seem unduly clear to you, you must have misunderstood what I said."[4] It was only after his retirement that the chairman's own lack of clarity was revealed. Speaking before the U.S. Congress in October 2008, Greenspan conceded his "shocked disbelief" regarding the role that lending institutions, deregulation, and other policies played in contributing to the financial crisis of 2008–2009.[5]

## What is Money?

It is common to think of money in terms of its material representations. Down through the ages, money has appeared to be a *thing*—in fact, an incredible variety of things. Monetary historian Glyn Davies created a near-complete alphabet with a selection of objects that have represented money in the past, starting with amber, beads, and cowries, and ending with wampum, yarns, and zappozats (decorated axes).[6]

A simple thought experiment, however, helps distinguish money from other things. Assume you are stranded alone on a deserted island. If you had a *thing*, say a knife, it is still useful as a knife. Yet, if you had a million dollars in whatever form—cash, gold coins, credit cards, or even zappozats—it becomes merely paper, metal, plastic, or whatever. But it no longer functions as money.

In short, although money has taken many material forms throughout history, *money is not a thing*.

What, then, is money?

Money may be defined as an *agreement*, within a *community*, to use some standardized item as a *medium of exchange*.[7]

As an *agreement*, money inhabits the same space as other social constructs, like marriage or lease agreements. These constructs are real, even if they exist only in people's minds. A monetary agreement can be made formally or informally, freely or by coercion, consciously or unconsciously. Most people do not consciously agree to use dollars or pesos, nor do we consider their nature. We just use them and in so doing, automatically enter into an unspoken agreement with all others with whom we conduct business.

A monetary agreement is only valid within a given *community*. Some monetary agreements are operational among only small groups of friends like chips used in card games, or within a larger community like the citizens of a particular nation, or for restricted periods of time like the cigarette medium of exchange among frontline soldiers during World War II. A community can be geographically disparate, such as Internet users, and can include large segments of the globe, as with the case of the U.S. dollar in its role as an international reference currency.

The key function that transforms a chosen object into money is its role as a *medium of exchange* for the trade of goods and services. Other functions of money include its role as a *unit of account*, that is, a standard numerical unit capable of measuring the value of goods and services; a *store of value* that can be reliably saved, stored, and retrieved; and finally, especially of late, as a *tool for speculation*. Not all currencies, however, necessarily serve all of these functions.[8]

In summary, the magic of money is bestowed on something when a given community agrees to use it as a medium of exchange. Conventional money and the monetary system are therefore not de facto realities like air or water, but are instead choices such as social contracts or business agreements. As such, they are subject to review and amendment.

Another long-standing mystery is how and where our money is made.

## MONEY CREATION

When asked why he robbed banks, American criminal celebrity Willie Sutton's reputed reply was, "because that's where the money is." To better appreciate our agreements about money, it is first necessary to understand the banking system, *not* because that is where money is kept, but rather because it is where money is actually *created*.

**Origins of the Western Banking System**

During the Late Middle Ages, gold and silver coins were established forms of money. Those most qualified to check the purity of these coins were the goldsmiths, who, coincidentally, also owned strongboxes to protect against thieves. It thus became a prudent practice to give one's excess coins to the goldsmith for safekeeping, who would issue a receipt for the coins and charge a small fee for the service.

When money was needed, owners could cash in the receipt, and the goldsmith would pay out the coins. It soon became more convenient to settle an account by paying with the receipt instead. If the goldsmith was known to be a trustworthy fellow, why risk moving the coins physically? The goldsmith's receipts thus became a promise of payment. Anyone who accepted such a receipt was implicitly entering into an agreement with the goldsmith. This was the origin of modern-day paper money.

In time, some enterprising goldsmiths saw that the bulk of the coins stayed put in their strong boxes. Depositors would rarely if ever retrieve all their coins at the same time. The goldsmiths could thus issue receipts in excess of the gold coins stored on behalf of clients, and increase their income by lending out money without having to increase actual reserves.

A gradual shift took place from money based on commodities such as gold or silver to money based on credit or loans in the form of paper receipts. The same basic arrangement exists to this day, with one major difference being that banks replaced the goldsmiths. Our lexicon reminds us of this link. The transactions between goldsmiths and their clients took place on Italian benches, or *bancos*, the origin of the word "bank."[9]

European banking and the credit-based monetary system were thus simultaneously born in 13th-century Italy. Many of the key ingredients were already in place: paper money as the counterparty's liability, the importance of a good reputation for that counterparty, and the ability of the bankers to create more money than the deposits they held in reserve. This latter process is today called the "fractional reserve system."

The remaining elements of today's banking system would be established several centuries later in pre-Victorian England.

**Our Monetary Agreements**

The late 1600s saw the dawn of the Industrial Revolution and the creation of modern-day nation states. These developments required substantial resources, including more sophisticated types of investments and monetary agreements. The arrangement that was reached provided that in exchange for a commitment to provide loans whenever governments needed money, banks secured the exclusive right to create paper money as "legal tender," that is, as the currency accepted by government in payment for taxes.[10]

The longest surviving agreement of this kind originated in 1668 with the license of the "Bank of the Estates of the Realm," Sweden's central bank (now known as the Riksbank). Two decades later, the Bank of England was founded on a similar model, "from where it spread around the world."[11] According to economist John Kenneth Galbraith, the Bank of England is "in all respects to money as St. Peter's is to the Faith. And the reputation is deserved, for most of the art as well as much of the mystery associated with the management of money originated there."[12]

The deal struck between the banks and government remains in effect to this day, and entitles banks to create new money for the deposits they receive. The new money is generated in the form of a loan to customers of up to 90 percent (a *fraction*) of the value of the deposit (held in *reserve*); hence the name "fractional reserve system."[13] That new loan— say, a mortgage to buy a house—usually results in another deposit made somewhere in the banking system, in this case by the seller of the house. The bank receiving that next deposit is, in turn, entitled to create a new loan for yet another 90 percent of that deposit, and the cascade continues from deposit to loan to deposit again and again throughout the banking system. This "money alchemy" is one of the most arcane secrets of our monetary system (see insert).

### Money Alchemy

Modern money alchemy is officially called the "fractional reserve multiplier." It starts with the injection of say, 100 million units of "high-powered money" into the banking system by the central bank of a nation, which issues a loan to pay for government bills for said amount. These funds are then deposited in the banking system by the recipient, which enables the receiving bank to lend out 90 million units (90 percent of the original 100 million units), while the other 10 million remain on deposit as "sterile reserves."

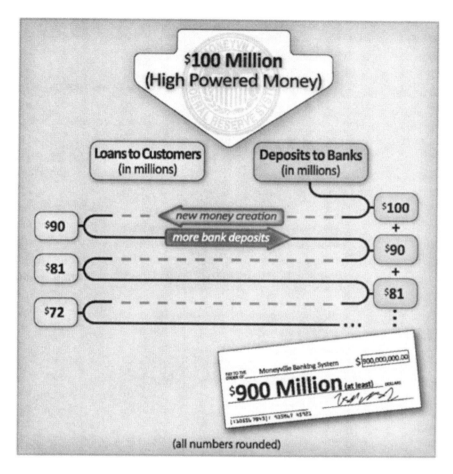

*Figure 4.1 – Money Creation through Bank Debt*

The new loan for 90 million units will, in turn, lead to another deposit for that amount somewhere else, enabling the next receiving bank to provide another loan for 81 million (which again represents 90 percent of the deposit), and so forth. This is how the original 100 million units will, after many iterations, generate 900 million units of additional "credit money" as it flows through the banking system.

This convoluted mechanism is the end result of the deal struck between banks and governments. It is the reason why money ultimately involves the entire banking system, and helps explain how money and debt are literally two sides of the same coin.

Note that this entire money-creation process hinges upon loans. *If all debts were repaid, bank money would simply disappear!* This is so because the entire process of money creation, as illustrated above, would reverse itself. This process of paying off all loans (on the left side of figure 4.1) would automatically use up all of the deposits (on the right side). Even the central bank's high-powered money would evaporate if the government were able to repay its debts.

This money-creation process is one of the more significant yet least understood aspects of the current monetary paradigm. With our money set up as loans, we are all debtors, indebted to those who create and loan us money—the banking system. The implications of this money-creation scheme are profound and far-reaching, as is examined in the next chapter.

## CLOSING THOUGHTS

Magic and mystery have surrounded money throughout its long evolution. Given money's key role in society today, it is vitally important that we become as familiar as possible with this all-important human creation. The first step is to understand that money is an agreement, and as such is open to amendment.

The current agreements we have regarding our monetary and banking systems date back to late 16th-century England. The banks were given the right to create new money from the deposits they received, which is now commonly known as the fractional reserve system. In this money-creation process, almost all of our money is debt money, derived from loans made by our banking system. This arrangement was made centuries ago in a very different place and time and under very different conditions. Is it possible that there are other types of money better suited to manage today's challenges?

## CHAPTER FIVE

# Money Is Not Value Neutral

*The most powerful force in the universe*

*is compound interest.*

~ATTRIBUTED TO ALBERT EINSTEIN

There is a long-held assumption in economics that money is *"value neutral,"* that is, money is simply a passive medium of exchange that affects neither the transaction nor the nature of the relationships among its users. This assumption is closely related to another traditional notion, "economic man," which claims that people invariably act with perfect rationality regarding economic decision-making in such a way that maximizes their personal utility or wellbeing.

It should be noted, however, that these notions date back to the 18$^{th}$ century, before many important discoveries and current understandings regarding the human psyche and decision-making. Each of these assumptions are rooted in a worldview that sought to fashion economics and much of society along the lines of Newtonian physics, and which held that the same order and predictability that defined plantary orbits would explain human behavior and investment patterns.

We now know that attempts to understand money and other complex socioeconomic phenomena through a mechanistic, value-neutral lens are inherently misguided. The countless instances of "irrational exuberance" and the boom-and-bust manias that have plagued our economies for centuries contradict the very idea of economic man. Likewise, money's supposed value neutrality is challenged by ample evidence showing that different types of monetary systems promote distinctly different values and have uniquely influenced societal behavior throughout history.

One of the key assertions of this work is that our money is *value-nonneutral*. Money is a major determinant in the nature of our exchanges and the relationships among currency's users. Each of money's constituent parts, from the manner by which money is created to whether or not a currency bears interest, strongly influences our behavior patterns and plays a determinant role in shaping the kind of economy and society we operate in.

All national currencies have the following key characteristics that persist as unquestioned features of conventional money:

- o   geographical attachment to a nation-state;
- o   creation out of nothing—fiat money;
- o   issuance through bank debt;
- o   incurrence of interest.

Below, we examine how these seemingly innocuous components of our monetary system wield a profound influence upon each and every one of us and on society-at-large.

## NATIONAL CURRENCIES

National currencies have proven to be a highly effective means of strengthening national identity, as they facilitate economic interactions with fellow citizens rather than with foreigners. Economist Charles Handy explains money's impact on identification within a given community: "A common currency translates into a common information system, so that its inputs and outputs can be measured and compared across the parts."[1] Money draws an "information border" between "us" and "them," making tangible boundaries that would otherwise be visible only in an atlas, reinforcing unity within the confines of a nation-state.

During the breakup of the Soviet Union, for example, one of the first acts by each of the newly independent republics was the issuance of their own national currency. The euro, the single currency that officially replaced more than a dozen national European currencies, had as one of its principal aims the creation of a European supranational consciousness and unity.

While it might be difficult today to imagine any currency other than those issued on a national or supranational level, the vast majority of historical currencies were actually privately issued by local rulers.

## FIAT MONEY AND BANK DEBT

The word *fiat* is found in the Latin version of the Bible. According to Genesis, *"Fiat Lux"*(Let Light Be) were the first words pronounced by God. The next sentence states, "And light was, and He saw it was good." Fiat implies the godlike ability to create something out of nothing (*ex nihilo*), through the power of the Word.

All conventional national currencies in the world today are fiat currencies. They are created by an authority that declares a particular medium of exchange as acceptable in payment of taxes—that is, as valid legal tender. As we have seen, these fiat currencies are created as bank debt under the hierarchical authority of a national central bank.[2]

The convoluted bank-debt, money-creation process described earlier resolves the apparent contradiction between two principal goals of pre-Victorian England: creating and supporting the nation-state on the one hand, while relying on private initiative and competition on the other. The monetary system provides a smooth way to privatize the creation of a national currency—theoretically a public function—via the private banking system, while simultaneously maintaining pressure on individual banks to compete for deposits.

Economists John Jackson and Campbell R. McConnell summarize an important aspect of bank debt and fiat monetary systems: "Debt-money derives its value from its scarcity relative to its usefulness."[3] In other words, money must be maintained artificially in shorter supply than the need for it. It is this built-in scarcity that keeps each of us doing what we must to obtain this vitally important commodity. From a banking perspective, failure to uphold this scarcity results in inflation and even hyperinflation, and erodes a currency's value.

The necessity of managing scarcity is one reason why today's monetary system is not self-regulating, but instead requires central banks' supervision. Central banks also compete among themselves to keep their own currencies in short supply, so that the relative value and scarcity of their currencies are maintained internationally. They accomplish this by raising interest rates whenever they need to tighten the money supply, thereby making it more expensive to borrow.

Among its many profound impacts upon society, this artificially-maintained scarcity creates strong incentives to compete rather than cooperate.

## INTEREST

Though loans and interest likely date back to pre-urban societies, the first written evidence of interest comes from ancient Sumer where it was known as *más*, which also meant "a lamb." This followed from the practice by which, in return for permitting a flock of sheep to graze on one's property, the landowner had the right to choose a lamb born from that flock. This denotes the original relationship between loans, interest, and rural produce.[4] According to Stephen Zarlenga, Director of the American Monetary Institute, "loans were made in seed grains, animals, and tools to farmers. Since one grain of seed could generate a plant with over 100 new grain seeds, after the harvest farmers could easily repay the grain with 'interest' in grain."[5]

But what will an ounce of silver or gold generate? Once interest was applied to money, a fundamental debate arose that has continued to this very day. One of the central areas of concern is how much interest should be applied to a loan.

### Interest and Usury

While usury is today considered an excessive interest rate, it was formerly defined as charging *any* interest on money. The practice of charging interest on money was not officially sanctioned in the West until the reign of England's King Henry VIII, who legalized interest in 1545 following his break with the Roman Church. Up until that schism, all three "religions of the Book" (Judaism, Christianity, and Islam) prohibited usury.[6]

### Usury and Religion

It is written in the Hebrew Scriptures: "Unto thy brother thou shalt not lend upon usury, that the Lord thy God may bless thee in all that thou settest thine hands to" (Deuteronomy 23:20). Islam is even more universal in its condemnation: "What ye put out as usury to increase it with the substance of others, shall have no increase from God" (Koran Sura 30:38).

Since the modern monetary system evolved predominantly under Christian influence, it is this religion's changing views of usury over time that merits particular attention.

The denunciation of usury as a mortal sin was one of the most persistent dogmas of the Catholic Church. Clement of Alexandria, an early church father, specified in his *Stromata,* Chapter XVIII, "the law prohibits a brother from taking usury; designating as a brother not only him who is born of these same parents, but also one of the same race and sentiments."[7]

The First Council of Carthage (345 CE) and the Council of Aix (789 CE) declared it reprehensible even for laymen to make money by lending at interest. The Canonical Laws of the Middle Ages absolutely forbade the practice.[8] The Council of Vienne (1311 CE) went so far as to declare that those who maintained that there was no sin in demanding usury, should themselves be punished as heretics.

The original doctrine against usury was finally questioned within the Catholic Church itself in 1822. The case involved a woman from Lyons, France, who was refused absolution unless she returned the interest she had earned. Clarification was requested from Rome, which responded: "Let the petitioner be informed that a reply will be given [to] her question when the proper time comes...Meanwhile she may receive sacramental absolution, if she is fully prepared to submit to the instructions of the Holy See." A forthcoming resolution was promised again in 1830 and for a third time in 1873. This promised clarification never came.

Thus, the sin of usury, which was never officially repealed by the Church, was simply forgotten.[9]

## Interest and Lending

Interest serves key functions during the lending process. Researcher Andrew Lowd points to three factors for reasonable interest rates: default protection, inflation, and opportunity cost.[10]

*Default Protection.* Interest protects lenders from potential loan defaults. Known as "risk premium," the interest in such cases acts as a precaution to ensure that the lender receives back at least the amount lent out to borrowers.

If, for example, 105 loans of $1,000 each are made, but only 100 are repaid, $5,000 is, in effect, lost. Not knowing which of the borrowers will default, the lender spreads the risk out over all the loans by charging a five percent interest charge to each borrower. The interest serves as a small borrower's fee for the convenience of making additional funds available as a loan.

*Inflation.* Defined here as a sustained increase in the general level of prices, inflation necessarily decreases the purchasing power or value of money over time. If a lender makes a loan with the inflation rate at three percent annually, the money automatically loses three percent of its value per year, even if the borrower is perfectly reliable and trustworthy. By charging an interest rate equal to the prevailing rate of inflation, lenders act to ensure that their money maintains its value.

*Opportunity Cost.* Money can be used as a means to make more money. By loaning money to a borrower, lenders forgo their own opportunity to make a profit. Charging interest compensates for the lender's missed opportunity.

What is of particular relevance here with regard to money's value-nonneutrality is the impact of interest on our behaviors.

## Behavioral Effects of Interest

Though the full implication of interest is seldom understood, its behavioral effects are pervasive and powerful. Three patterns directly related to this built-in feature of our monetary system include:

1. encouraging competition;
2. fueling economic growth;
3. concentrating wealth.

### 1. Encouraging Competition

Charging interest—one effect of money created as bank debt—forces competition beyond that which would occur naturally.

Consider bank loans. When a bank creates money, say by providing a $100,000 mortgage, it only creates the principal for that loan. The bank does not create the interest on that loan, but expects a return of some $200,000 over the next 20 years or so. The bank requires the borrower to earn this second $100,000.

The following story illustrates how interest is woven into the fabric of the monetary system and how it stimulates competition.

## The Eleventh Round

Once upon a time, there was a small village where people knew nothing about money or interest. Each market day, people would bring their chickens, eggs, hams, and breads to the marketplace. There they entered into the time-honored ritual of negotiations and exchange for what they needed.

One market day, a stranger with shiny shoes and an elegant hat came by and observed the process with a smile. When one farmer ran around to corral six chickens needed in exchange for a ham, the stranger could not refrain from laughing.

"Poor people," he said. "So primitive."

Overhearing this, the farmer's wife challenged him: "Do you think you can do a better job handling chickens?"

The stranger replied: "Chickens, no. But I do have a much better way to eliminate the hassles. Bring me one large cowhide and gather the families. I will then explain this better way."

As requested, the families gathered, and the stranger took the cowhide, cut perfect rounds in it, and put an elaborate stamp on each. He then gave ten rounds to each family, stating that each round represented the value of one chicken. "Now you can trade and bargain with the rounds instead of those unwieldy chickens," he said.

It seemed sensible. All were impressed by the stranger.

"One more thing," added the stranger. "I will return in one year's time, and as a token of appreciation for the improvement I made possible in your lives, I want each of you to bring me an extra round, an eleventh round."

The wife was concerned. The eleventh round was never created; it was never cut from the cowhide. She then asked, "but where will that round come from?"

"You'll see," replied the stranger with a sardonic smile.

As the stranger suggested, it was far more convenient to exchange rounds instead of chickens on market days. But this convenience had a hidden cost: the eleventh round generated a systemic undertow of competition among the participants. One out of every 11 families would have to lose the equivalent of all its rounds in order to pay the stranger, even if every villager managed their affairs responsibly.

The eleventh round and the competition it generated impacted another age-old tradition as well. During harvests, or when someone's barn needed repairs after a storm, the villagers simply helped one another, knowing that if they themselves should one day have a problem, others would in turn come to their aid.

But when a storm threatened a few of the farmers the year following, there was an uncharacteristic reluctance to assist neighbors. Families were now wrestling with one another over that eleventh round. The introduction of interest-bearing money actively discouraged the long-held tradition of spontaneous cooperation among the villagers.

The Eleventh Round is a simplified story for non-economists. The impact of interest was isolated from other variables by making the assumption of a zero-growth society: no population increase, no production increases, and no increases in the money supply. In practice, all three variables (population, output, and money supplies) do change over time, further obscuring the impact of interest. The point of the Eleventh Round is that, all other things being equal, the artificial competition to obtain the money necessary to pay the interest is structurally embedded into the current system.

So how does a loan whose interest is never created get repaid? Interest repayment requires the use of someone else's principal. Scarcity is generated by *not* creating the money required to pay interest. It forces people to compete with each other for money that was never created, and penalizes them with bankruptcy should they not succeed. When a bank checks credit worthiness, it is really verifying a customer's ability to compete successfully in the marketplace to obtain the money required to reimburse both the principal *and* interest. Ultimately, someone must always lose. *Scarcity is the hidden engine that drives our bank-debt monetary system.*

In the current national currency paradigm, one reason why so much attention is paid to central bank decisions is that increased interest rates necessitate more bankruptcies in the future. The economic pie must grow that much faster just to break even. The monetary system therefore obliges us to incur debt and then compete with others through our exchanges to pay the resulting interest to the banks or lenders. No wonder "it is a tough world out there," and those who live within a competitive monetary system readily accept Darwin's supposed "survival of the fittest."

An ever-mounting body of evidence, however, supports a less harsh and even wholly contrary interpretation of the natural world.

Kinji Imanishi, the late professor of biosociology from Kyoto University, challenged the stereotypical Darwinian vision of nature as a struggle for life. The survival-of-the-fittest model is completely blind to the many frequent cases of symbiosis, joint development, and harmonious coexistence that prevail in all domains of evolution. Even our own bodies would not be able to survive long without the symbiotic collaboration of billions of microorganisms in the digestive tract.[11]

Evolution biologist Elisabet Sahtouris points out that predominantly competitive behavior is a characteristic of a young species during its first forays into the world. In contrast, in a mature system like an old-growth forest, the competition for light, for instance, is balanced by intense cooperation among species. Those species that do not learn to cooperate with others with whom they are codependent invariably disappear.[12]

Although the theories of Social Darwinism—a 19th century movement that advocated "survival of the fittest" as applicable to human society—have long been debunked, some of their tenets still linger. Many people maintain that competition and cruelty are natural and inevitable tools for survival, and are inherent to human nature. Yet, contrary to popular belief, Charles Darwin himself did not see competition as the foremost tool for continued existence in the evolution of humankind (see insert).

### Darwin, Loye, and Survival of the Fittest

Evolutionary systems scientist David Loye, in his books *The Great Adventure* and *Darwin's Lost Theory of Love,* points us back to the very source of Darwinism itself: Charles Darwin. After *On the Origin of Species* (1859), Darwin wrote another book, *The Descent of Man* (1871), in which he points out that the brutal and bloody theory in *Origin* pertains only to prehuman evolution.

Loye explains that in *The Descent of Man*, which deals primarily with human evolution, "Darwin actually writes only twice of survival of the fittest—and one of these times is to apologize for exaggerating the importance of this idea in *Origin of Species!*"[13]

Furthermore, "in this book of 848 pages in fine print, he [Darwin] writes only 12 times about selfishness, which by now hordes of sociobiologists, evolutionary psychologists, and best-selling books have assured us is the central survivalist motivation for human evolution high and low."[14] The misunderstood theory of evolution simply does not apply to the evolution of human society, because once human consciousness comes into play everything changes. As Loye points out, what Darwin is actually writing about in *Descent* can be clearly inferred by the word count:

- survival of the fittest, 2 times;
- selfishness, 12 times;
- moral sensitivity, 92 times;
- love, 95 times;
- habit, 108 times.

More surprising still, as Loye uncovers, Darwin wrote in *Descent* more than a century ago:

As important as the struggle for existence has been and even still is, yet as far as the highest part of our nature is concerned there are other agencies, which are more important. For the moral qualities are advanced, either directly or indirectly, much more through the effects of habit, by our reasoning powers, by instruction, by religion, etc., than through natural selection.[15]

*Descent* was completely overlooked, not because it was less valid than *Origin*, but rather because it contradicted the bias of the age in which Darwin lived. That competitive bias is still reinforced in the world today by the monetary system, especially through the built-in feature of interest.

## 2. Fueling Economic Growth

The key assumption of the Eleventh Round is that everything remains the same, one year to the next. In reality, we do not live in a world of zero growth. Population, production, and the money supply all grow at varying rates, making it more difficult than in the Eleventh Round to notice what is taking place.

Perpetual growth is not just another fact of life. The monetary system acts like a treadmill requiring sustained economic growth, even if the average real standard of living remains stagnant. The interest rate determines the average rate of economic growth needed just to remain at the same place.

Presently, the monetary system takes the first slice of the ongoing growth to pay for interest. Agrarian societies customarily sacrificed the first fruits of the harvest to their gods, while we instead now give the first yields of our toils to the institutions that manage our money.

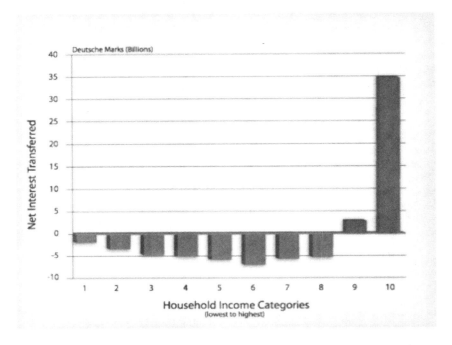

*Figure 5.1 - The Transfer of Wealth Via Interest (Germany, 1982)*

## 3. Concentrating Wealth

A third effect of interest is the continual transfer of wealth from the vast majority to a small minority. The wealthiest receive an uninterrupted profit from whoever needs to borrow money.

A revealing study on the transfer of wealth via interest from one economic group to another was performed in West Germany in 1982 (Figure 5.1).[16]

Germans were grouped into ten income categories of about 2.5 million households each. During that year, transfers between these ten groups involved a total of DM 270 billion in interest payments (approximately $120 billion at the time). A stark way to present the process is to graph the net interest transfers (interest earned minus interest paid) for each of these ten household categories.

The net effect is that the top ten percent of households received a net transfer of DM 34.2 billion in interest from the remaining 90 percent of society during the year in question. The greatest sums of interest were transferred from the middle classes (categories three to eight), each of which transferred about DM 5 billion to the top ten percent of the households (category ten). Even the poorest households transferred a substantial DM 1.8 billion of interest each year to the wealthiest group.

The graph illustrates this systemic transfer of wealth from the bottom 80 percent of the population to the top 20 percent, and especially to the top ten percent. This transfer occurs independently of the cleverness or industriousness of the participants—a classical argument often used to justify differences in income—and is instead a direct result of the type of money in use.

Is it mere coincidence that once interest became legal, all democratic countries created income taxes and income redistribution schemes to counteract at least part of this wealth transfer process?

No equivalent study isolating the effects of interest payments on the concentration of wealth yet exists for other countries. This process is, however, occurring everywhere, as by definition interest payments transfer wealth from those who have to borrow to those who can afford to lend money out. Available data, for example, suggests that economic disparity is even more dramatic in America than in Germany, with the U.S. middle class particularly adversely affected. The share of wage income earned by those in the 20–80 percentiles fell by one-fifth between 1966 and 2001. Those in the 80–90 percentile income group instead maintained their percentage of earned income, while those in the 95–99, 99–99.9, and 99.9–100 percentiles earned 29 percent, 73 percent, and 291 percent more, respectively.[17]

This concentration-of-wealth mechanism is, strictly speaking, a structural issue. Nonetheless, its behavioral effects are quite significant. Consider, for example, that the vast majority of us must work ever harder to maintain our middle-class lifestyles. This same mechanism not only corroborates the perception that the rich keep getting richer; it reveals that this concentration of wealth is an ongoing, self-perpetuating, systemic reality that endures despite our efforts to address it.

Interest-bearing money and the transfer of wealth it perpetuates have many important consequences, including the steady erosion of one of the key elements required for societies to function—*trust*. Today's societies are instead plagued by mistrust in our hopes for the future, in our leaders and institutions, and ultimately, in one another. It is trust that backs our money and allows a free nation to function optimally. And it is the corrosive effects of a deficit of trust that ends relationships, divides nations, and has undermined entire civilizations down through history.

Much of today's focus is placed on the accumulated negative consequences of industrialization, such as pollution, global warming, and our economic woes. It should be understood, however, that it is not interest-bearing money that is the principal cause of these and other troubles, but rather that it is the *only* type of money available to us at present. What kinds of economic and behavioral patterns could be engendered if there were different types of currencies working side by side with central bank-issued money?

The importance of money's non-neutrality and the extent to which it is linked to the human condition is examined further in Part III of this work. Suffice it to say here that money's impact on society is of vital importance. Our ability or failure to understand this seemingly obscure feature of money may very well determine our capacity to successfully navigate the challenges of our age and realize a better future.

It may be difficult to imagine monetary systems other than the one currently in use, or how they might function and what effects, if any, they would have on society. Fortunately, we now have sufficient information to piece together the monetary paradigms of several past ages, as well as the different economic and social patterns they generated. One such epoch is explored next.

## CLOSING THOUGHTS

Money is not value-neutral, but instead profoundly impacts the kind of society we live in. Interest-bearing national currencies were the hidden engines that propelled civilization into and through the Industrial Revolution. Both the best and the worst of what the Modern Age has achieved can be directly or indirectly attributed to the architecture of our money and the values they encourage, including: competition, the need for perpetual growth, and unrelenting wealth concentration. By intelligently engineering money, we can encourage different kinds of behavior and produce different societal outcomes.

## CHAPTER SIX

# Back to the Future

*The icons of old are the coding of tomorrow.*

*And tomorrow holds the promise of recovery of forgotten wisdom.*

~JEAN HOUSTON

Historical evidence informs all our social, cultural, and economic knowledge. In economics, however, it is only very recent data that tends to be considered, based on the assumption that experiences from past ages are not relevant to contemporary economic issues. Yet, our banking and monetary systems have remained fundamentally unchanged for centuries. Failure to examine the more distant past prior to the inception of the current paradigm risks overlooking potential insights useful for today.

One historical period of particular relevance is explored herein.

## THE CENTRAL MIDDLE AGES

Once upon a time, there existed an age blessed by an uncommon prosperity that enriched each segment of society. There was work for all, with favorable working conditions and abundant time for family, community, and personal pursuits. This age was also characterized by significant advancements in science, technology, education, literature, music, arts, craftsmanship, and more. Its ethics included cooperation, an unusual civic pride, and long-term thinking. The many unusual traits of the period culminated in the creation of some of the most beautiful and enduring public works the world has ever known.

Though seemingly like some fairy tale, this age not only existed, but endured for centuries. It flourished in the very same region from where our current monetary and banking systems originated—Western Europe.

This epoch came into being, however, long before the advent of our present monetary paradigm, and a millennium hence, offers unique lessons for today.

The Middle (or "Medieval") Ages were so named because it was the expanse of European history in the "middle" of the high civilizations of Rome (ending in the mid-400s CE) and the Renaissance (beginning in the late 1400s). This period is also commonly referred to as the "Dark Ages," as popular belief regards it as one of dismal poverty and primitive lifestyles, crowned by the horrific plague. The term medieval is still used today as a derisory label to dismiss something as hopelessly primitive.

Many of the opinions regarding this period, however, date back to 19th century assertions, which have since been proven to be incomplete or mistaken. The Middle Ages spanned more than 1,000 years. Recent scholarship has unveiled key distinctions regarding what transpired over this long expanse of history.

A dismal view certainly remains justified for the period following the collapse of the Roman Empire—the Early Middle Ages (5th–8th centuries)—and is much more accurately descriptive still of the dramatic closing medieval centuries. It is in fact the particularly appalling Late Middle Ages (14th–15th centuries) that provided much of the fuel for the dark image that future generations would project, inaccurately, onto the vast entirety of the medieval millennium.

There were, however, two and one-half centuries during the medieval millenium when something quite different took place. This middle period is the "Central Middle Ages."

## Highlights of the Central Middle Ages

Toward the middle of the 10th century, a marked shift in consciousness paralleled dramatic economic improvements in many areas of Western Europe. The progress spanning 1040–1290 is noted by medieval scholars as the "First Modernization," the "European Takeoff," and the "True European Renaissance." Between 1180 and 1230, for instance, the first wave of universities was founded in Europe.[1] Abstract sciences, such as mathematics, once thought to have developed in the official Renaissance of the 16th century, occurred instead centuries earlier during this period.[2]

The Central Middle Ages were also characterized by a very uncommon prosperity.

*Prosperity for All*

The prosperity of this age was quite unusual not only in quantitative terms, but also by the extent to which it benefited the general populace. A number of contemporary medievalist historians report that the quality of life for ordinary people in the 12th century may very well have been the highest in all of European history, comparing favorably in important respects even to present-day conditions. Workers, for example, seldom had less than four courses at lunch or dinner and enjoyed three or even four meals a day. Daily caloric intakes, estimated at 3000 calories in developed countries today, was instead 3500–4000 calories in the Central Middle Ages.[3]

Working hours were limited as well. When the dukes of Saxony tried to extend the workday from six hours to eight, workers in the region rebelled. Sunday was the "Day of the Lord" and the appointed day for public matters, while the so-called "Blue Monday" was designated as a free day, set aside for the general public to attend to their private affairs. In addition, there were at least 90 official holidays annually. In some regions, there may have been as many as 170 holidays in a single year!

In addition to favorable working conditions, the working class also enjoyed a remarkable level of economic independence. As medieval economic historian Guy Bois explains: "In the agricultural sector, for the first time the small landowners as a group become much more productive than the Seigniorial holdings. In short, Europe becomes more and more a world of small producers with the family unit as its fundamental engine."[4]

A number of medieval historians offer testimony to the expansion and improvement that took place in virtually every dimension of Central medieval society. Medievalist Marcel Bloch claims that increased private ownership is accompanied by "the largest increase in cultivated agricultural land in the entire span of the historical record."[5] Guy Fourquin reports that, "not only did the land available expand, but also the average yields more than doubled in most cases."[6] F. Icher writes: "Between the 11th and 13th century, the Western world experiences a high level of prosperity that is reflected concretely by a demographic expansion without precedent in history."[7]

Between 1000 and 1300, Europe's population is generally estimated to have increased an unprecedented twofold, one expression of the increased capacity to feed and maintain the population. Moreover, as Guy Bois writes, "growth isn't limited to a demographic explosion combined with a strong agricultural expansion. A flourishing commercial expansion was its third dimension."[8]

Medievalist Jean-Pierre Bayard reports that, "ordinary life is revolutionized: coal is used for heating, candles for lighting, eyeglasses for reading, glass is used more and more commonly, paper is manufactured on an industrial scale."[9] Robert L. Reynolds writes, "[There is] a growing manufacture of textiles, pottery, leather goods, and many other things. The products get better and better. Prices go down in terms of man hours because of more efficient management, improvement in tools and machinery, and better transport and distribution."[10] According to medievalist R. Phillippe, at the beginning of the 12th century there were in operation in France alone no fewer than "20,000 water mills, which represented the energy of 600,000 workers. Such technologies liberated massive amounts of labor."[11]

Urbanization, previously thought to take off with the Industrial Revolution of the 1700s, instead began during the Central medieval period. Frances and Joseph Gies write, "Europe was turning from a developing into a developed region. The growth of industry meant the growth of cities, which in the 12th and 13th centuries began to abandon their old roles of military headquarters and administrative centers as they filled with the life of commerce and industry."[12] Robert Lacey and Danny Danzinger report that, "Warwick, Stafford, Buckingham, Oxford—most of the county towns of modern England originated in the tenth century."[13]

Guy Bois summarizes:

> One can only be impressed by the extraordinary vitality and power of the changes that occurred during those three centuries. Whether one considers the demography, the urbanization, the techniques, the relationships between labor and money, every one of these aspects of society was completely revolutionized...One will have to wait five hundred years to live another wave of transformation of that scale: the capitalist Industrial Revolution.[14]

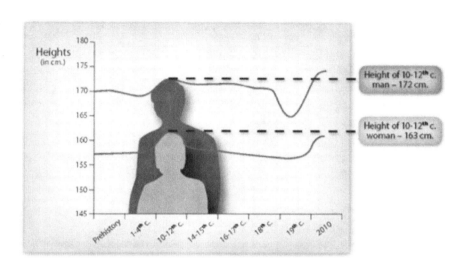

*Figure 6.1 – Heights of Londoners, prehistory to present-day*

## Heights

Confirmation of the unusual prosperity of this age comes in an equally unusual form of physical evidence: bodily remains.

It is well known that today's generation is substantially taller than the previous one—better nutrition and care, particularly in youth, is credited with this process. In a study of the skeletons of bodies in the same geographical area—London—informative findings emerged. The women of London were taller on average during the 10th–12th centuries than any other period in recorded history, measuring a whopping 7 centimeters taller than her Victorian counterpart and even 1 centimeter taller than today! Regarding males, it is only within the past fifty years that they have caught up to and, by 1998, finally outgrown their medieval counterparts, by a mere two centimeters (see Figure 6.1).[15]

The increased height of Londoners of the Central medieval period appears to reflect the greater quality of life for men and women of that time.

*Age of Cathedrals*

This medieval epoch has also been referred to as the "Age of Cathedrals,"[16] as nearly all of the cathedrals of Europe were built at this time. Historian Sacheverell Sitwell writes that, "it was the greatest period of building activity that there has ever been, and no mere catalogue of names and places can convey any idea of the strength and quality of its products."[17]

It is estimated that by 1300 CE there were almost 1,000 cathedrals in Western Europe, alongside 350,000 churches and several thousand large abbey foundations. Yet, the total population back then is estimated at only 70 million, which calculates to an average of one Christian place of worship for every 200 inhabitants. The ratio was even higher in parts of Hungary and Italy: one church for every 100 inhabitants![18]

This medieval building phenomenon is more remarkable still given that there was no central authority, church or otherwise, in charge of initiating or funding the construction of these cathedrals. Contrary to popular belief today, these structures were neither built by nor belonged to the church or nobility.[19] Local nobility and royalty customarily did make contributions, but these monuments were typically owned and financed by the citizens of the municipalities where they were built.[20]

The cathedrals embody some of the most beautiful gifts of Western history. These monuments stand as a strong statement of faith, ingenuity, and generosity. From a narrower economic viewpoint, they also offered a viable long-term income strategy for the community (see insert).

### Cathedrals: an Investment Forever

Besides their symbolic and religious roles, the cathedrals served another key function. Attracting currency into a community has clear economic advantages, as those living in proximity to today's tourist attractions such as Disney World will confirm. In medieval times, this was realized by attracting pilgrims, who played a similar economic role to that of today's tourists. A proven way to draw pilgrims was to build the most accommodating and spectacular cathedral in the area, which may help explain why medieval communities built cathedrals that could house two to four times their own population.

Additionally, these cathedrals, which were built to last forever, created cash flow not only for the population of the time, but for many future generations. The bulk of the businesses in Chartres, France, for example, still thrive today from tourists coming to visit its medieval cathedral 800 years after its construction.

Few contemporary medievalists doubt the extraordinary economic and building boom of the Central Middle Ages. One fundamental matter, however, remains unresolved: "The medieval blossoming has been described many times in its manifestations, its chronology, and its many facets, but never explained. Its mechanism remains an enigma."[21]

The economic mechanism that justified the remarkable blossoming of that period remains unclear. Where did the resources come from to fund hundreds of building projects on the scale of cathedrals? Faith and devotion alone cannot explain this construction any more than they can explain the remarkable prosperity of the ordinary people.

One medieval feature has, however, been almost entirely overlooked—the monetary system. This previously ignored element may help to explain the atypical dynamics of that period.

*The Invisible Engine*

Two different types of currencies functioned in parallel to one another throughout much of Western Europe during the Central Middle Ages. One type of currency consisted of centralized royal coinage, with many features in common with present-day national currencies. Its usage was primarily for long-distance trading and for the purchase of luxury goods. The second type of currency consisted of an extensive network of different local currencies, used primarily for community exchanges.

Many of the local currencies had a peculiar feature—a *demurrage* charge. Similar to a negative interest on money, the demurrage feature functions like a parking fee, which is levied for holding onto the currency for too long without spending it.

The demurrage was implemented through a general recoinage practice, enacted during the transfer of power to a new lord, usually due to the death of one's predecessor. As a rule, four old coins were handed in and exchanged for three new ones, each with the same individual value of the coins that they replaced. This tradition, called "renovatio monetae," amounted to a 25 percent tax payable by anyone in possession of dated coins at the time of recall. The uncertainty about the duration of a lord's life (and thus, the functional lifespan of the currencies) acted as an incentive for users to spend or invest rather than save such coins.

In technical terms, when demurrage is applied, money continues to function as a "medium of exchange" but no longer serves as a "store of value," that is, something worth hoarding. Though saving was very much encouraged, it was not done by storing currency, but took the form of productive assets. Examples of such investments were land improvements or high-quality maintenance of equipment such as water wheels and windmills, or enduring investments in the community such as the cathedrals. The specifics of how demurrage was applied differed from region to region, but generally speaking, provided a built-in incentive to invest in this way.

Written records from the period offer testimony to the benefits of this kind of savings. A significant number of mills, ovens, winepresses, and other heavy equipment were improved upon or even completely rebuilt each year. "They did not wait until anything was breaking down...On average, at least ten percent of all gross revenue was immediately reinvested in equipment maintenance."[22] No other period since then has encouraged such intensive preventive maintenance.

In effect, a pattern of longer-term investments became the norm rather than the exception. For those with demurrage currency to spare, investing in the cathedrals was likely an ideal way of demonstrating one's faith while also providing benefits for the community. The medieval cathedrals, still standing today and continuing to receive visitors from around the world, are enduring testimonies to the long-term vision of that former age.

Demurrage-charged complementary currencies also help to explain the particular Central medieval economy. Given that savings were inherently discouraged by demurrage, these currencies would remain in circulation and were exchanged with far greater frequency at all levels of society, in contrast to other forms of money. The greater velocity of circulation (a higher frequency of transactions with the same given coin) enabled the less-privileged classes to engage in substantially more transactions, which significantly improved their standard of living.

Medieval stone masons in action, using a variety of tools: a windlass with radiating spokes, a plumb line, a level, axes, and an adze. Jean Gimpel estimates that in less than three centuries millions of tons of stone were extracted in France alone, more than in Egypt over its entire history of more than three thousand years (notwithstanding that the Great Pyramid of Gizeh represents 2.5 million cubic meter of stone by itself).

## THE END OF AN AGE

This remarkable age came to a brutal end at the closing of the 13th century. The plague, otherwise known as the Black Death, is customarily blamed for causing the misery that subsequently befell Europe. Recent findings offer a different account.

Though usually cited as the cause of the later medieval horrors, the outbreak of the plague did not occur until 1347–1349. Yet, the population started plummeting two generations beforehand. Mostly overlooked is the fact that the pandemic was preceded by decades of economic and social devastation.

A major economic crash occurred during the period of 1280–95. A majority of the population, urban as well as rural, ended up being reduced to living at subsistence levels in the last decade of the 1200s. This economic downturn was then followed by widespread famines, epidemics, and extensive loss of life from 1300 onwards, decades prior to the outbreak of the deadly pestilence. From 1315–1322, the noted Great Famine took place. Historian Henry S. Lucas estimates that hunger killed ten percent of Europe's population.[23]

Accounts from the period describe the severity of conditions: "So many men and women died every single day from all social classes— wealthy, middle class and poor—that the priests couldn't bury them fast enough, so that the stench in the air was everywhere."[24] A London chronicle reported that, "the poor people ate for hunger cats and horses and dogs…some stole children and ate them."[25]

Again, all these events took place decades prior to the first outbreak of the plague. Historian Daniel Power writes that, "one needs, I believe, a lot of blindness to describe the outbreak of the Black Death as an accidental and exogenous event. Isn't it most surprising that this disaster happened only after 60 or 70 years of total misery?"[26]

It is now known that more than a half century prior to the pandemic, disastrous monetary changes were implemented.

**Political and Monetary Chnges**

A historic power shift occurred in Western Europe during the 13th century, whereby the doctrine of "King by Divine Right" was taken to its extreme. Local governments and administrations were overrun by strong, rapidly expanding central authorities with commanding kingdoms and large armies. The dual currency system was abolished and replaced by the imposition of a monopoly of royal coinage. King Louis IX of France specified that only royal mints had the right to issue coins in the realm.

Though it would take several decades, the elimination of local currencies eventually became sufficient for the monetary contraction to have an overall economic impact.

The final kiss of death to the "good" monetary period in Central medieval France came in 1294–98 when, in preparation for war, King Philip IV, resorted to the *debasement* of royal money to meet his urgent income requirements. Debasement is a process in which the precious metal content of a coin is significantly reduced. By taking this expedient debasement road, and by doing so on a significant scale, Philip IV set into motion severe inflation and economic disaster.

In practical terms, these monetary changes of centralization and debasement resulted in a double economic hit—monetary contraction followed by inflation. With the abolition of the local currencies, there was now complete dependency on the official, centrally issued coinage. The debasement in the late 1290s resulted in massive inflation. Existing contracts or monetary agreements became, in effect, meaningless. A modern parallel would be the Great Depression of the 1930s, in which the money supply shrank, followed immediately by hyperinflation, as occurred in 1920s Germany and in 1970s Brazil.

The medieval economic crisis led to a general societal breakdown and decades of famine and death. The physical weakening of the population was sufficiently extensive to render conditions ripe for the plague to become one of the worst pandemics in all of history. The Late Middle Ages that followed were indeed dark.

As Guy Bois explains, "this depression would be a long one—it would last one and a half centuries; it would be painful to a degree that we still have difficulty imagining. No aspect of social life would be protected from this collapse."[27]

Although a small number of local currencies managed to survive until the 18th century, the medieval experiment with complementary currencies would not be repeated on such a scale. Complementary currencies never again reached the critical mass needed to significantly impact the standard of living of Western society.

### Twice and Thrice Upon A time

Support for the role played by the particular monetary framework in the realization of this golden age, as well as its demise, is offered by a nearly identical scenario found in another ancient civilization—Dynastic Egypt.

Egypt enjoyed one of the highest standards of living of the ancient world. Its economy afforded Egypt the capacity to be the first known civilization to offer assistance in the form of foreign aid to other societies. Like its medieval counterpart, Egypt had a dual monetary system, with long-distance currencies much like our own national currencies, together with demurrage-charged local currencies that enabled local exchanges among the working classes.

Unlike the Central Middle Ages, however, Egypt's economy and dual monetary system endured not hundreds but rather thousands of years. The end of ancient Egypt's golden age, like that of medieval Western Europe, coincided with the introduction of a currency system similar to today's national currencies, which was imposed on the Egyptians by the conquering Romans.

Another example of an unusual economy and monetary system that dates back to the medieval period, but which continues in part to this very day, is found in Bali. Though its monetary system has undergone changes in recent decades, Bali maintains at least some of the traits found in Central medieval Europe and Dynastic Egypt. The economies, monetary systems, and societal conditions of Bali, the Central Middle Ages and Dynastic Egpyt offer important insights about how we might improve conditions in our world today, and are the subject of further investigation in Part IV of this book.

## CLOSING THOUGHTS

The complementary currencies of the Central Middle Ages came and went without any awareness of their role in shaping the investment patterns that created a golden age. Yet, when local currencies disappeared, cathedral building also stopped. What changed? It wasn't people's faith: there is no evidence that Europeans were less devout in the 14th century than in the 12th.

In this light, the Central Middle Ages reveals two important characteristics of money: its value-nonneutrality and its potential for addressing large-scale social issues. It is only a millennium after the fact that are we beginning to understand how local currencies, particularly those using demurrage, induced long-term investment and cooperative behavior patterns that benefited both the local economy and the entire population, regardless of socioeconomic levels.

## CHAPTER SEVEN

# A Change of View

*We take a handful of sand*
*from the endless landscape of awareness around us*
*and call that handful of sand the world.*

~ROBERT PIRSIG

It is not simply that our banking and monetary systems are centuries old that makes them problematic. It is the fact that these two systems are the key replicators and propagators of a set of beliefs, perceptions, and objectives that do not accurately reflect many of the core values, realities, and requirements of society today.

The creation of these two influential systems was part of a massive wave of change that swept over Western European society during the 1700s, from secularization, democratization, and the creation of new nation-states, to commercialization, the rise of a middle class, and more. The Industrial Age and its socioeconomic order were accompanied by novel beliefs and perceptions regarding the world and humanity's place in the cosmic scheme of things. That emerging worldview— Modernism—has informed our ways of being and doing from centuries past until now.

Today, we are in the midst of another period of transformation, perhaps the most profound in human history. Our understandings, many collective beliefs, objectives and realities have shifted dramatically, particularly in recent decades. Yet, the same systems and institutions that helped shape society in the 1700s, continue to function in similar fashion to this day, and enforce ways and means that no longer accurately reflect present-day conditions.

There is an obvious need and a growing consensus from around the world for reform. But we must ask ourselves how this is to be pragmatically accomplished. How do we transform our systems and institutions to better reflect our core values and today's changing requirements?

We examine below how the conditions, objectives, and limited understandings of a former age coalesced into a single dominant worldview; how that set of perceptions influenced our economic tenets and practices; and the consequences upon our world of those systems born under the influence of Modernism.

We begin with a brief look at societal conditions in Western Europe following the demise of the Central Middle Ages, the reaction to which gave root to the modernist perspective.

## SEEDS OF CHANGE

The late medieval and premodern periods from the 1300s to 1600s involved dramatic reversals to the widespread economic prosperity and social progress enjoyed throughout much of Western Europe during the Central Middle Ages.

The economic downturn of the late 1200s led to centuries of extreme hardship for the masses and concentrated wealth for a privileged few, with little or no opportunity for upward mobility. With the rare exception of a small, developing urban middle class of burghers, the overwhelming majority of people were born into and remained trapped in poverty.[1] The late medieval status quo maintained its sociopolitical and religious repression through an authoritarian Church and titled upper class. This class system was supported by the prevailing belief of a universal order in which, just as the planets and sun rotated around the Earth, one's station in society's pecking order was fixed at birth and remained constant throughout one's life.[2] The underlying pretext for this social order was rooted in the old notion that man was "a stranger to himself, incapable of self-knowledge; thinking himself good and virtuous, but in reality full of pride and disordered loves."[3] In essence, the populace was deemed incapable of governing itself and, for its own worldly good and eternal salvation, must submit to religious authority and the supposedly divinely ordained rule of monarchy.

Mounting tensions and calls for religious and social reform eventually found support in the form of a new technology—the printing press. The Ninety-Five Theses of Martin Luther in 1517 and other works of dissent were disseminated in the vernacular of the masses and helped bring about the Protestant Reformation. Printing also led to the publication of new scientific journals. Inventors and researchers could now share findings and learn from one another as never before. This led to an epoch of unprecedented discovery—the Scientific Revolution.[4]

In 1543, Nicolaus Copernicus placed the Sun, not the Earth, at the center of the solar system. The works of Galileo, Johannes Kepler, Isaac Newton, and others followed. Of more lasting importance than any particular finding, however, was the establishment of a new, more reliable method of inquiry. The scholar Joseph Needham noted that, "during the Renaissance in the West, in the time of Galileo...the most effective method of discovery was itself discovered."[5]

For centuries, life's mysteries had been defined by the process of "Revealed Truth,"—presumed direct communication from the divine. The medieval world was widely perceived as "inhabited by angels and demons, spirits and souls, occult powers and mystical principles. Some medieval scientists spoke about the 'soul of a magnet' as easily as they spoke about its mass."[6] Scientific inquiry changed all that.

Investigation and the acquisition of knowledge could now be obtained through observable, empirical data, experimentation, and the testing of hypotheses. Conclusions were reproducible and often enjoyed precise mathematical backing. Kepler's findings on Mars' elliptical orbit, for instance, were accompanied by nine hundred pages of computations. Newton's laws of motion and universal gravitation were supported by another of his inventions—calculus.[7]

The implications were profound and extended far beyond physical principles and planetary motions. An exquisite order to the natural universe was being uncovered, not by revelation, but by scientific inquiry. Evident, as well, was the ability of people to think and reason far beyond medieval notions of humankind's prelapsarian fallen state.

Copernicus' heliocentric theory, for example, raised the seditious question: Could humanity's place in the great order of things also be mutable? Doubts mounted regarding the supposed infallibility and presumptive authority of the Church and nobility. Hope and confidence grew that critical thought could be applied to other domains, and to the formation of a more just society governed by and for the people.

Western society was at the dawn of a comprehensive transformation.

## The Advent of Modernism

New discoveries and abhorrence of past societal conditions contributed to sweeping changes in Western Europe with the Age of Enlightenment.[8] Pioneered by such intellectual leaders as John Locke, Voltaire, Jean-Jacques Rousseau, Adam Smith, Benjamin Franklin, and others, modern society emerged in a whirlwind of brilliant philosophy and a noble outpouring of revolutionary ideas. Its nascent worldview—Modernism— underscored a dedication to freedom, reason, critical thought, and a new sense of humanity's place in the universal order.

Ideas led to demands and, on occasion, rebellion. In 1688, England's Glorious Revolution curbed the power of the king, produced a Bill of Rights, and ushered in modern parliamentary democracy, making that country's government the first model of Enlightenment thought. Other independence movements and constitutional reforms followed in America, France, and elsewhere. To help insure against past abuses, measures such as the separation of church and state were constitutionally enshrined.

The emergence of this new age and social order was enabled by a new monetary system, and was accompanied by a new social science— economics—which provided a technical foundation and school of thought for money's dissemination.

## Monetary and Commercial Changes

Sociopolitical change was accompanied by historic banking, monetary, and economic reforms. As noted, the central banks of Sweden and England were formed in the 1600s.[9] Each bank obtained the exclusive right to create paper money as legal tender in exchange for its commitment to provide the funds required by sovereigns and governments. These measures brought about the institutionalization of the fiat-based, interest-bearing, bank-generated national currency system in use today. Though the immediate purpose of the structural monetary changes in both Sweden and England was to raise sufficient funds in preparation for war (against Denmark and France, respectively),[10] these reforms eventually enabled many of the changes that defined this age.

The new nation-states and the Industrial Revolution required enormous capital investments for improvements to infrastructure, including the construction of roads, canals, railways, large factories, and expanding urban centers. Increased trade and colonization by maritime nations also required large sums of money for shipbuilding and exploration.

To help stimulate private investment into these novel and often risky financial ventures, a new business entity was created—the joint-stock company—which "limited the liability of investors to the extent of their personal investment without endangering their other properties."[11] New commercial laws and civil arbitration facilities were established as well, to also help ensure investments and economic progress.

Another key monetary issue was standardization. Up until this period, a myriad of trading currencies were in use, including ducats, florin, noble, guinea, and grosh, but they lacked a standard of value. An essay in 1717 by Newton purportedly inspired the founding of the gold standard, which fixed a unit of account to a precise weight in gold.[12] Among its many advantages, the gold standard greatly facilitated international trade.

Economic matters were given extensive consideration during the Enlightenment. Its leaders were not just philosophers, but pragmatic businessmen who understood that ideals such as inalienable rights and the pursuit of happiness must include economic and financial reforms. Property rights, free trade, and enterprise were seen as vital interacting pieces in a holistic drive towards the liberalization and maturation of society. Voltaire said, "where there is not liberty of conscience, there is seldom liberty of trade, the same tyranny encroaching upon commerce as upon religion."[13] Adam Smith argued that with each individual and nation free to improve their own economic position, and with economic systems designed to encourage and utilize the best skills of all, everyone in society benefited.

Indisputable economic benefits were realized through industrialization. It provided greater assurance and regularity of wages in comparison to the erratic harvests, outright crop failures, and other vicissitudes of agrarian-based economies. Many new jobs, professions, and opportunities for upward mobility emerged that were previously unavailable. Economist

Alec Tsoucatos explains that prior to modernization, the principal means of enrichment "was through war, by plunder, inheriting it by death, or acquiring it through marriage. For the first time, money and wealth were now possible through work and enterprise."[14]

Economic progress was gradually accompanied by a host of social improvements. These included lower infant mortality, decreased death from starvation, eradication of some fatal diseases, universal primary education, the birth of the middle classes, and eventually, though accompanied by many struggles and sacrifice, more equal treatment of people from different backgrounds.[15]

Yet, for all the improvements it wrought, modernization and its accompanying worldview were laden with limitations. Many of today's critical issues can be traced back to the shift to this dominant intellectual framework, and to the fact that it was not only progressive but also reactionary. Modernism set its sights on the future while denying many important and valuable elements of our past. It would take centuries to realize that a more optimal approach to healthy transformation was possible, achieved not by a process of reaction and denial, but rather by inclusion, integration, and a deeper appreciation for the power and influence of systems.

## A Rational New World

Modernism was rooted in the determination to form a new society based on reason and the precision of 18th-century empirical science. It was also fashioned by a resolve to prevent a return to the conditions that had plagued former centuries. This resulted not just in many innovations, but in an extensive process of exclusion as well. Practically anything premodern or nonscientific in nature came to be considered primitive, antiquated, and inferior. "If something couldn't be measured, it was considered irrelevant."[16] Entire realms of human experience that did not lend themselves to modern analysis or quantification were partially or wholly discounted. Discounted as well were many time-tested customs and the notion that the past could contribute in any meaningful way to the formation of modern society. This precluded any insight into the role that complementary currencies played during the Central Middle Ages. There was, in fact, little if any common knowledge regarding the very existence of a medieval golden epoch.[17]

*"Are you just pissing and moaning, or can you verify what you're saying with data?"*

Similarly, the prevailing mindset of the time did not lend itself to inquiry into the functional dynamics of money, especially the notion that different types and particular features of money could induce specific behavior and investment patterns. Different types of money and their impact upon society were simply not taken into consideration. The principal focus vis à vis the new monetary system was that it be streamlined, efficient, and codified.

These exclusions point to one of the great ironies regarding Modernism. Though it developed in reaction to the narrow, rigid mindset of another age, the modernist worldview assumed its own insular monopoly of legitimacy in the interpretation of reality.

Modernism's new, supposedly rational understanding of the world was tainted by a skewed hyperrationality, referred to as the Technocratic Materialistic Mechanistic (TMM) model.[18]

Three of TMM's leading myths include:

o Modernism is the only legitimate approach to knowledge;

o Modernism is innately superior as it alone is capable of understanding and knowing everything;

o it is possible to be absolutely logical, rational, and objective.

It was in this reductionist, mechanistic milieu that a one-type-fits-all national currency system emerged, which, by design or happenstance, reflected the prevailing worldview of the period. It is also under the influence of this same mindset and its inherent limitations that the development of Traditional Economics—the set of ideas that has dominated economic thinking and practices—came into being, as discussed next.

## CLOSING THOUGHTS

Our present-day banking and monetary systems arose as part of a massive societal shift during the 1700s in Western Europe. The new banking and monetary paradigms that emerged during the Enlightenment enabled industrialization, nation-states, the emergence of a middle class, secularization, and commercialization. The new accompanying worldview was itself a reaction to the pre-scientific, religious mindset that preceded it. Though Modernism brought with it many benefits, it's new mode of inquiry rejected many of the beliefs and customs that preceded it. Ironically, by pursuing knowledge in this analytical manner, substantial pieces of human experience and history were ignored, including many valuable monetary insights and practices that benefitted society in the Central Middle Ages.

# CHAPTER EIGHT

# Economic Myopia

*Economics has never been a science.*

*And it is even less now than a few years ago.*

~PAUL A. SAMUELSON

Economics participated in a unique, profound way in the transformation of modern society. Like the current monetary system, economics was not only influenced by, but became a key replicator of, the modernist perspective and the quest for a society based on Enlightenment ideals.

Following the great scientific discoveries of Newton and others, efforts were made to transform economics into a science and strip it of the kinds of inquiries and concerns that it upheld previously as a field of applied moral philosophy. This was accomplished mainly through the fields' attempted integration with mathematics. From the Scientific Revolution onwards, mathematical language was increasingly used to describe an ever-growing range of natural phenomena. "Problems that have baffled humankind since the Greeks, from the motions of planets to the vibrations of violin strings, were suddenly mastered."[1] There was hope that, fueled by precise empirical data, economics could provide modern society with the same predictability and order as was found in physics.

At the time of its founding in the mid-1700s, however, economics was limited to algebra and a few numerical examples, nothing more. Advanced mathematics and economic theory did not converge until the latter half of the 1800s in conjunction with the concepts of supply, demand, balance, and the equilibrium theory.

## THE EQUILIBRIUM THEORY

From Smith's day to our own, economists have studied how the supply and demand for goods and services affect their price. Many economists argued that in a free, competitive marketplace, the quantity of goods demanded by consumers, and the amount supplied by producers, would come into balance with one another.

This concept of balance was of particular interest to late-19th century economist Léon Walras, who saw a parallel between equilibrium points in physics and balancing points in economic systems. He asserted that given the available resources, participants in a free and fair market economy trade their way to a state of equilibrium—a natural resting point where supply equals demand, resources are allocated to their most efficient use, and the welfare of society is optimized. Walras also believed that this equilibrium point could be mathematically computed.

Using sophisticated, physics-based differential equations, Walras immortalized the equilibrium theory in his magnum opus, *Elements of Pure Economics* (1874). This work became foundational to the ideas and mathematical direction that have dominated traditional economic theory for more than a century. Unfortunately, the math and many of the assumptions used to formulate the equilibrium theory were fundamentally flawed.

The equations derived entirely from the First Law of Thermodynamics (Conservation). This law states that energy can be converted from one form to another, but it is neither created nor destroyed. This first law is, however, only one part of the thermodynamic story.

Entirely missing from Walras's formulation was the Second Law of Thermodynamics, which states that entropy—a measure of disorder in a system—is always increasing. Over time, all structures and patterns break down and decay. "Cars rust, buildings crumble, mountains erode, apples rot and cream poured into coffee dissipates until it is evenly mixed."[2]

Entropy is inevitable in systems that are self-contained, at rest, and in equilibrium, that is, closed. But we now know that the economy is anything but in equilibrium, at rest, or closed. It evolves, adjusts, expands, contracts, and is inextricably linked to a changing environment, absorbing massive amounts of energy from outside the system (such as solar, mineral, human, and animal inputs) and emitting equally massive byproducts into the universe (such as gases, waste, and pollution). The economy actually has little in common with mechanical models found in Newtonian physics. The economy instead exhibits many traits and emergent properties common to complex, adaptive, open systems found in nature and the biological sciences.

Additionally, to ensure that his mathematical theories worked, Walras made use of impractical idealized assumptions. These included perfectly functioning free markets, perfectly efficient corporations, brilliant players who knew everything taking place in the markets, and more. In reality, however, corporations, shareholders, and many others who constitute the marketplace and economy are, at best, interacting in a complex, imperfect, ever changing, dynamic world.

In his book, *The Origin of Wealth: Evolution, Complexity, and the Radical Remaking of Economics* (2006), Eric Beinhocker details many of the inherent misconceptions in the equilibrium theory and in Traditional Economics—the economics found "in university textbooks, discussed in the news media and referred to in the halls of business and government."[3]

Among the many important consequences of the misclassification of economics and the exclusive use of the First Law of Thermodyamics was the assumption that new wealth, like energy, is neither created nor destroyed. Rather, "the world begins with a finite set of commodities that are allocated among users."[4] Citing Philip Mirowsku of Notre Dame, Beinhocker writes that, "in general equilibrium models, the economy can't create new wealth any more than a lump of coal can reproduce."[5]

With respect to Walras's implausible assumptions, Beinhocker cites Axel Leijonhufvud, an economist at the University of California, Los Angeles, who comments that, "[Traditional Economics] models incredibly smart people in unbelievably simple situations while the real world is in fact more accurately described as 'believably simple people [coping] with incredibly complex situations.'"[6]

Walras, like his contemporaries, was driven by noble intentions—to imbue economics with mathematical certitude and to provide society with a field of science to ensure order, stability, and predictability in the marketplace. But these lofty ends were never realized. The misclassifications and reductions inherent in the general equilibrium theory instead, "acted as a straightjacket, forcing economists to make highly unrealistic assumptions and limiting the field's empirical success," leading Beinhocker to conclude that, "Walras' willingness to make tradeoffs in realism for the sake of mathematical predictability would set a pattern followed by economists over the next century."[7]

The same pattern of reductions found in the general equilibrium theory and in traditional conomics would also come to inform our systems of national accounts.

## THE GNP, GDP, AND THE FLOW OF MONEY

The crash of 1929 and the depression that followed forced economists and nations to question their assumptions about how the economy actually worked. In 1932, the U.S. government hired a young economist and statistician to develop a set of measures on which to base a new national accounting scheme. Simon Kuznets created the Gross National Product (GNP).

The GNP computed the value of goods and services produced by businesses and citizens, both at home and abroad. Though more comprehensive and sophisticated than any previous accounting system, its underlying assumptions reflected the same type of reductionist thinking as that found in the general equilibrium theory.

The GNP assumes that all economic activity can be measured simply and accurately by price and value, and thus by the flow of money. Accordingly, the lone criterion used by the GNP to indicate the economic wellbeing of nations is the use of money. In 1991, the GNP was replaced by the Gross Domestic Product (GDP), which modified slightly who is included in the metrics, but not what it measures—monetized transactions.[8]

According to the rationale of the GDP, each and every monetary transaction is considered a gain, while any exchange of a good or service that does not involve the direct use of money is disregarded. Barter exchanges, for example, are not tracked. Nor are domestic care and volunteer work taken into account. Yet, the same work performed by someone paid in dollars (or any other national currency) is measurable and, therefore, does count. It has been estimated, for instance, that if parents were paid for all the services rendered in raising a child, they would bring in $134,000 a year.[9] This figure compares with average annual earnings of $52,000 by a registered nurse and $34,000 by a firefighter.[10] The dramatic difference in wages is not due to higher pay per hour for parents, but to the extra hours of work they put in.

The consequences of not taking into account nonmonetary activities are unfortunate and significant. Many such exchanges are critically vital to the social fabric of society and comprise a significant portion of overall economic activity in communities and nations. Yet, they remain invisible to conventional economics because no money changes hands.

The decline of a nonmarket economy, such as the social breakdown of a family or community, is a negative prospect for society. Yet, from a strictly monetized economic perspective, it is not measured and therefore has no value. If the breakdown gets to the point where paid intervention is needed, however, the *costs* of social decay are then registered as *profit*.

As economists Clifford Cobb, Ted Halstead, and Jonathan Rowe have pointed out, "the GDP not only masks the breakdown of the social structure and the natural habitat upon which the economy—and life itself—ultimately depend; worse, it actually portrays such breakdown as economic gain."[11]

Costs associated with psychological counseling, social work, and addiction treatment, which arise from the neglect of the nonmarket realm, are tallied as economic gains. Crime adds billions to the GDP due to the need for prison buildings, increased police protection, and repair of property damage. Similarly, the depletion of our natural resources, the clean up and medical treatments associated with industry's toxic byproducts, the costs of ecological disasters such as the Exxon Valdez and recent British Petroleum oil spills, the terrorist attacks of 9/11, relief efforts following Hurricane Katrina, the devastation caused by wars, and the hundreds of billions of dollars allocated in emergency stimulus packages—all register as improvements to a nation's economy by the curious standards of the GDP.

Economists and politicians alike have long been aware of the shortcomings in our economic accounting systems. Criticism can be traced back to the 1930s, and to the GNP's principal architect, Simon Kuznets, who cautioned that, "the welfare of a nation can scarcely be inferred from a measure of national income. If the GNP is up, why is America down? Distinctions must be kept in mind between quantity and quality of growth, between costs and returns, and between the short and long run."[12]

Seven decades later, critical analysis continues. Former World Bank economist Herman Daly put it this way: "the current national accounting system treats the Earth as a business in liquidation."[13] Many others have echoed similar sentiments (see insert).

### Robert F. Kennedy and the GNP

The following critique of the GNP was given by Robert F. Kennedy at a Friends of the Earth rally in 1963. It was reechoed in large part by the Senator in one of his last speeches in March 1968.

"The Gross National Product includes air pollution and advertising for cigarettes, and ambulances to clear our highways of carnage. It counts special locks for our doors, and jails for the people who break them. GNP includes the destruction of the redwoods and the death of Lake Superior. It grows with the production of napalm and nuclear warheads...and if GNP includes all this, there is much it does not comprehend.

"It does not allow for the health of our families, the quality of their education, or the joy of their play. It is indifferent to the decency of our factories and the safety of our streets alike. It does not include the beauty of our poetry or the strength of our marriages, or the intelligence of our public debate or the integrity of our public officials...GNP measures neither our wit nor our courage, neither our wisdom nor our learning, neither our compassion nor our devotion to our country. It measures everything, in short, except that which makes life worthwhile."[14]

Despite the obvious limitations of our accounting schemes, and the availability of more relevant measurement tools such as the *Calvert-Henderson Quality of Life Indicators*,[15] the GDP endures. So too do the questionable practices it helps legitimize by means of their portrayal as gains to the nation. This same accounting scheme has now been adopted worldwide, with predictable results. Indonesia, for example, has been a huge success story since the 1970s according to the standards of the GDP. "But it achieved this status by clearcutting its forests, exhausting its soil, and selling off precious nonrenewable mineral wealth. In short, it sold off its future to pay for accounting measures of success."[16]

According to Clifford Cobb, Ted Halstead, and Jonathan Rowe, the GDP endures because, "[it] serves deep institutional cravings, combining the appearance of empirical certitude and expert authority with a readymade story line."[17] That story line, that money activity and concomitant economic growth result in happiness and security "is so entrenched that it now defines our consumer driven Western society."[18]

*"Tell me the fairytale about the economy."*

The GDP's continued use is explained further by the fact that, given the confines of the mindset from which it emanated, the national accounting scheme appears to make sense; that is to say, it accurately reflects the rationale and entrenched reductionist strains from which it and our economic and monetary paradigms emanated. When, for example, economists refer to "the economy" or to "the market," they often intend only that portion of the economy or market that is readily measureable, not the entire economy. It is only when economic thought is linked up to real world outcomes and the whole economy that the flaws in our thinking and practices become obvious.

It was under the influence of this same industrial-age mindset that our monetary system and economic tenets took root. But given what is currently taking place, and what is now needed, it is high time to review and amend our modern beliefs, tenets, and systems with the same strength, conviction, and purpose as Enlightenment leaders did with premodern European society.

## CLOSING THOUGHTS

The general equilibrium theory and the GDP are emblematic of a mindset that, with all good intentions, sought to make perfect sense of a world by taking into account only limited, readily quantifiable aspects of our lives and activities. The tradeoffs and omissions that were made in the quest for mathematical certitude and economic predictability, however, contributed instead to limited understandings and many unintended, often costly consequences.

The same externalities that were excluded from traditional considerations constitute many of the very practices and issues that now threaten the environment and society. Additionally, the solutions that are required to address our concerns and bring about improvements are simply not to be found within the confines of traditional economic thought and its limited set of tools. It is only by broadening our understanding and by venturing outside, that solutions become both apparent and available.

# CHAPTER NINE

# Lessons from a Depression

*A man is wise with the wisdom of his time only,*

*And ignorant with its ignorance.*

~HENRY DAVID THOREAU

In 2008, the world economy went belly-up. Tens of millions of jobs and trillions of dollars of wealth were lost. Few analysts saw the crisis coming. Preceding the recession, many economists were instead congratulating themselves over the success of their field. Nobel laureate Robert Lucas, for instance, declared in his 2003 presidential address to the American Economic Association that, "[the] central problem of depression-prevention had been solved."[1] Lucas was not alone in his assessment. Nobel laureate, Paul Krugman, notes that leading up to the downturn, many economists were "blind to the very possibility of a catastrophic failure in a market economy."[2]

A few short years following the most severe downturn in seven decades, and the predictive failure by the overwhelming majority of experts, confusion about the economy abounds. As occurred in the early stages of the Great Depression, each hint of economic improvement is hailed by governments, banks, and regulators as evidence of the "end of the crisis." Such pronouncements, however, now as in the past, are influenced by the apprehension that saying otherwise would only aggravate the situation. As *The Economist* noted in its lead story on October 11, 2008: "Confidence is everything in finance."[3]

But confidence in today's supposed economic recovery is not shared by all. At least some of the countless millions of recent additions to the ranks of under- or unemployed, who continue to struggle to find jobs, are not likely to feel so optimistically inclined. They are joined by other concerned citizens from around the world, and by a small but growing assembly of noted economists, including Krugman, who, by mid-2010 stated on record that we are "in the early stages of a new depression."[4] Supposed signs of recovery are instead seen by at least some experts as misleading and transitory, reminiscent of what occurred during the 1930s.

History shows that periodic economic surges did occur in the early 1930s, but were short-lived. It was not until years after the 1929 stock market crash that a depression was understood and acknowledged to be taking place. Policymakers, Wall Street giants, economists, investors and many others back then had failed to appreciate what was unfolding and misinterpreted each fleeting advance as the hoped-for turnaround of the markets. But hope proved no match for faulty assumptions about how the economy actually works, or the failures in policy that derived from such notions. The Great Depression would persist for a decade and degenerate into the most catastrophic bust in modern history. In a number of disconcerting ways, history is now repeating itself.

In the above-cited 2008 article regarding the downturn, *The Economist* went on to say that, "with a flawed diagnosis of the causes of the crisis, it is hardly surprising that many policymakers have failed to understand its progression."[5] This is indeed the case, although in a more profound way than is generally appreciated.

A lot of energy and ink has been spent trying to allocate the blame for the recent disaster. Greed in the financial sector, lack of oversight by regulators, policies that over-emphasize deregulation, and incompetence at various levels, have all been cited. Any or all of these may have played a role, but at the core we are dealing with a much deeper systemic issue related to our monetary paradigm.

While the global recession is the biggest one since the 1930s, it isn't the first such crisis. Economic troubles are, in fact, all too common. The World Bank has identified no less than 96 banking and 176 monetary crises in one 25-year-period alone, beginning with the floating exchange regime introduced by President Nixon in the early 1970s. Additionally, long before this period, banking and monetary crises were, in the words of historical economist Charles Kindleberger "hardly perennial."[6] Kindleberger inventoried no less than 48 massive crashes between the 1637 tulip mania in Holland and the stock market crash of 1929. According to the U.S. National Bureau of Economic Research, 47 recessions have befallen the United States alone since 1790, a dozen of which occurred in the decades following the Great Depression.

These repeated breakdowns in different countries and times, under different regulatory environments, and in economies with very different degrees of development can be seen as telltale symptoms of an underlying systemic, structural problem.

If such a deeper systemic issue is in fact involved, it would explain why each new set of regulations achieves, at best, a reduction in the frequency of banking and monetary crises, without getting rid of them or their horrific socioeconomic and political costs. A deeper structural problem would also explain why even some of the brightest and best educated people on the planet have not been able to avoid major financial catastrophes, however diligently they do their work, whether on the regulatory or on the financial services side. Finally, if our monetary system is actually a structural accident waiting to happen, then even if it were possible to perfectly control greed through innovative and tight regulations, such measures would only defer when the next disaster will hit.

Until and unless there is review and amendment regarding these critical matters, we cannot expect an end to ongoing and costly financial disruptions, or realistically hope for lasting improvements to our economies.

In support of our claims regarding the monetary paradigm and the relief that is possible with new initiatives, we offer the following all-but-forgotten accounts regarding the role of complementary currencies during the difficult Depression years in Europe and the United States.

## COMPLEMENTARY CURRENCIES AND WORLD WAR II

Scores of complementary currencies were in operation during the 1920s and 1930s, and included initiatives from Germany, Austria, France, Italy, the Netherlands, Sweden, the Baltics, Canada, Mexico, China, the United States, and other nations from around the world. Many programs were undertaken in response to the dramatic conditions of the period, with the inability of communities large and small to meet their socioeconomic needs. Two popular initiatives in Germany and Austria, and the U.S. response to complementary currencies in the leadup to World War II, are explored next.

## German Hyperinflation and the Wära System

The German economy and its currency had been in trouble for years prior to the depression. In 1913, prior to the outbreak of World War I, one U.S. dollar was worth 4.2 German marks.[7] By the time Germany's inflation peaked a decade later in November 1923, the exchange rate for one dollar reached an untenable 4.2 trillion marks. A postage stamp cost billions and a loaf of bread required a wheelbarrow full of money. Almost one hundred million trillion German marks were then in circulation.[8] Daily salary negotiations preceded work, wages were paid twice per day, and earnings were typically spent within the hour.

Sparked by these desperate conditions, people looked for alternative means to meet their needs. This led to growing interest in complementary currencies, which was inspired in large part by the teachings of Silvio Gesell, a merchant-turned-social activist and economist. Gesell founded the principles of modern demurrage and advocated its use as a means to help ensure money's circulation (see insert).

### Silvio Gesell, Demurrage, and the Wära

Much of the credit for the understanding and use of demurrage in the 20th century is attributed to Silvio Gesell, who provided a modern theoretical framework for this practice.

Gesell's interest in economics and money derived from his own personal experience with downturns. In 1887, he moved from Europe to Buenos Aires where he went to work in his brother's business. But a depression in Argentina hurt the enterprise and led him to reflect upon the structural problems caused by the monetary system. In 1891, Gesell released his first writing on this topic: *The Reformation Of The Monetary System As A Bridge To A Just State*, followed by *Nervus Rerum* and *The Nationalization Of Money*. He returned to Europe in 1892, where he studied economics and worked for decades on monetary reform.

Gesell's ideas regarding demurrage derived from railroad and shipping vessel practices. The quicker a freight train or cargo ship could be unloaded and reloaded, the greater its earning power. To encourage quicker turn-arounds, a charge was levied for the time the train or vessel remained unused, beyond an allotted time for unpacking. The term coined for this purpose was demurrage (from the French verb, *demeurer*, to delay).

An organization based on Gesell's teachings was formed in Germany in 1929. Its name was the Wära ("VAIR-a") Tauschgesellschaft (or Wära Trading Company).[9] The founders coined the term "Wära," which is a combination of the German words "Ware" (goods) and "Währung" (currency). The aim of the Wära Trading Company was to "fight stagnation of the market and unemployment."[10] It issued a currency—the Wära bill—which had a small monthly demurrage charge in the form of a stamp fee to ensure that the currency would circulate and not be hoarded.

The Wära stamp scrip (a currency with a stamp fee) drew international attention after its success in the German community of Schwanenkirchen.

Up until hyperinflation, the largest employer and economic mainstay of Schwanenkirchen had been the local coalmine. But like many other businesses in Germany during the 1920s, it was forced to file for bankruptcy. Operations were shut down and the coalmine went on sale for 8,000 reichsmarks, far below its estimated value.

One former production engineer wanted to purchase the mine, but could not get a bank loan. Max Hebecker instead decided to apply the concept of the Gesell-inspired Wära stamp. Hebecker gathered the miners, local shopkeepers, and others that would be affected by the new local currency. He explained to all that the coalmine could be reopened, but only if each were willing to accept payment in Wära scrip in replacement of the virtually worthless national currency. The coal inventory extracted from the mine would provide the backing for the scrip. Following a lively exchange, all parties finally agreed.

The decision to accept the complementary currency turned out to be economically very sound. During a time when many other businesses and communities in Germany were struggling to survive, the Wära not only saved the coalmine and revitalized the local economy, but also began to circulate nationally. Over 2,000 businesses throughout Germany soon accepted and paid one another with Wära scrip. Many banks even opened Wära accounts. The Wära's great success, however, also turned out to be its demise.

*Figure 9.1 - Wära Stamp Scrip, front and back*

Germany's central bank, the Reichsbank, grew concerned over the popularity of the Wära and other local currencies then in circulation. The relief to businesses during the difficult downturn, and the longer-term potential benefits provided by these complementary currencies to the national economy (and to the banking system itself), were outweighed by their perceived threats to the hegemony in the issuance of money by the central bank. Consequently, in October 1931, through legislative action, the Wära and other complementary currencies were declared illegal in Germany.[11]

Two years following the banishment of complementary currencies, as the economy continued to plummet, a dramatic shift took hold of the German political landscape.

*Rise of the Nazi Party*

The repression of complementary currencies, together with other anti-inflationary decisions by the Reichsbank, led to a sharp decline in the German money supply.[12] This loss of liquidity resulted in the shut down of the Schwanenkirchen mine and hundreds of other businesses. This resulted in soaring unemployment.

Given that the reigning monetary monopoly made it increasingly more difficult for people to help themselves on a local level, advocates of centralized solutions gained appeal. In the beer halls of Bavaria, an obscure Austrian immigrant began drawing audiences to his fiery speeches, with promises of a return to jobs and glory. His name was Adolph Hitler.

Some may consider the simultaneous ban of complementary currencies, deterioration of economic conditions, and the rise of radical authoritarian political ideology as unrelated coincidental occurrences isolated to Germany. It should be noted, however, that a nearly identical set of circumstances was taking hold concurrently in neighboring Austria.

## Austria and the Wörgl

When Michael Untergugenberger was elected mayor of Wörgl, Austria, he faced high unemployment and a near-penniless constituency. He had a long list of projects he wished to accomplish, along with many willing and able people to do the work. But only 40,000 shillings remained in the bank...just enough to pay the salaries of about 20 people for one month, a pittance compared to the cost of what was needed.

Rather than spend the last of the limited funds on a long list of projects, the mayor instead put the limited money supply on deposit with a local bank as a guarantee for 40,000 shillings' worth of Wörgl's own complementary "labor certificates," officially termed Banknotenausweis, which soon came to be referred to simply as the Wörgl ("VUR-gul"). Like the German Wära, the Wörgl was a stamp scrip that included a "relief tax," which was actually a demurrage charge applied through a stamp affixed each month at 1 percent of face value. As with other demurrage charges, this relief tax acted as an incentive to keep the currency in circulation. Those paid in Wörgl made sure to spend it quickly. The extra money in circulation led to additional employment opportunities in the community.

The Austrian Wörgl, like the German Wära, was a dramatic success. Wörgl quickly became the only town in Austria with full employment. This was made possible through the rapid circulation of the local stamp scrip, which was estimated to have created eight times more employment than national shillings would have. The demurrage-charged, anti-hoarding feature proved particularly effective as a spontaneous work-generating device.

Swiss essayist Alex von Muralt, who investigated the Wörgl at the time, reported the mayor's delighted comments that, "taxes were eagerly paid...in a number of instances in advance."[17] Following his investigation, Von Muralt concluded:

*Figure 9.2 - Wörgl Stamp Scrip, front side*

This eagerness to pay taxes may be, in my opinion, simply owing to the fact that the businessman who finds at the close of the month that he holds a considerable amount in relief money [Wörgl], can dispose of it with the greatest ease and without loss by meeting his parish [local tax] obligations. A change of attitude has manifestly taken place. If formerly the paying of taxes was deferred to the last, now it occupies first place.[18]

Word of the Wörgl's success soon spread. More than 200 other towns and villages in Austria wanted to adopt this complementary currency system to address their own economic concerns. The French Prime Minister, Edouard Dalladier, made a special visit to see first-hand "the miracle of Wörgl."

It was at that point that the Austrian central bank reacted. Like its German counterpart, the central bank decided to assert its monopoly rights, making it a criminal offense to issue the currency. The complementary currency was banned and in a very short span of time following, the town of Wörgl returned to 30 percent unemployment. Predictably, as in neighboring Germany, Austria's economy continued to decline.

During the Anschluss of 1938—the occupation and annexation of Austria into Nazi Germany—many Austrians openly welcomed Adolph Hitler as their economic and political savior.

**America's Fateful Decision**

The success of the Wörgl soon caught the attention of U.S. policy makers, who were then struggling with the Great Depression and massive unemployment. Conversations ensued between Yale professor and noted economist Irving Fisher, Harvard economics professor Russell Sprague, and Undersecretary of the Treasury, Dean Acheson. Each became convinced that the Wörgl model offered a clear and prompt way out of the Depression. Fisher stated for the record: "The correct application of stamp scrip would solve the Depression crisis in the United States in three weeks!"[19]

The three men met with President Roosevelt, in which a Wörgl-type scrip was recommended. Fisher reported that though Roosevelt was himself impressed, the final decision regarding complementary currencies was left to advisors who instead favored a series of new centralized programs for which political credit could be more easily claimed. These new programs included the expansion of the Reconstruction Finance Corporation and large-scale work-creation projects managed by the Federal government, all part of what would eventually become popularly known as "The New Deal."

The "emergency currencies," the code name given for complementary currencies, were banned by executive decree. This ban applied to any and all such currencies then in existence and any that might be proposed. No official reason was given for the ban. The end result, however, was that the United States failed to take advantage of such monetary innovations to address the economic crisis of the 1930s.

Contrary to popular belief, the centralized initiatives taken by the Roosevelt administration did not actually pull the United States out of the Great Depression. Certainly, the public works programs that were enacted did provide employment opportunities to many and built vast, vital public infrastructure. But most economic historians today agree that the U.S. economic recovery was due mainly to the war effort. Roosevelt himself declared this to be the case, stating that, "it was Dr. Win-the-War, not Dr. New Deal, that ended the Depression!"[20]

It bears noting that the disregard of such a solution by the United States is ironic, especially given the particular history and struggles of this nation regarding monetary matters. Complementary currencies were in widespread use in the American colonies prior to its struggle for independence from Great Britain. "Colonial scrip," the term given to these currencies, was issued in each of the thirteen colonies, beginning with Massachusetts in 1669 and ending with Virginia in 1755. The suppression of this scrip with the Currency Act of 1764 by the English Parliament was cited as one of the major grievances that led to the American Revolution.[21]

## Social and Political Lessons

What may initially appear to be boring technical decisions related to banking and currency matters are found to hold profound social and political implications. It cannot be irrefutably proven that Hitler would not have been elected, or that Anschluss and World War II would have been avoided, had complementary currencies such as the Wära and the Wörgl been allowed to flourish. Many other variables certainly impacted as well upon such sweeping phenomena. Nonetheless, historical records do show that the suppression of these popular grassroots initiatives had a significant negative impact on employment and the economy in both Germany and Austria. It is also clearly evident that deteriorating economic conditions contributed directly to the degeneration of these two democracies into ruthless dictatorships that went on to embroil the world in conflict.

Monetary crises invariably provoke fear, despair, and anger. This is an explosive social mix that reckless demagogues can and do exploit, even today. What started as a monetary problem in the former Yugoslavia, for example, was aggravated by the IMF readjustment program, and degenerated into intolerance toward "others." Minorities were used as scapegoats by ethnic leaders to redirect anger away from themselves and toward a common enemy, providing the sociopolitical context for extreme nationalist leaders such as Milosevic in Serbia to reassert their power. Within days of the 1998 monetary crisis in Indonesia, mobs were incited to violence against Chinese and other minorities. Similarly, in Russia, discrimination against minorities was aggravated by the financial collapse of the 1990s.

Just months prior to such economic disturbances, few among the intelligentsia in these countries had imagined the possibility of such dramatic social turmoil. Yet, particular monetary decisions dramatically impacted the economies and sociopolitical framework of their societies.

It is often forgotten that until the monetary collapse of the 1920s and the takeover by the Nazis, Germany was among the most advanced, educated, and cultured nations on Earth. Outlawing their local currencies likely contributed to the tragic events of that period.

Monetary issues are often painted in purely technical terms, supposedly to be left for so-called experts to resolve. But, as has been amply demonstrated down through history, monetary and financial concerns are a most explosive powder keg with potentially formidable social and political consequences. Given its impact upon each of us and the whole of society, money matters require as much understanding and awareness as is possible by one and all.

## CLOSING THOUGHTS

A seemingly endless series of financial crises have plagued the world's financial system for centuries. The fact that these crises recur in all kinds of economies and nations on a continuing basis, points to a systemic root issue.

Highly successful complementary currency initiatives in the years preceding WWII offer us important lessons. The Wära and Wörgl each produced nearly miraculous results in turning around the local economies at a time when the national economies were in dramatic decline. In America, similar complementary currency programs were advocated on a national basis to deal with the ongoing depression. Eminent economist Irving Fisher estimated that such measures would bring about the end of the contraction in a matter of weeks. But President Roosevelt instead opted for the New Deal and America languished economically until WWII.

Economic concerns have important social implications. The lessons of Germany, Austria, and many other nations serve as important historical reminders for us all. Money matters are intrinsically linked to many important societal concerns.

# CHAPTER TEN

# The Blind Spot

*The real voyage of discovery*

*consists not in seeking new landscapes,*

*But in having new eyes.*

~MARCEL PROUST

The human eye has a biological blind spot, a place in the visual field of the retina through which the optic nerve passes, where we literally can't see anything. Traditional economics has a collective blind spot as well regarding one of the most coveted and influential of all human creations—money. This blindness is directly linked to many of our most vital concerns.

Some of the many consequences of this collective blind spot are briefly examined below, along with a few of the mechanisms for this condition's existence and continuance. We begin with a look at how our lack of understanding regarding money impacts the enduring divide regarding intervention in the marketplace.

## ECONOMIC DOCTRINE AND MONEY

One of the many profound effects of the Great Depression was the specter of doubt it cast upon the predominant classical notion that an economy functions best when left to its own devices. Neoliberal free market orthodoxy has long maintained that public intervention into the private marketplace is misguided and unnecessary because intrinsic market forces can and will self-correct any disruptions such as the periodic ups and downs of the economy, especially over the long run. This perspective dominated economic thought prior to the 1930s.

A rare dissenter to such free market notions was the celebrated depression-era economist John Maynard Keynes. The job losses and prolonged suffering of the period prompted Keynes' famous quip: "The long run is a misleading guide to current affairs. In the long run we are all dead."[1]

It bears recalling that the drastic decline of the world economy during the 1930s persisted for the better part of a decade in many countries, and finally came to an end only due to a world war. In stark contrast to free market beliefs, the revolutionary idea of Keynes was that in the event of a significant market disruption, timely and sufficient intervention was mandated to restore the economy. He further argued that the only entity with the capacity to intercede in a sufficient manner was government.

A bit of review, however, reveals how our collective blindness with regard to money calls into question key underlying assumptions on both sides of this long-standing economic divide between neoliberal non-interventionists, and neo-Keynesian interventionists.

With regard to free market theory, a marketplace that is restrained by a monopoly in the issuance of money, with the predominance of one type of bank-debt money, should be considered *anything but free*. Our centuries-old monetary and banking paradigms continually reinforce a circumscribed set of industrial-age values and a narrow range of predictable outcomes, including: widespread scarcity, the concentration of wealth, short-term investment patterns, the amplification of the business cycle, and the resultant lack of not only meaningful work but sufficient job opportunities of any kind. Moreover, and again contrary to commonly-held notions of free markets, today's globalized economic reality demands increasing conformity by virtually all its many participants, no matter their particular and oftentimes diverse socioeconomic requirements or aspirations. In essence, our monetary state of affairs not only pre-empts the possibility of a genuinely free market, but instead mandates strict compliance and the continued intervention by central banks and government to try and restore stability to an inherently unstable system. Free market doctrine in fact endorses a free market for virtually everything *except the structure of the monetary system itself*, and instead accepts the monopoly of bank-debt-based money as an economic fact of life.

The same blind spot regarding money also undermines Keynesian-type interventions into the marketplace. It has been argued, for instance, that the emergency measures undertaken by the Bush and Obama administrations, with the Troubled Assets Relief Program (TARP) and historic stimulus packages were necessary to prop up the banks and avert a general economic meltdown. But to what end? The influx of trillions of dollars to the banks and other financial giants has not significantly impeded any of the high-risk activities by Wall Street that contributed to the most recent crash. Nor have these interventions resulted in notable job creation or increased liquidity to Main Street, several years later. These packages have instead diverted already-scarce public funds from other important socioeconomic concerns. Additionally, this allocation of taxpayers' money, by definition, comes in the form of interest bearing, bank-debt currency, which was borrowed by government—and at a time when deficit spending was already dangerously high. The obligation to repay these loans with interest only serves to further aggravate the already-heavy burdens on the current population, and is likely to adversely affect future generations of taxpayers as well.

With regard to repayment liabilities, it should be noted that whenever a bank deemed "too big to fail" gets in real trouble, the recipe has been the same since the 1930s: the taxpayers end up footing the bill, thus allowing these banks to start all over again.

For each of the 97 major banking crashes around the world in recent decades, taxpayer bailouts have been the answer in every instance. The U.S. Reconstruction Finance Corporation from 1932-53, for example, was funded by government by way of taxpayer money. The U.S. government repeated the exercise from 1989-95 with the Resolution Trust Corporation for the Savings and Loan crisis, and once again with TARP in 2008. Other recent examples include the Swedish Bank Support Authority from 1992-96, and the Japanese Resolution and Collection Corporation, still ongoing, which started in 1996. During the 2008 crisis, among the first institutions "saved" in this manner were Bear Stearns in the United States and Northern Rock in the United Kingdom. Likewise, in October 2008, European governments pledged an unprecedented 1.873 trillion euros, combining credit guarantees and capital injections into banks, all by means of taxpayer money.

In essence, having overlooked the structure of the monetary system itself, each side of the economic chasm unwittingly contributes to outcomes that are inconsistent with its own cherished ideals and stated objectives. Supposedly free markets wind up requiring burdensome and expensive intervention. Keynesian-type deficit measures instead leave in their wake massive debt, oppressing taxpayers and society. Our collective blind spot renders traditional economics incapable of addressing the deeper systemic issues that contribute to our many repeated financial and economic crises.

How did this blindness come to be, and why does it persist?

## Collective Conditioning

Our modern monetary and banking paradigms were not arbitrary designs that merely came into being without context. These systems are, as previously mentioned, reflections of a set of perceptions, beliefs, values,

THE BLIND SPOT   [99

and objectives that emerged in Western Europe with the Enlightenment and the industrialization model that followed, and which, centuries later, continues to spread around the world. The particular competitive, hierarchical, and wealth-concentrating orientations of these systems, however, are not exclusive to our modern age, but can be seen as well in the monetary systems and the cultures of civilizations down through the ages, including ancient Sumer, Babylon, Greece, Rome, and Western society from the Renaissance all the way up to today.

Each of the aforementioned societies had in common a patriarchal emphasis accompanied by a monopoly of a single currency. That currency was imposed from the top down, was hierarchically issued, was either naturally scarce or maintained such scarcity artificially, and carried positive interest rates. The particular forms of these currencies varied widely, from standardized commodities and precious metals to pieces of paper and electronic bits. But each society held in common the crucial agreement that only their one specific currency could be used for payment of taxes, that this currency could be stored and accumulated, and that borrowing of the currency required payment of interest.

It bears noting that even societies and economies with very different ideologies, such as communism and capitalism, nonetheless share at least one trait in common—they all impose a monopoly of bank-debt money. The one main difference between the two ideologies with regard to their monetary and banking paradigms is that the banks in communist countries are state owned, while the banks in capitalist nations are privately held, with the occasional exception occurring during bank-related crises when governments must step in, as occurred with the downturn of 2008. While the ideological warfare between capitalism and communism has placed considerable emphasis on the myriad ways in which the two systems differ, their nearly identical monetary paradigm has been almost totally overlooked. This oversight is yet another expression of our long-standing, collective monetary blind spot.

Down through history, societies that instead tended toward a *matrifocal* orientation—whereby feminine values are honored as well, with a greater balance between feminine and masculine perspectives— were more inclined to make use of very different monetary structures.

Several prominent matrifocal civilizations are known to have embraced a dual-currency system instead of a monoculture of one type of money. The first currency was used for trading long distance with foreigners, and was very similar to those used by more patriarchal societies. The second type of currency was, however, quite different, as it was mainly exchanged within and created by the local community, was issued in sufficiency, and didn't bear interest. In the more sophisticated cases, this local currency even had a demurrage fee that, as mentioned, systematically discouraged accumulation, and instead promoted ongoing circulation of this currency as a pure medium of exchange, and not as a store of value. This was the case, for instance, with the wheat-backed currencies used for more than a millennium in Dynastic Egypt during the time of the Pharaohs, and was one of the secrets of that ancient society's remarkable wealth. Another example, as noted, is the Central Middle Ages in Western Europe, whereby various local currencies contributed substantially to the remarkable collective wealth and wellbeing of the period. The link between the money and cultural values of these societies are examined in greater depth in Part IV of this book.

## Institutionalized Status Quo

Sometime during the 18th and the 19th centuries, a decision was made that the monopoly of a single currency issued through bank debt should be institutionalized. The particular body charged with that role in each country is its own central bank, with the IMF and the World Bank each added to the panoply following ratification of the Bretton Woods agreement in 1945. These institutions have important and useful tasks in preserving the integrity of the overall financial system. They are also the guardians of the prevailing monetary orthodoxy and its core tenet that: achieving the objective of monetary stability requires safeguarding the monopoly of the existing money creation process as well as that of a single national currency, one in each country or group of countries.

Though created to safeguard the economy, these institutions are nonetheless afflicted by the same collective blindness regarding money. Thus, they preserve the very orthodoxy that has gotten us in trouble time and again, which spawns and then protects banks that might become too big to fail, and which dispels any action to review and amend our monetary and banking systems. This institutionalized status quo serves to insulate us not from harm but from detection and amendment of this collective blind spot regarding money. Consequently, the ongoing industrial-age paradigm continues to reign mostly unquestioned.

Challenging the status quo in any field is always a daunting business, and is particularly the case with money given its power and the collective lack of understanding in its regard. But it is precisely because of its unique influence, as well as its inherent potential for improvement to our world, that we must endeavour to better understand and make greater use of this remarkable human-made creation.

## CLOSING THOUGHTS

From its very inception, traditional economics has suffered from a blind spot with regard to money. This failing is attested to by the fact that, while the vast majority of economists universally regard monopolies as destructive, the monopoly of one type of money has continued unchallenged from the time of Adam Smith onward. This collective blindness with regard to money, shared by layperson and expert alike, is the source of a number of concerns and consequences, catalogued in this Part I.

Our money journey continues in Part II with a look at some of the many monetary tools that are available to help address important issues of our day, and the pragmatic possibilities that exist to create a better world by rethinking money. As it happens, growing numbers of communities from around the world are doing just that. Their efforts are helping to show us innovative, pragmatic ways and means by which to match unmet needs with unused resources.

## PART II

# NEW MONEY

*Society will, only a few generations from now,*
*be as different from modern industrial society*
*as that is from a society in the Middle Ages.*
~WILLIS HARMAN

# CHAPTER ELEVEN

# Great Change

*Every few hundred years in Western history, there occurs a sharp transformation. Within a few short decades, society—its worldview, its basic values, its social and political structures, its arts, its key institutions—rearranges itself...We are currently living through such a time.*

~PETER DRUCKER

In 1900, there was not a single airport, television set, or credit card. There was no theory of relativity, no quantum mechanics, and no GDP. Genetics, immunology, and endocrinology did not yet exist, and hormone was not even a word. Hollywood was a bunch of farms and the sun never set on the British Empire. The life expectancy was 47.6 years for Caucasian-Americans, while for African-Americans it was a mere 33.0 years.[1] The world's 1.7 billion people lived and worked mostly in rural surroundings,[2] and the overwhelming majority of women around the world could not vote.

A generation or so ago, there was no e-mail, no laptops, or DVDs; no ATMs, subprime mortgages, or euro. China's economy was mostly agricultural, Eastern Europe was under the grip of the Soviet Union, and apartheid continued its reign in South Africa. There was not yet a single reported case of AIDS, the concepts of sustainability and climate change were first beginning to enter mainstream awareness, and the world's population had more than doubled since 1900.[3]

In early 2007, Japan's industrial output reached an all-time high,[4] Lehman Brothers was the fourth-largest U.S. investment bank,[5] and for the first time ever, a woman led in an American presidential primary. By late 2008, Japanese output sank to its lowest level on record, Lehman Brothers was bankrupt,[6] and the U.S. presidential elections made history.

Other milestones in 2008 included: the worst quarterly losses by one corporation ($61.7 billion by AIG),[7] the greatest annual earnings by another corporation ($45 billion by Exxon Mobil),[8] tens of millions of job losses, the lowest interest rates by the Bank of England since its founding in 1694,[9] and the most dire warnings to date regarding climate change.[10] In early 2009, a century or so after the first Wright Brothers flight of 120 feet in 12 seconds, NASA launched the Kepler Mission in search of other habitable planets in our galaxy, while here on Earth, President Obama took office, inherited the worst economy since the Great Depression, and signed off on the largest stimulus bill in history.[11]

As 2012 approached, political, social, and economic tensions mounted around the world. Regime changes swept across the Middle East and North Africa as part of the so-called Arab Spring. Austerity measures aimed at dealing with the growing debt crisis led to protests in Greece and other parts of Europe. The Indignants Movement in Spain called for radical economic and political reform. The Occupy Movement, which began in Kuala Lumpur, spread to Wall Street and more than 2,300 towns and cities around the world. The major campaign issues in the upcoming elections in the United States and elsewhere would center on job creation and the economy. And human population had more than quadruppled since 1900 to 7 billion.

We are living in a time of epic transformation. Though extraordinary in its breadth, scope, and potential, many of the undercurrents of societal change have happened before. Such shifts, referred to as *Big Change*, are described by systems scientist and nonlinear dynamicist Sally Goerner as, "like a seventh wave swollen with streams from many directions, sweeping away the social reality and worldview that was, leaving new ones in their wake."[12] Former instances of Big Change include the fall of the Roman Empire, the rise and fall of the Central Middle Ages, and the Age of Enlightenment.

As in the 1700s, many entrenched ways of being and doing are found to be increasingly in conflict with the realities and requirements of our time. This is particularly the case with our industrial-age economic tenets, financial institutions, business practices, and banking and monetary paradigms. As in the past, there are mounting calls for reform and change.

But what types of reforms? What manner of change?

*"There, there it is again—the invisible hand of the marketplace giving us the finger."*

Though there is growing recognition that we are in the midst of a postindustrial shift, many questions remain about what this will mean in practice. Consensus on how to tackle the issues of our day is also lacking. Whatever measures are taken must speak to a number of inconvenient truths.

Author and educator Duane Elgin notes:

> Never before has humanity been on the verge of devastating the Earth's biosphere and crippling its ecological foundations for countless generations to come. Never before has the entire human family been required to work together to build a sustainable and meaningful future. Never before have so many people been called to make such sweeping changes in so little time.[13]

In addition, history cautions us that societal transformations are often associated with tumult and loss. The philosopher Alfred North Whitehead observed that, "it is the first step in sociological wisdom to recognize that the major advances in civilization are processes which all but wreck the society in which they occur."[1]

Though accurate, Whitehead's reflection is, however, not uniformly true and applies mainly to those who still cling to former belief structures. The shift into the Central Middle Ages, for example, appears to have been a mostly peaceful, constructive process that improved conditions on a broad scale. A similar prospect exists in our time.

Notwithstanding the enormity of the task before us, there are whispers of cautious optimism by a small-but-growing body of respected scientists, sociologists, economists, and others. Each has identified in today's shift the potential not only to address our many concerns, but to realize vast improvements for the whole of humanity. It is one of today's many great ironies that at the very moment we find ourselves confronted by a host of unparalleled challenges, there is concurrently the potential for the greatest positive transformation in all of recorded history. The key word, however, is *potential*. A better future is not assured us but will depend heavily upon an informed general public and leadership that together make informed decisions.

In Part II, we look at some of the many obvious and not-so- obvious reasons for hope in our time. We will focus on insights and strategies, particularly within the monetary and economic arenas, that can help bring about significant revitalization. We will also examine some of the many reasons why the current societal shift is the first instance in recorded history of a phenomenon we refer to as *Great Change*.[15]

## TOWARDS GREAT CHANGE

Today's shift distinguishes itself from others in myriad ways, including its extent and impact. Its epicenter is not restricted to any one people or region but is instead erupting in many places at once, influencing the full spectrum of human and natural habitats, from Wall Street, Main Street, and the remote villages of the developing world to virtually every living system on Earth. Everyone and everything is affected.

This shift is accompanied as well by an epic progression in perceptions. As noted, our seemingly vast and ever-abundant planet, whose great mysteries were once explained by myth and dogma, was widely held to be the center of the universe. Scientific inquiry and a new modernist worldview came into being and transformed many things, from our understanding of planetary orbits, governance, and economics to humanity's place in the cosmic order.

As yet another perspective takes hold, today, change is upon us once again. With many times more people, greenhouse gases, peak oil, shrinking forests, and other diminishing resources, our world appears more finite, vulnerable, and far more complex. Physicists are now seriously postulating an intricate, quantum multiverse, composed of infinitesimal strings, space, and energy, with many more than three dimensions. We are discovering that biological systems, humans included, are governed not only by DNA but by a genetic setting that includes billions of microbes and trillions of viruses living in symbiosis within each of us, "all working together in ways that leave our mind mysteriously free to focus on getting our bodies to the office and wondering what's for lunch."[16] Additionally, we are discovering that human biology is governed not only by inherited genetics but by attitudes and lifestyle choices, as revealed by the newly-named discipline of *epigenetics.*

In short, we are living with multiple potential realities simultaneously coexisting at the same point in time. This changes many things, including a new multidimensionality and framework in the acquisition of knowledge. Systems analyst Jamshid Gharajedaghi writes:

> There is a shift in our understanding of the nature of the beast from a mindless mechanical system to a multi-minded socio-cultural system...[and] in our way of knowing: from analytical thinking, the science of dealing with independent sets of variables, to systems thinking, the art and science of handling interdependent sets of variables.[17]

In a radical departure from Modernism, with its dismissal of entire realms of inquiry, a new, greatly expanded and dynamic framework is emerging. This new inquiry retains the rigor and empiricism of modern science while greatly expanding and enhancing the picture. It allows one to go into almost any field of inquiry and organize "outlier insights" that include and integrate information from a much broader range of sources: past as well as present; Eastern as well as Western; traditional as well as contemporary; intuitive and experiential in addition to empirical and mathematical; interdisciplinary, multidisciplinary, and transdisciplinary as well as conventional areas of inquiry. Whereas modern science has been built around materialism, reductionism, linear causality, and disorder, "new science" is oriented towards energy flow, inclusion, complex causality, and "systemic patterns that hide beneath the chaos of local vicissitudes."[18] Hardly anything appears quite the same.

The medical realm is one example, and helps to illustrate the broader shift now taking place.

## Integrative Medicine

Modern medicine views patients, illness, and disease in material terms, with emphasis on the physical body separate from the mind and spirit. It directs treatment accordingly around surgery, pharmaceuticals, and germicides. Its orientation is analytical, mechanistic, and reductionist, not systemic. As a result, modern medicine has not been very successful in dealing with system-based diseases, including three of the leading causes of death: cancer, diabetes, and heart disease.

Integrative medical programs instead complement conventional techniques with alternative therapies such as acupuncture, Ayurveda, biofeedback, chiropractic, yoga, and diet-based strategies, each of which conceptualizes the body as matter/energy/flow systems. This new framework takes a holistic, systems approach toward the understanding, treatment, and prevention of illness and disease.

Decades ago, few patients or practitioners in the West knew much about nontraditional therapies. This is no longer the case. In Britain, 42 percent of all physicians now routinely make referrals to homeopaths.[19] Most European pharmacies dedicate more shelf space to herbal medicines than to pharmaceutical drugs. In America, there are more visits to unconventional therapy providers than to primary care physicians.[20]

John Astin of Stanford University's School of Medicine offers the following interpretation for this shift:

> Users of alternative health care are more likely to report having had a transformational experience that changed the way they saw the world...They find in [alternative therapies] an acknowledgment of the importance of treating illness within a larger context of spirituality and life meaning...The use of alternative care is part of a broader value orientation and set of cultural beliefs, one that embraces a holistic, spiritual orientation to life.[21]

The grassroots movement toward holistic medicine began in the face of once considerable opposition to alternative methodologies by conventional medicine. A similar phenomenon is occurring presently in the monetary and economic realms.

## Monetary, Economic, and Social Change

For years preceding the global financial crisis, Wall Street enjoyed stunning windfall profits, seemingly affirming the logic of the reigning neoclassical orthodoxy. Yet, despite boom numbers, soaring indicators such as the GDP, and the certitudes of an impressive list of free market adherents, a groundswell of disenchantment grew in opposition to the direction of the economy, as smaller players, developing countries, and the environment struggled. One expression of the growing divide was a grassroots explosion of complementary currency initiatives, from a mere handful in the 1980s to thousands today in diverse communities globally.

With regard to current economic policies and direction, dissatisfaction appears to be at a record high. In late 2009, twenty years after the fall of the Berlin Wall, a BBC poll conducted across 27 countries showed that only 11 percent of those questioned said that the dominant economic framework was working well.[22] Though these opinions were very likely influenced by the recent downturn, discontent with the economic order has been mounting steadily for decades.

In the largest survey of its kind ever undertaken, with cumulative surveys involving 100,000 adult Americans and 500 focus groups conducted over a 13-year period, a significant portion of the U.S. population was found to hold views that diverged from mainstream thought and the economic status quo. Unlike the aforementioned BBC poll, this study was conducted years prior to the recession, during a period of relative stability (1987 to 1999). As reported by researchers Paul Ray and Sherry Anderson in *The Cultural Creatives: How 50 Million People Are Changing the World*,[23] the findings indicated that the value orientation of tens of millions of Americans was not adequately reflected in mainstream business, finance, politics, and culture. The many issues cited included:

o  concerns with big business and the means used to generate profits;

o  practices that exploited resources and poorer countries;

o   the effects of globalization;

o   the lack of meaningful work;

o   mass consumption;

o   materialism;

o   women's issues in business and other realms;

o   and a number of quality-of-life concerns.

There was a willingness to pay higher taxes for improvements and a desire that government spend more money on education, community programs, and support for a more ecologically sustainable future. Political affiliations varied, but many of those surveyed considered themselves independents, not aligned with any political party.

No detailed survey similar to that of Ray and Anderson's has yet covered the globe. In 1997, however, the European Union's monthly Euro-Barometer surveyed all its member nations, employing the same values-based questionnaire.[24] The findings mirrored those cited above, with at least as many Europeans sharing values similar to those of their American counterparts. Similar results were obtained elsewhere and were as strongly felt in developing countries as in developed ones.[25]

Many of those who share similar views are likely participants in what author and social activist Paul Hawken more recently referred to as the largest and fastest growing social movement in history. In his book, *Blessed Unrest: How The Largest Movement in the World Came Into Being and Why No One Saw It Coming* (2009), Hawken estimates that several million organizations, mostly nonprofits (NGOs), are working to tackle economic, social, environmental, and other concerns in communities of virtually every nation around the world.[26] Without much fanfare, their efforts, ingenuity, and creativity are addressing many issues not being attended to by government. These findings mirror Ray and Anderson's depiction of a new culture being created. As this subgroup's numbers of this subgroup steadily climb, so does its impact on civil society and the transformation now taking hold.

In essence, a new worldview is emerging. Its perspective embraces input from many diverse points of view, and is aligned with a new stage of science increasingly identified as *integral science*.[27] This moniker proclaims a profound relationship between values orientation and emerging science.

The integral approach is providing insights and benefits in many domains. In medicine, for example, it has led to breakthroughs in the treatment and prevention of a wide range of disorders.

The same holds true for new monetary choices and economic reforms. For the first time in history, using the same precision and language demanded by scientists, it can now be shown why complementary monetary initiatives and the financial reforms demanded by mounting numbers of concerned citizens are not only popular but empirically valid. This indeed changes many important things.

New approaches now make it possible to demonstrate why:

o   it is far better for the economy to engage in sustainable development rather than mere growth;

o   a healthy economy requires *resilience*, not just efficiency;

o   policies that favor Wall Street over Main Street are contraindicated on the grounds of counterproductivity;

o   a vibrant, stable economy depends as much, if not more, upon many healthy smaller players as it does upon a small number of big guys;

o   and caring for our young, the elderly, our environment, and natural resources are not just morally sound, but are also empirically and economically the appropriate choices.

New evidence also explains why an assortment of currencies working alongside and *complementing* our national currency system is of benefit to all, and why monopolies of any kind—particularly a monopoly in the issuance of money—is neither sustainable nor in our collective interest.

In essence, the integrative scientific and economic framework affirms:

o   the triple bottom line approach of building social, economic, and environmental health;

o   the rediscovery of Adam Smith's original vision of free enterprise networks;

o   and the vital role played by complementary currencies towards the realization of the kind of sustainable vitality that reliably maintains and enhances the health and well-being of all levels of our global civilization.

For these reasons alone, the current shift is quite important. But other elements add to the enormity of what is taking hold, and deserve brief mention here.

## A Milestone for Humanity

In historical terms, a new worldview is a very rare occurrence and as such, represents in and of itself a significant shift. But the advent of an integrative culture implies an even greater milestone for humanity. Unlike the old changing of the guard, with the replacement of the medieval religious mindset by Modernism, what is occurring now is more than a simple reaction to and substitution of one worldview by another.

In the words of John Astin:

> The appearance of this integrative culture is about healing the old splits: between the inner and outer, spiritual and material, individual and society. The possibility of a new culture centers on reintegration of what has been fragmented by Modernism: self-integration and authenticity; integration with community and connection with others around the globe, not just at home; connection with nature and learning to integrate ecology and economy; and a synthesis of diverse views and traditions.[28]

What appears to be unfolding is a reemergence and healing of human energies and values that have long been repressed in society. The evolutionary shift from modernist to integrative values is of such importance that it can only be compared with the move toward reason in classical Greece, with one significant difference—the current transformation is bound to be much faster. Greek rationalism took centuries to spread to other areas of the Mediterranean world. Civilization had to wait many more centuries still for the Renaissance and the Enlightenment to finally mainstream these concepts into everyday life and spread them around the world. In contrast, as events in our present world and societies demonstrate, the shift toward integrative values is already occurring at the speed of a veritable tidal wave.

Given the dimensions and qualities of what is now taking place, the current transformation may well be the first instance of Great Change. The implications for humanity of the current shift are still being assessed and will take decades to understand more fully. What is already apparent, however, is the potential for fundamental improvements to the human condition and the renewal of our natural life-support systems.

To this end, to the revitalization that is readily possible, we examine in the following chapters of Part II the highlights of a new economic framework, and some of the many monetary initiatives that are now available to communities and society-at-large.

## CLOSING THOUGHTS

We are in the midst of the most comprehensive societal transformation in recorded history. All human systems and all living systems are in the process of being affected. Part of this Great Change is a new scientific inquiry that is providing a more holistic approach to the pursuit of knowledge. This integrative inquiry is already revolutionizing our understanding in many important domains, from ecosystems and medicine to economics and monetary systems. Some of the many implications for economics are considered next.

# CHAPTER TWELVE

# Efficiency, Resilience, and Money

*The very process of the restoring the land to health*

*is the process through which we become attuned to Nature*

*and, through Nature, with ourselves.*

~CHRIS MASER

Our perceptions have undergone significant changes over the centuries. Evolving views of our planet, for instance, have matured from a stationary orb at the center of a divinely conceived order, to an immense world in a mechanistic universe, to a living planet with limited resources suspended in a multidimensional, energy-based cosmos.

This progression in understanding mirrors the continually evolving expressions of governance, economic rules, and monetary paradigms that have taken place: from a premodern, theocratic, agricultural-based society, in which most financial exchanges took the form of barter; to modern democracies and industrialized economies, with increasingly concentrated financial wealth dominating a monetized, global marketplace; to an emerging postmodern landscape in search of more sustainable ways and means of meeting the requirements of the world's many diverse peoples and natural ecosystems.

In support of humanity's epic journey and 21$^{st}$ century objectives, we explore herein a conceptual framework that offers new understandings and solutions towards sustainable development, with relief for both the economies and living systems of this planet.

## FLOW SYSTEMS AND ECONOMICS

Advancements in recent decades in a number of domains—from systems theory, complexity theory, and information theory, to the study of natural ecosystems and what makes them sustainable—have contributed to a new theoretical scaffold for economics. This integrative, empirically backed model likens economies to complex, adaptive, living systems in which matter, energy, and information continually flow.

Flow systems exist throughout nature. Our circulatory system, for example, provides a nourishing supply of blood to every cell in the human body, without which we would quickly die. Similarly, ecologists view natural ecosystems as energy and flow systems, in which the natural food chain is actually a streaming network of matter, information, and energy built of complex relationships among organisms. Energy radiates from the sun onto the planet. Plants capture the sun's energy through photosynthesis and transform it into biomass. Animals eat the plants and one another in a chain up to the top predator, only to die and decompose. Bacteria and other microorganisms recycle their decomposed remains.

Economies, like natural ecosystems, are also complex flow networks. They consist of millions of businesses and productive activities whereby outputs of one entity serve as inputs to others and to consumers, in a vast web that processes and circulates energy, information, and resources through practically the whole planet.[1]

Though complex, some structural patterns of these networks are predictable and independent of the nature of what flows through them, be it biomass in an ecosystem, information in an immune system, electrons in an electrical distribution system, or money in an economy. What makes these patterns predictable is the universality of their structures.

Theoretical nonlinear physicist Predrag Cvitanović explains:

> The wonderful thing about this universality is that it does not matter much how close our equations are to the ones chosen by nature, as long as the model is in the same universality class...as the real system. This means that we can get the right physics out of very crude models. The existence of such universal patterns and dynamics explains why similar energy-flow concepts and analysis methods apply to economic systems as well as natural ones.[2]

In essence, understanding how ecosystems and other complex flow networks maintain sustainability allows us to apply this same knowledge to economic systems. A summary of the findings is described below. With the aforementioned caveats in mind regarding the application of mathematical proofs to real-world situations, interested readers may refer to the relevant paper.[3]

## EFFICIENCY AND RESILIENCE

It is now known that long-term sustainability in real world networks such as ecosystems depends on an appropriate balance between two opposing requirements—efficiency and resilience.

*Efficiency* in a complex network is defined as a network's capacity to process volumes of whatever flows through it in a sufficiently organized and streamlined manner so as to maintain the integrity of the network over time.[4]

*Resilience* is that same network's rebound capacity, that is, the ability to retreat elegantly and safely to fallback positions, to access a diversity of options to meet the needs of unexpected disturbances, and to spawn innovations for ongoing development and evolution.[5] For any complex flow system to sustain itself over time, it thus needs to not only be efficiently organized but must also be resilient, able to withstand changes in its environment, be it drought or disease in a natural ecosystem or downturns in an economy.

Two structural variables of any complex system govern the degree of efficiency versus resilience. One such element is *diversity*, the existence of different types of agents acting as nodes in the network. The other is *interconnectivity*, which measures the number of pathways between the given agents. Diversity and interconnectivity play key roles in the efficiency and resilience of any complex system, but in opposite directions.

All other things being equal, a system's resilience is enhanced by both greater diversity and connections, as they provide more agents and channels to fall back on in times of trouble or change. Efficiency, on the other hand, increases through streamlining, which typically implies reducing diversity and connectivity. A dynamic push-pull between efficiency and resilience is crucial to the long-term health of a system whose optimal fitness requires a specific balance between these two poles.

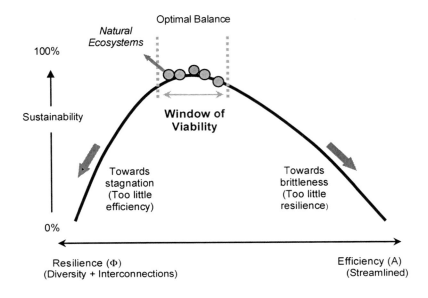

*Figure 12.1 – Simplified Sustainability Curve of a Natural Ecosystem[6]*

A predator animal, for instance, may eat a variety of species, or depend instead on only a single species for its food supply. In the latter case, this hunter will likely be more skilled when it comes to catching its favorite prey, but find it hard to adapt if that one food supply becomes scarce. Consequently, the feeding network of this predator, while efficient, is not very resilient, and is at risk of dying off with unfavorable changes to its environment.

Efficiency and resilience are both controlled by diversity and connectivity. Since diversity and connectivity can each be precisely measured, the fitness and sustainability of any given complex flow network can be mathematically determined as well. In all real-life sustainable systems, the relationship between sustainability, resilience, and efficiency follow a conceptual curve that is illustrated in a simplified manner in Figure 12.1.

Note that in nature, *the optimum point whereby sustainability is maximized invariably lies closer to resilience than to efficiency.* Moreover, all sustainable ecosystems have their most critical parameters within a very specific and narrow range, which can be computed with precision. This range is referred to as the "Window of Viability."[7]

Healthy ecosystems keep their diversity and numbers of pathways within a certain range that is neither too much nor too little. This is because flow networks that are overly efficient tend to become too brittle, whereby one small break may cause the whole system to collapse. On the other hand, overly diverse networks tend to become stagnant, in which energy, resources, and information wander through a tangle of meandering pathways that lead to nowhere.

Let us emphasize that the relationships between efficiency and resilience, the role of the structural variables of diversity and interconnectivity, and the "window of viability," are all requirements and emergent properties of not only natural ecosystems but of any complex flow network system.

The concept of efficiency is so deeply ingrained in our thinking today, especially in engineering and economic thought, that it may be difficult for most of us to imagine how anything could be too efficient. But the lesson of recent crises is precisely that—over-efficiency. Consider, for example, the blackouts of entire electrical distribution networks that have occurred in the Northeastern United States and other parts of the world.[8] These failures followed decades of engineering optimization for greatest efficiency, an unintended consequence of which was that these distribution systems became brittle.

The same principle of a balance between efficiency and resilience also applies to the viability of enterprises and economies. To address multiple contingencies and survive challenging times, organizations must be adaptable and resilient, able to change their ways as needed. Healthy businesses must maintain resilience by creating and maintaining appropriate systems of production, marketing, delivery, accounting, and training. But organizations must also maintain competitiveness by honing the efficiency of their processes, which is typically accomplished by streamlining.

Today's emphasis on maximizing efficiency underscores the current general belief that all improvements need to proceed further in this same direction. But when managers over-emphasize streamlining and other short-term efficiencies at the expense of long-term resilience, they may be sacrificing viability. Such an orientation keeps driving us further away from sustainability.

One dramatic example of what can happen when efficiency is pushed too far comes from global supply chains that revealed themselves incapable of dealing with the aftershocks of the Japanese 2011 disaster. For instance, two Japanese companies that have damaged factories produce 90 percent of the market of a speciality resin used to bond parts of microchips that go into all smartphones. These lean, "just-in-time" supply chains should be reviewed with a "just-in-case" approach.

These considerations have direct relevance to our monetary and banking paradigms and to the credit crunch of the last several years.

## Money, Efficiency, and Resilience

Money—the codified agreement that circulates throughout our global economic network—is maintained as a monopoly of a single type of bank-debt, fiat-based, interest-bearing currency. The technical justification for this monopoly is to optimize the efficiency of price formation and exchanges in national and international markets. Massive legal and regulatory mechanisms are in place to ensure and maintain this monopoly, mainly through the requirement that only national currencies are acceptable as legal tender for payment in taxes.

The current monetary paradigm is, in effect, equivalent to a planetary ecosystem where only one single type of plant or animal is tolerated and artificially maintained, and where any diversity is eradicated as an inappropriate competitor because it would reduce the efficiency of the whole. Only one end result is possible in such a scenario—the collapse of the system as a whole.

## Complementary Currencies and Resilience

The solution that leads toward monetary sustainability defies conventional economic thinking, which mistakenly assumes monopolies for national currencies as a given. Sustainable ecosystems demonstrate that flow systems require sufficient diversity and connectivity at different scales covering all levels.[9] A monopoly of one type of centralized currency, particularly one that requires artificial scarcity to maintain its value, is not compatible with such a role. A monoculture of bank-debt national money may have been appropriate—perhaps even necessary— for an industrial-age world to emerge. But this paradigm is without question far too limited for a 21$^{st}$-century pluralistic society seeking innovative, sustainable, postindustrial economic solutions.

Even some of the more simple complementary currency systems can empower people. The use of these monetary tools allows many more people to participate in exchanges, and provides a richer interconnectivity among the constituents of an economy. Complementary currencies thereby serve to prod the overall system back towards more sustainability.

Complementary currencies improve the resilience of the whole economy by providing greater diversity in exchanges; they enable transactions that otherwise wouldn't occur, through connections that otherwise wouldn't exist. Though traditional economics tends to dismiss the contributions of complementary currencies on the grounds that they are less efficient, systems thinking demonstrates the fundamental flaws in that argument. Though complementary currencies may reduce overall efficiency, they increase resilience and engender a more sustainable economy. When diverse types of money reach every level of society, a richer socioeconomic fabric is inevitably woven that is far more pliant, able to better withstand and deal with multiple contingencies and changes to the environment. The system thus becomes more stable. This is the structural lesson of natural ecosystems.

New understandings regarding complex flow systems and the need for resilience points a way towards the long-term health of our economies. It also helps clarify why today's pressure for ever-greater efficiency actually destabilizes the economy by relentlessly repressing diversity. The lack of diversity erodes businesses, communities, and the wellbeing of the billions of people that interact through our economies.

## CLOSING THOUGHTS

A new way of understanding any type of complex flow system is now available. A continuous exchange of energy, matter, and information outputs from one part of a system serve as inputs to another part of that same system. Importantly, understandings gained from any one kind of flow system are applicable to all others *with the same structure*, be they ecosystems, electrical distribution systems, human immune systems or entire economies.

Flow systems that are optimally sustainable enjoy a dynamic balance between efficiency and resilience. Excessive efficiency occurs in the case of too little diversity or too few connections, and can result in the sudden collapse of a network. Resilience is instead enhanced by increasing diversity and connections. These findings have vital implications for our financial, economic, and monetary systems.

# CHAPTER THIRTEEN

# Sustainable Development

*Growth for the sake of growth*

*is the ideology of the cancer cell.*

~EDWARD ABBEY

Understanding the need for a balance between efficiency and resilience, together with the ability to measure a network's structure, allows for a deeper, more accurate assessment of a number of vital contemporary issues. One such issue, and a key factor related to most of our current socioeconomic and environmental concerns, is that of sustainable development.[1]

## ECONOMIC DEVELOPMENT VERSUS GROWTH

Traditional economic thought and practices have placed great emphasis on continued economic growth. Widely considered to be synonymous with development, economic growth is the main criterion used to determine overall economic vitality and is a key objective in economic planning and policies. Yet, many accepted assumptions regarding the concept of growth reveal themselves to be just that—assumptions.

Even the most basic questions regarding growth defy simple answers. How, for example, do we define economic growth? Which criteria and methods should be employed to measure it? What kind of growth is actually good for the long-term health or sustainability of an economy? Confusion and misconceptions associated with this subject matter have contributed instead to policies and practices that exacerbate ongoing economic instability, inequities, hardship, and ecological devastation…hardly expressions of health or sustainability.

For decades, mounting numbers of concerned citizens have intuitively understood and identified many supposedly growth-oriented economic activities as deleterious to society and the actual economy of peoples and nations. Such concerns, however, lacked the kind of supporting empirical evidence deemed acceptable by traditional economic protocol. Consequently, growth has persisted as a key objective and desired outcome in most economic pursuits.

Fortunately, new findings—particularly with regard to flow networks, resilience, and sustainability—enable a much clearer understanding of what actually constitutes healthy development, and the means by which to differentiate it from mere growth. We now know, for example, that a large ecosystem that lacks sufficiently diverse nutrient pathways, such as the lack of ample waterways or nourishing topsoil, is not properly prepared to withstand challenges such as drought or disease. Size alone does not make ecosystems sustainable. The same structural rules apply to any type of flow system, including our economies.

An economy that lacks resilience cannot be considered to be optimal, no matter how seemingly big or efficient it may be. Even Simon Kuznets, the principal architect of the original GNP national accounting scheme, cautioned that economic wellbeing cannot be determined by volume or growth alone. Theoretical ecologist Robert Ulanowicz points out that the long-term sustainability of any type of flow system depends on a judicious balance of size in conjunction with internal structural development. These insights regarding flow systems, together with advancements in our understanding of money, allow for a much clearer and more accurate assessment of the conditions needed by free-enterprise networks to produce the kind of economic vitality that enhances the wellbeing at all levels of our global civilization.

In economies, volume is measured by Gross Domestic Product (GDP). In ecosystems, size is generally measured by the Total System Throughput (TST), which gauges the total volume of nutrients, biomass, or energy moving through a system. Both GDP and TST are, however, poor measures of sustainability in that they each measure only size (volume), while ignoring the agents and pathways needed to process resources and circulate energy in a network structure to all parts of the whole. This leaves metrics such as the GDP unable to distinguish between the kind of frenetic growth that occurs in a bubble economy and that of healthy development in a resilient economy.

## Sustainability in Natural Ecosystems

A simple ecosystem example from Dr. Ulanowicz clarifies how tradeoffs among efficiency, resilience, and growth affect a flow-system's long-term health. The following study observed the American alligator in one of its natural habitats, the Cypress wetlands of South Florida.[2]

One of the alligator's important sources of biomass (carbon flow or food) is freshwater prawns. The alligators do not, however, normally feed directly on the prawns themselves, but obtain this biomass indirectly by instead consuming other predators that in turn feed on the prawns. Three such intermediate predators include: large fish, turtles, and snakes.

In this example, the most efficient pathway between prawns and alligators is via large fishes. If, as is often the case in economics, efficiency were taken as the sole criterion for vitality, then the flow path through the fish would grow at the expense of less efficient routes until it completely dominated the transfer. In such a scenario, the increase in efficiency almost doubles and also creates a 20 percent jump in volume (available biomass). A comparable economic event would be a massive increase in productivity and efficiency that leads to a dramatic leap in GDP and growth, which is then conflated with healthy development.[3]

In this ecosystem scenario, the resilience for this highly efficient system vanishes completely. The alligators are now strictly dependent on large fish as their only food source. Should some catastrophe occur to these now overly efficient predators, like a virus wiping out the fish population, all transfer from prawns to alligators would cease, with potentially cataclysmic consequences for the predator species. The growth that would have taken place is based on a shaky foundation and is not sustainable.

Dr. Goerner points out that this natural ecosystem situation mirrors what occurs in the marketplace. The surges in GDP growth that often accompany increased efficiency may give the appearance of economic vitality but could mask increasing brittleness. One example of systemic fragility is found in the energy sector, with global dependence on oil as the primary source of fuel, whose production and supply is limited to a few, very large suppliers. Any disruption here bodes ill for the economy at large due to the absence of viable contingencies and alternative sources to turn to. In other words, there is a lack of resilience.

Global dependence on large agribusinesses presents a similarly serious threat. A mere ten to twelve companies now control over 80 percent of the world's food supply of cereals, grains, meat, dairy, edible oils, fats, and fruits.[4] Such consolidation may, as some economists claim, represent the most efficient path from resource to consumer. But the global food system is left with few options should political, economic, microbial, or climate-change-induced events disrupt one or more major pathways. Consolidation of this kind puts all of one's eggs in a single basket; it errs on the side of efficiency and courts disaster by eliminating resilience.

Systems that, in contrast, maintain proper resilience during growth are more likely to adapt to crises in ways that largely protect TST. In the alligator biomass transfer example, healthy populations of turtles and snakes would provide alternate pathways and allow the system to adapt while maintaining flow in case of a fish virus outbreak. Though the loss of large fish does cause sustainability to drop by almost half, the TST volume only drops a modest 2-3 percent, and the efficiency loss is slight as well. Most notably, total collapse of the system is avoided. The alligator still receives a plentiful supply of biomass.

Such numbers substantiate diversity's role in supporting a soft-landing response to the booms, busts, and other periodic disturbances that inevitably befall an economy. The ability to quantify resilience also provides an empirical basis and new appreciation for the small, diverse economic networks that make up the bulk of any economy, and lends support to concerns about, for instance, the plight of small farms that provide vital, alternate food-supply pathways for the global food-security crisis (that many experts argue lies on the horizon). In short, understanding the need for resilience discredits the idea that focusing on highly efficient big businesses is the surest path to economic health.

## Sustainability and Positive Feedback

Understanding the tradeoffs required for long-term economic vitality helps us aim policies toward a more appropriate balance between efficiency and resilience. There is, however, more to this story, especially in trying to grasp phenomena such as the booms and busts of the business cycle. For this, we must turn to positive feedback circuits that take the form of centripetal pull.

The following example, named after one the world's largest corporations, helps illustrate how self-reinforcing or autocatalytic forces draw ever more resources into their sway, like an expanding whirlpool that sucks all surrounding flows into itself.

## The Walmart Effect

Walmart runs a large U.S. discount department store chain and membership-required warehouse outlets. The "Walmart Effect" is one in which large, highly efficient companies, supported by local economic development offices, tend to erode surrounding economic networks even as they increase GDP.

For decades now, most economic development offices have focused on creating incentives to lure big corporations to set up shop in their locale in hopes that jobs and taxes would best trickle down from there. This approach skyrocketed because of increasing emphasis on GDP growth, and resulted in mutual-benefit deals between the giant, deregulated corporations and allied economic development officers, academicians, and politicians.

Support for "big-box" retailers seemed sensible. Greater economies of scale means lower prices, which naturally and progressively pulls in more consumers and money. This centripetal pull causes corporate and government coffers to swell along with the GDP. The benefits of this centralizing circuit appeared as much undeniable as it was self-perpetuating. Those who supported the process were rewarded, while those who did not were simply removed.

Champions of such policies failed, however, to consider the price paid for this in social and economic erosion.

As noted in the documentary *Walmart: The High Cost of Low Prices*,[5] the efficient, big-box retailers drive smaller, more diverse local enterprises out of business, mainly through lower prices. These same retailers then take advantage of this situation by lowering worker wages, removing benefits, and finally increasing prices after local competition has been weakened. Main Street shops—one of the prime losers in this process—disappear one by one, leaving the center of town run-down and unsafe, and begging for another publicly funded "urban renewal" effort. Much of the money and benefit of large-scale efficiency are ultimately drained from the local economy and siphoned off to distant headquarters.

A 2002 study in Austin, Texas showed that for every $100 local consumers spent at a national bookstore, only $13 was spent in the local economy; but the same $100 spent at local bookstores instead yielded $45.[6] A 2003 study of Mid-coast Maine expanded this finding, showing that big-box retailers spent just 14 percent of their revenue locally, mostly in the form of payroll; while local businesses spent 54 percent of their revenue (in goods, professional services, wages, benefits, etc.) within Maine.[7]

This centripetal drain from the local community to corporate coffers erodes the social and economic vitality of a community. The ultimate costs to local governments far outweigh the tax revenues that the big retailer adds. The overall impact in lost jobs, lower wages, over-extended infrastructure, and the erosion of community wellbeing can be dramatic.

The innocence with which this process proceeds explains why strategies that are intended to increase economic health often erode it instead. An autocatalytic circuit grew out of natural desires for progress in the form of economic growth, the kind that GDP numbers celebrate. More and more resources from the local community were pulled into this loop, which resulted in the loss of diversity, jobs, profits, and local resilience. Policies that promote centripetal economic growth have in common a wealth-concentrating vortex that simultaneously breeds brittleness at its periphery and unsustainable surges at its center.

The 2008 banking and financial crisis, initially triggered by the mortgage derivative bubble, illustrates how this very process works on a broader scale than what has been described thus far.

## Autocatalysis and the Global Downturn

In the period leading up to the global downturn of 2008, a profit-driven circuit had been well established, formed by deregulated bankers in search of new sources of income, stockbrokers in search of hot new products to sell, and big institutional investors in search of higher returns. Gains in any one part of this self-amplifying circuit benefitted other segments of the same internal circuit, but to the detriment of the resilience of the economy-at-large. This autocatalytic loop grew rapidly by drawing in resources from the greater economy through ever more-efficient, though dangerous, "pull" techniques, mainly in the form of risky derivative instruments, which served to concentrate or pull wealth into the hub. This was accompanied by a kind of rigid group-think that dismissed traditional risk assessments, which was realized via intense selection pressures that lavishly rewarded those who increased gains, and eliminating the jobs of those who did not.

While the derivative mess helped trigger the crisis, the erosion of other sectors created an underlying systemic risk in the form of brittleness. Not only was the broader economy left increasingly vulnerable, but the banking and financial sectors were also left exposed. The most vital factor behind this erosion and brittleness traces right back to the same epicenter—to the banking and monetary systems themselves.

The crash of 2008 predictably devolved from a financial crisis into a liquidity crisis, in which the banks and financial sector, needled by the pressure to rebuild their balance sheets and reacting to the shift in economic climate, did what they usually do in such risky circumstances. At the very moment when Main Street needed it most, the large financial institutions reduced lending. Lacking credit, businesses and consumers were simply forced to tighten their belts and economic activity slowed down. As occurred in the 1930s, many businesses were forced into insolvency and massive unemployment ensued.

Our ongoing monetary and banking paradigm amplifies the business cycle. It helps drive a good economic period into a potential inflationary boom, and a difficult period into a bust. It does this by making more credit available when it is least needed during high times, and by making credit less accessible when it is direly needed during periods of contraction. Central banks try their best to counteract this cycle, but have limited success, at best.

The increased instability caused by this amplification of the business cycle is abetted further still by the destabilizing autocatalytic centripetal phenomenon, which pulls resources in from the greater economy, be it through subprime mortgages, derivatives, or other means. Both the amplification of the business cycle and autocatalysis contribute to the kind of loss of resilience that helped escalate the downturn of 2008-2009 into the worst recession since the Great Depression.

Joseph Tainter points out in *The Collapse of Complex Societies* that autocatalytic economic circuits follow a path similar to that of the Roman Empire: they grow, dominate their surroundings, reach their limits, and if left unchecked, end in collapse due largely to erosion of small farmers, local governments, and other non-epicenter networks.[8] Understanding this process empirically grounds the age-old claim that monopolistic concentration, insider trading, speculation, and sheer greed are each detrimental to economic health. Some regulations, like the Glass-Steagall Act of 1933, counteracted this by barring Wall Street investment banks from owning community savings banks. Such measures were effective because they blocked too much autocatalytic alignment. This act was, however, repealed (under the Clinton administration) after intense lobbying by the banking system, and is another manifestation of the same recursively self-serving process.

Structurally, this autocatalysis is compounded by the current monetary and banking paradigms, with a monopoly in the issuance of money; that is, by the very same sector that wields such enormous influence on all else in our monetized economy, including the booms and busts of the business cycle. The continued lack of reassessment and amendment to these paradigms, together with unchecked autocatalytic circuits, are as dangerous a mix of ingredients as one can imagine with regard to the sustainability of our global economy. Until and unless addressed, this perilous status quo virtually ensures continued lack of resilience, instability, and ongoing crises.

## RETHINKING THEORY AND PRACTICE

Current economic theory rests on the assumption that economic laws, such as standard supply-and-demand dynamics, hold true regardless of the resilience of the underlying networks. But GDP growth only counts the volume of monetary exchanges; it ignores whether such exchanges actually contribute to or destroy economic resilience. Supposed growth, as gauged by this primitive accounting scheme, may instead mask declines taking place in various parts of the economic web by allowing massive gains in one sector, such as hedge funds, to be conflated with health for the whole. As noted, this blindness to network health renders traditional economic theory incapable of understanding, much less predicting, bubbles, which, in the context of this economic framework constitutes growth without underlying structural development. The various schools of traditional economics are also unable to foresee the kind of widespread economic instability that now threatens the world.

The lack of attention to the erosion of lower-scale networks has opened the door to policies that have accelerated destruction at every level of the economy. Reigning economic thinking of the last several decades, which is devoted to regulating capital, has removed many of the impediments to wealth concentration long known to create harm. Blind faith in market efficiency and the seeming correctness of maximizing profits regardless of the costs to anyone or anything else, has bred disdain for moral concerns, including harm to smaller economic actors.

Where an underlying stability once supported the monetary domain, our collective blindness has now inevitably caused that stability to collapse. The damage done to people—as consumers, laborers or operators of small businesses—and the continued onslaught upon the environment caused by predatory practices, externalization of costs, toxic products, as well as a lack of monetary choices, were all rationalized as necessary collateral damage and creative destruction. But the destruction factor now impacts the whole of the economy and virtually every living system of this planet, and seriously compromises our future prospects.

A long list of critics (including Joseph Stiglitz,[9] Robert Pollin,[10] John Saul[11]) point to the more than 100 major banking crises,[12] the increasing concentration of wealth and power,[13] the elimination of good jobs,[14] and the erosion of civil liberties, public health, and democracy,[15] all of which have accelerated between the 1970s and today. Each is an expression of the inherent unsustainability of our present economic regime.

This combination of blindness and disregard leads to widespread brittleness that, as the ongoing economic crisis shows, threatens big and small alike. It also highlights the fallacy of other common assumptions, including:

o   increasing efficiency always improves economic health regardless of the harm that financial efficiencies can cause to people, communities, and our planet's ecosystem;

o   highly skewed distributions of wealth, power, and size do not affect economic health;

o   money is value neutral, and our fiat-based, bank-debt monetary system can meet all of humanity's many diverse needs.

Another road to socioeconomic vitality is available to us. A whole currency innovation movement has emerged over the past decades, thanks in large part to the efforts of pioneers from many countries. In the

United States, much of the credit goes to innovators such as Hazel Henderson,[16] Edgar Cahn,[17] Paul Glover,[18] Thomas Greco,[19] Sergio Lub,[20] Susan Witt,[21] Wilson Riles, Arno Hesse, Guilllaume Lebleu, Nipun Mehta, Matthew Edwards, Charlie Rebich, as well as hundreds of grassroot activists too numerous to mention here. The next chapters will document some of the results.

## CLOSING THOUGHTS

Traditional economics places a great deal of emphasis on "growth." This parameter, as measured by GDP, is widely assumed to be synonymous with healthy economic development. Recent findings, however, derived in large part from our understanding of flow systems, calls into question many long-held growth-related assumptions and activities.

One of the many ways in which growth is conflated with overall sustainability is how current policy and activities benefit dominant players at the expense of the greater economy. The present monetary and banking paradigm, together with the phenomenon of autocatalysis, enables large institutions to become ever larger, thereby reducing connections and diversity in the system.

This relentless emphasis on GDP gains, efficiency, and growth, at the cost of resilience, together with the lack of diversity embodied in our monetary paradigm, constitutes a structural cause for the instability of our economies. A balance between efficiency and resilience is essential for sustainable development.

## CHAPTER FOURTEEN

# LETS and Time Dollars

*How wonderful it is that nobody need wait a single moment*

*before starting to improve the world.*

~ANNE FRANK

As in other major societal transformations, monetary changes are a vital component of today's Great Change. Prompted in large part by the inability to address issues by traditional means, and spurred on as well by low-cost computing, more and more communities are getting involved with new complementary currencies. Only a small handful of such currencies were known to be operational during the 1970s. Today several thousand systems are operational worldwide.[1] A very conservative estimate of the rise in the number of systems is illustrated in figure 14.1.

It bears noting that only those social-purpose complementary currencies identified as operational in a dozen countries as of 2009 are represented. Excluded from the figure are the thousands of "loyalty currencies" (discount coupons, airline miles, etc.) used for commercial purposes and the countless social-purpose currencies that do not advertise their existence outside of their immediate geographical environment.

Two of the most popular complementary currency systems operational today are LETS and Time Dollars. Each of these currencies is an example of a mutual credit system, designed to help facilitate exchanges in communities in which national currency is either lacking or otherwise inadequate to meet local needs. A brief description of each system follows, beginning with the most ubiquitous and one of the most easily adopted of all social-purpose currencies—LETS.

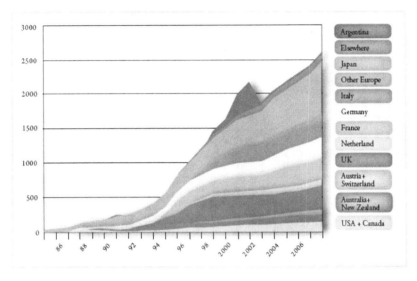

*Fig 14.1 - Growth of Complementary Currencies (1984-2009)*

## LETS

There are many flavors of Local Exchange Trading Systems—or LETS. One example is LETSystem, which originated in a once-prosperous fishing community near Vancouver, Canada during the 1980s. The community had fallen on hard times; local unemployment persisted at nearly 40 percent despite the presence of a large, skilled labor force and the continued demand for goods and services by the local population. LETSystem was created to help facilitate the local trade of goods and services. As LETSystem's founder Michael Linton observed, the missing link was *money*. Without it, transactions simply could not take place. According to Linton:

> The greatest deficiency of conventional money is that for too many, it is simply not available. By its very design, there is only a limited amount of it created. And, as conventional money must come from somewhere outside the local community, it inherently doesn't understand or concern itself with the needs of a particular community.[2]

Exchanges in the LETS system take place using either LETS money alone or in combination with national currency. A gardener or car mechanic, for example, might ask only LETS money in exchange for services rendered, or accept partial payment in both LETS and in national currency. The proportion of LETS and national currencies used in each exchange is determined by the participants themselves on a case by case basis. The *material* inputs used in most LETS exchanges, for instance, fertilizer or car parts, are customarily paid for using *national* currency. The *service* inputs tend to be paid in LETS.

LETS is a *mutual credit system*, whereby the currency to be used in a particular exchange is created at the time of a transaction. When an exchange takes place, the account of the individual supplying the goods or service is credited, while the recipient's account is debited. Credit balances indicate that an individual has provided goods or services to fellow community members in excess of the amount of goods or services redeemed, and vice versa for debit balances.

This system ensures that the supply of LETS within a community is sufficient and self-regulating. Like other mutual credit systems, LETS enables participants to benefit from whatever resources are available within the trading community. It thereby overcomes the systemically imposed scarcity of a national currency.

In contrast to conventional money, a negative balance in LETS is not a problem but instead is an indication that this particular member has purchased more goods and services from other members. Those with a negative balance are simply called upon to offer goods or services in return, further increasing the community's collective wealth. Some LETS programs set debt limits to avoid abuses, but there is generally a common understanding that debts will be repaid.

Because open records are customarily kept of both credits and debits, those LETS users who refuse or fail to repay their debts (by serving or supplying goods to fellow community members) can be identified easily and barred from future participation. This built-in transparency ensures checks and balances, and engenders greater trust among users. Thus it is a self-regulating system.

One important advantage of LETS compared to conventional money is that it promotes the use of skills and services that are otherwise less likely to be considered for trade, such as having someone else perform one's cooking, driving, web designing, gardening, etc.

James Taris writes in *The LETSaholic TWIST*:

> Having a limited income meant I could only afford to pay for the essentials in my life; everything else became a luxury. But all that changed with LETS ... Very soon I was mowing lawns, removing rubbish and painting rooms. Later I was also designing business cards, brochures and newsletters. And in return, I received massages, piano tuition and restaurant meals, computer support, computer software, and web design services. I would have reluctantly bypassed all of these goods and services if I had to pay for them in cash. LETS made them all possible.[3]

Typically, the value of one LETS unit is equivalent to one unit of whatever national currency is used in that community. Setting up a local LETS exchange is a straightforward process. Its few requirements include: a basic agreement to use LETS amongst participants, a user-accessible, transparent accounting mechanism, and the creation of a member directory listing each respective member's offers and needs priced in LETS units.

LETS programs are currently operating in many different parts of the world. In Australia, there are an estimated 200 different LETS programs. England has more than 300 programs. A partial list of other nations with LETS programs includes: Argentina, Austria, Belgium, Brazil, Canada, Chile, Colombia, El Salvador, Finland, France, Germany, Hungary, India, Indonesia, Ireland, Israel, Japan, New Zealand, Nigeria, Norway, Poland, South Africa, Switzerland, Thailand, and the United States.

## TIME DOLLARS

Time Dollars, also known as Time Banking, was created by distinquished American attorney Dr. Edgar Cahn, who observed that formally paying people—by whatever means—empowers them. He emphasizes that, "counting what people do is a way of valuing what they do."[4] Given the inherent scarcity of national currency, Cahn conceived of using time as a medium of exchange. The basic unit of account is a Time Dollar, equivalent to one hour of service, which can be spent for goods and services available within a given community.

Time Dollars works in the following manner, as explained on the Time Dollars website:

> At its most basic level, Time banking is simply about spending an hour doing something for somebody in your community. That hour goes into the Time Bank as a Time Dollar. Then you have a Time dollar to spend on having someone doing something for you. It's a simple idea, but it has powerful ripple effects in building community connections.[5]

Time Dollars, like other complementary currency systems, link a community's unmet needs (the services requested) with its unused resources (community members with time and services to render). Like LETS, Time Dollars facilitates transactions that likely would not take place otherwise. Time Dollars can be as simple as a group of moms getting together to share carpooling of kids, grocery shopping, taking care of elderly parents, walking dogs, or helping out with homework.

Time Dollars builds and strengthens relationships within its community of users. In one ten-year, $51 million joint study, researchers from Harvard, Columbia, and the University of Michigan endeavored to identify what helps make neighborhoods safe.[6] The multimillion dollar answer was not additional police officers or more government assistance. Rather, the study concluded that community safety depended on "collective efficacy," a fancy term for neighbors looking out for each other's kids to curtail destructive behaviors. Time Dollars improves collective efficacy—and local resilience as well.

The acknowledgement of services via a currency also reinforces volunteerism. Research conducted at the University of Maryland's Center on Aging demonstrated that roughly one third of Time Dollars participants had never volunteered before. The same research showed that the use of a complementary currency induces people to continue volunteering over time. The dropout rate, which typically reaches 40 percent in purely volunteer-based programs, is only three percent in these "hybrid voluntarism" programs that provide modest payment in complementary currencies.[7]

The Time Dollars system is being applied to address a host of issues. Elderplan, a health insurance company located in Brooklyn, New York, accepts 25 percent of the premiums for its senior health programs in Time Dollars. Preventive measures, such as fixing a broken bathtub rail, are provided through Elderplan's Care Bank, a Time Dollar exchange.[8] The Elderplan model is now available in all five boroughs of New York City.

Another successful application is the Time Dollars Youth Court. Founded in 1996, it has become a cornerstone of the juvenile justice system in Washington, D.C. Juveniles accused of nonviolent offenses are tried before a jury of their peers, that is, other juveniles who have been convicted of similar offenses. Those found guilty must make a requisite apology and submit to life-skills counseling and a combination of community services, such as tutoring of younger students or service on a Youth Court jury. In return for rendering these services, tutors and Youth Court jurors earn Time Dollars, which can be redeemed for recycled computers, savings bonds for college, educational trips, special events, and more.[9]

The program's effectiveness has attracted significant attention. *Participation in the Youth Court has reduced first-year recidivism by half.*[10] The Youth Court now processes approximately 60 percent of nonviolent, juvenile offenders' first cases. The program has been officially sanctioned by the D.C. Superior Court to work with the criminal justice system in a "partnership for the purpose of jointly developing a diversion program which provides a meaningful alternative to the traditional adjudicatory format in juvenile cases."[11] Similar programs are being implemented in South Africa and Jamaica.

In some Chicago schools, a Time Dollars program incentivizes tutoring of younger students by older students. The hours spent tutoring can be used to obtain, for example, refurbished computers. A Time Dollars credo states that, "you have something your community needs, you should be rewarded for offering it."

Another application that makes us of Time Dollars is a prison program, currently operational in the United States and Great Britain. Inmates are offered the opportunity to earn Time Dollars by refurbishing bicycles. The Time Dollars earned can then be used by the families of participating inmates for their own needs, while the bicycles are sent to Africa as part of an aid program.

The cost of starting a Time Dollars program is minimal; communities can use a blackboard or a piece of paper to keep a tally. For larger-scale projects, a timekeeper computer program can be downloaded for free from the Internet. Time Dollars is also scalable to accommodate any level of participation. Its scalability, cost-effectiveness, ease of use, and benefits to community members make Time Dollars a popular choice among students, retirees, and the unemployed.

There are approximately 350 Time Dollars programs now operating in 22 countries on six continents. In the United Kingdom, where the system is referred to as "Fair Shares" or "Time Banking," an estimated 79 programs are currently in operation with another 80 now in development. In both the United States and Japan there are 65 to 70 established Time Dollars programs. Other countries that have recently adopted the system include Senegal, Ghana, and New Zealand.

Both Time Dollars and LETS cater mostly to the needs of individuals and are designed specifically for smaller, lower-income communities where, for whatever reason, there is insufficient national currency.

In recognition of the social contributions offered by Time Dollars, three separate Internal Revenue Service (IRS) rulings make this complementary currency officially tax-exempt in the United States.[12]

## COMPLEMENTARY CURRENCY REFLECTIONS

An understanding of LETS, Time Dollars, and similar mutual credit complementary currency designs helps shed light on matters associated with money, including: money's value-nonneutrality; currency designs and inflation; and the important advantages of money and complementary currencies, as compared to barter.

### Currencies and Behavioral Changes

In keeping with the value-nonneutrality of money, currency designs have the potential to elicit specific behavior patterns. Complementary currencies promote exhanges and attitudes not customarily associated with our national currency model.

LETSystem founder Michael Linton observes:

> Community currencies seem to engender different attitudes. Fear disappears. People aren't overly concerned about individual trade balances or who "benefits" most in a particular transaction. A different type of exchange comes into existence. Local currencies go round and round and come back: Joe does this for Mary, Mary does this for Jim, and Jim helps Joe. Life is

cyclical, I serve my neighbor then another neighbor serves me. Community currencies encourage people to support each other, which is really the business of life. And it slowly restructures the economy into a more benign form, generative of quality of life, social capital, and common wealth.[13]

What is the reason for the occuring behavioral differences when conventional money or community-oriented mutual-credit systems are used?

As the Eleventh Round story in Chapter Five illustrates, the interest feature built into conventional money drives the competition for a scarce currency. Most complementary currencies instead do not bear interest, and some make use of a demurrage. Within mutual credit systems, artificial scarcity need not be maintained; the currency is automatically created in sufficiency when an agreement to trade is reached. Thus, the two hidden mechanisms that promote competition in conventional money (scarcity and interest) are both absent in complementary currencies.

This structural difference helps explain why mutual credit and other social currencies engender cooperation and a sense of community among their users. These systems are simply a formalization of the tradition of helping each other, as in gift exchanges among neighbors that were embedded in almost all past societies. In southern France, for example, these activities were called *aller aux aïdats* (coming to the aid).

## Complementary Currencies and Inflation

The structure of well-designed complementary currencies also clarifies why, in contrast to what some economists might suspect, this form of money does not add to inflationary pressures. Inflation risk would be valid if, and only if, the complementary currency were designed as a fiat currency, like the dollar, euro, pound, and other national currencies. LETS and Time Dollars are *not* fiat currencies; they are each mutual credit systems, in which money is created only when an agreement is made, with a simultaneous credit and debit charged to the parties involved. This ensures that just enough money is created specifically for the transaction at hand—and no more. In this way, all mutual credit currencies automatically create their corresponding supply of goods and services when they are put into circulation.

It is essential to understand that most complementary currencies are intrinsically different from fiat currencies and are intentionally designed to avoid contributing to inflation. All our notions regarding inflation emanate from a traditional economic perspective, which implicitly assumes a monopoly of one single fiat currency in use within a given country or region. This perspective holds that inflation results whenever there are not enough goods and services produced for the quantity of money in circulation. Such a premise is, however, simply not applicable to well-designed complementary currencies.

## LETS, Time Dollars, Money, and Barter

LETS and Time Dollars are both money, and like other complementary currencies, enjoy the full functionality of money. They should not be mistaken for barter exchanges, in which goods and services are swapped bilaterally without any standardized medium of exchange. An inherent limitation of barter exchanges is that they require a "double coincidence of wants;"[14] resources and needs must match up perfectly between two parties for a transaction to take place. In a barter transaction, if one person needs shoes and another food, the exchange can only be completed if each possesses the particular item wanted by the other.

As money, LETS and Time Dollars overcome the limitations of barter. Each system provides an *internal currency*—a medium of exchange used by all members within a given LETS or Time community—which permits participants to select from a much wider variety of goods and services. LETS, Time Dollars, and other complementary currencies enable many exchanges that would not otherwise take place and allow communities and society-at-large to better meet their many needs.

Many other social-purpose complementary currency designs are possible, two of which are examined in the next chapter.

## CLOSING THOUGHTS

There is no lack of work to be done in the world. There are children to be educated, shelters to be built, ecological systems to protect, sick and the aged to be cared for—the litany is endless. In addition, there are hundreds of millions of unemployed or underemployed people who are ready, willing, and able to work.

What has been lacking is money, especially different types of money. We can easily make agreements to interact and assist one another. We do not need gold to back our currencies; garbage was turned into money in Brazil. LETS and Time Dollars demonstrate that in crafting monetary agreements, we are limited only by our imagination and competency to make use of these new monetary tools, and the courage to innovate.

Our national currencies are but one form of money. Just as no single tool can build a house, no single type of money, no matter how ingenious or robust, can be designed to address each and every one of the many and sometimes divergent requirements of society. Moreover, given the particular architecture of our current money, with its artificially maintained scarcity, there will never be sufficient sums of national currency available to meet our many and ever growing demands. A one-type-fits-all monetary design makes as much sense as artificially limiting our use of tools to hammers when so many other specialized means are readily available for practical use right now.

## CHAPTER FIFTEEN

# Social-Purpose Currencies

*There is a loftier ambition than merely to stand high in the world.*
*It is to stoop down and lift mankind a little higher.*

~HENRY VAN DYKE

An all-too-common reality of most societies today is the inability to adequately address an extensive list of social concerns, in no small measure due to the chronic lack of necessary funds. In stark contrast to the trillions of dollars made available by governments to the financial sector during the banking crash of 2008, hard-fought battles must be continuously waged to raise even the most basic sums necessary to address a wide range of health, education, and welfare issues in most developed and virtually all developing nations around the world. This struggle is not an accident, but is instead the logical outcome of a society shaped and constrained by our centuries-old monetary and banking systems. These systems currently maintain a virtual monopoly with regard to the money in play, and place almost exclusive emphasis on industrial and commercial interests.

It must be reemphasized that our national currencies are but one type of money. No single monetary design is capable of addressing the full spectrum of both societies' commercial and social requirements. Fortunately, there is a growing recognition of the necessity for different currency designs that, working alongside the dominant currency system, can address a much greater range of today's vital needs.

In the following pages, two social-purpose currency designs are showcased as examples of what becomes possible by rethinking money. Unlike LETS and Time Dollars, each of which are basic complementary currencies applicable in a generic way to a variety of different applications, the two currencies examined herein are more specifically designed to help address particular sectors of social concern for a society, namely health care and education. The following initiatives also serve to illustrate how important social needs can be met in the face of limited public funds.

We begin with the ongoing economic struggles in one of the world's leading economies and its endeavors to provide adequate health care for its mounting elderly population.

## JAPAN AND THE FUREAI KIPPU

Although sometimes mischaracterized as a nation of imitators, Japan is unquestionably a leading innovator of complementary currency initiatives.[1] Consider the following:

- o Japan has the largest number of complementary currency systems in the world today, with more than 780 operational systems.

- o Japan also has the largest diversity of ongoing complementary currency experiments. More than 260 different types of systems have been tested nationwide. This represents an almost 100 percent increase in Japan since 2002 and amounts to more types of systems than the rest of the world combined![2]

- o Japan additionally led post-World War II complementary currency efforts, beginning with a visionary, award-winning article by Teruko Mizushima in 1950.[3] Mizushima developed the core ideas of a time-based currency and a time bank, and went on to establish her own "volunteer labor bank" in Osaka in 1973, which is still in operation today.[4]

But, why is such a vast and diversified complementary currency movement happening in Japan?

### Japan's Meltdown and Currency Experiments

In 1990, Japan hit an economic wall, similar in effect to what the crisis of 2008 meant for the United States. Triggered initially by a real estate crash, this economy has been plagued by declines for the better part of the last two decades. The total wealth lost in Japan during the first five-year downward period alone, from 1990-1995, is estimated in excess of

$10 trillion, resulting mostly from real estate and stock market losses. This loss represents two years of the Japanese GDP at the time—the equivalent of the total losses incurred by Japan during the entire span of World War II!

Until 1995, most Japanese believed what they were being told—that just as in any other business cycle, things would get better after a few years of tough times. But every conventional recipe was tried to relaunch the economy: dropping interest rates (all the way to zero), gigantic public work projects (by encasing in cement 60 percent of the Japanese shoreline), tax cuts; massive deficit spending (to the point where governmental debt represents 200 percent of annual GDP!), and a desperate attempt to increase consumption through a coupon system. None of these conventional solutions succeeded in getting the economy back on track. The effects have been devastating and in a growing number of cases, fatal. For example, in Japan there is a suicide every 15 minutes, mostly involving men with families who are taking their own lives due to financial stress.[5]

Gradually, the government and grassroots circles began to look at less conventional solutions. It is in this context that the blossoming of Japanese complementary currencies was started.

From the mid-nineties onwards, the Japanese government began to quietly but ambitiously experiment with complementary currency innovations. Under the guidance of Toshiharu Kato, the former head of the Services Department of the Ministry of Economy, Trade and Industry (METI), dozens of new currencies were designed. A number of nongovernmental initiatives also began at the grassroots level.

Rui Izumi, an associate professor at the School of Economics, Senshu University in Tokyo, points to government support as a major contributor to the growth in complementary currencies:

> The central government and many local governments are supporting local currencies in positive ways. For example, they have given financial support to some organizations, and [both] the Minister of METI and the president of the Bank of Japan have made several encouraging remarks publicly about these systems.[6]

These government-sponsored projects were implemented in communities of very different scales, ranging from small villages to entire prefectures (roughly equivalent to a U.S. county), and involved millions of people. The trials ran for a period of three years or so, and the results were carefully observed. The purpose behind the currency experiments, the cost of which was estimated at over $10 million per year, is to understand as fully as possible what works best and under which circumstances.

In accordance with the well-known Japanese decision-making tradition, before a significant change is made and publicized, it must first reach an approval through consensus. This process is still taking place, and consequently, the currency initiatives have not yet been implemented to scale.

In the midst of this unusual Japanese research and development phase, hundreds of currencies were privately initiated. One family of such systems is the Fureai Kippu, a health care system designed to help address the economic consequences of an aging society.

## The Fureai Kippu

Two-thirds of all humans who ever lived to 65 years or older are alive today. The nation with the largest aging population in the developed world is Japan, with some 1.8 million elderly or handicapped citizens currently in need of daily care. The number of elders is expected to double over the course of the next decade.

Traditionally, two strategies have been used worldwide to try and deal with the economic consequences of this Age Wave:

o   trying to honor the financial promises that were made to the retired and elderly at the risk of fiscal bankruptcy, as seen, for example, in some Scandinavian countries;

o   gradually cutting support to the elderly to match available funds, as seen in the United States and Great Britain.[7]

Tsutomu Hotta, a highly respected former Minister of Justice in Japan, realized that these two principal conventional strategies were unsatisfactory. In 1991 he decided to tackle Japan's Age Wave using a different approach. He created a new complementary currency system, the Fureai Kippu, whose literal translation is "Caring Relationship Tickets." The Sawayaka Welfare Foundation further developed this idea in 1995.

The Fureai Kippu system provides the elderly and handicapped with many services not covered in the official national health care program. Its units are accounted for in hours of service. Various kinds of services have different valuations. Assistance with bathing, for example, can be given a higher hourly rate than shopping.

In what amounts to a health care time-savings account, those who care for the elderly in the Fureai Kippu system accumulate credits and may draw on them in a variety of ways. Caregivers may elect to electronically transfer part or all of their Fureai Kippu credits to parents or relatives who may live in another part of the country, or may instead make use of these credits if they themselves get ill. Such options ensure that ever more people are cared for. Electronic clearinghouses perform these credit transfers.

The elderly receiving care report strong preferences for the services offered by Fureai Kippu caregivers to those who are instead paid in conventional national currency. The main reason cited is the qualitative difference in the relationships. Fureai Kippu recipients consider the care to be more personal. Many of the caregivers involved in these programs report similarly that they often perceive the elders they treat as surrogates for their own parents. In short, the relationship is different!

An estimated 387 Fureai Kippu systems are now operational in Japan.[8] The economic savings are substantial; the human support network makes it possible for the elders to stay in their own homes longer or return home sooner after a medical intervention, rather than remaining in far more costly clinical or hospice settings. The savings, the human interaction involved, and the greater sense of community that is engendered benefit all. And, as in the case of Curitiba, Brazil (see Chapter One) these benefits are derived without having to raise taxes or divert funds from other vital programs. No one is burdened for the improvements.

Takeo Hiranuma, a former head of Japan's METI, stated in no uncertain terms that, "the use of complementary currencies can bring an end to the long-lasting deflation of the Japanese economy by supplying additional monies of various types at the local level."[9]

To give some sense of the sheer magnitude of the initiatives now taking place in this prominent world economy, the following maps of Japanese complementary currency initiatives are offered. Keep in mind that the 387 branches of Fureai Kippu have not been included, as they would simply overwhelm the map to the point of making it unreadable.

## TRENDS IN COMMUNITY CURRENCIES IN JAPAN
Rui, IZUMI
(As of April, 2002)

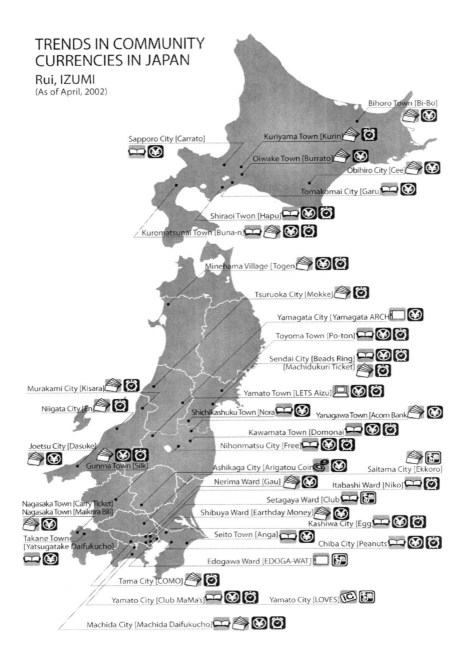

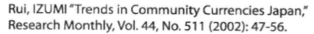

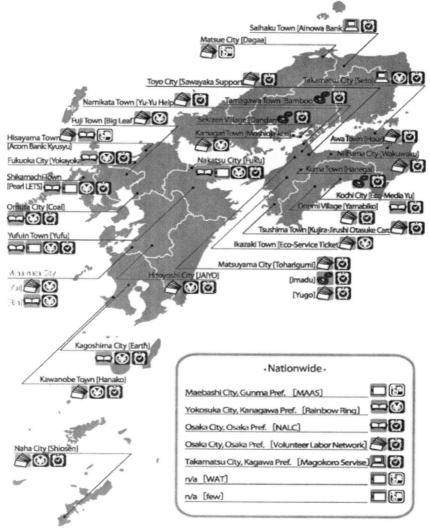

Rui, IZUMI "Trends in Community Currencies Japan,"
Research Monthly, Vol. 44, No. 511 (2002): 47-56.

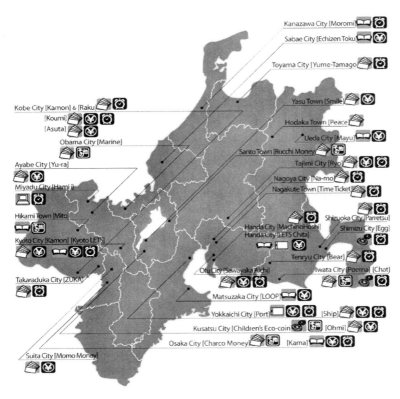

Kanazawa City [Moromi]

Sabae City [Echizen Toku]

Toyama City [Yume-Tamago]

Yasu Town [Smile]

Hodaka Town [Peace]

Ueda City [Mayu]

Santo Town [Rucchi Money]

Kobe City [Kamon] & [Raku]

[Koumi]

[Asuta]

Obama City [Marine]

Ayabe City [Yu-ra]

Miyadu City [Hami ]

Hikami Town [Mito]

Kyoto City [Kamon] [Kyoto LETS]

Takaraduka City [ZUKA]

Tajimi City [Ryo]

Nagoya City [Na-mo]

Nagakute Town [Time Ticket]

Shizuoka City [Parretsu]

Handa City [MachinoHoshi]     Shimizu City [Egg]

Handa City [LETS Chita]

Tenryu City [Bear]

Ofu City [Sawayaka Aichi]     Iwata City [Poema] [Chat]

Matsuzaka City [LOOP]

Yokkaichi City [Port]     [Ship]

Kusatsu City [Children's Eco-coin]     [Ohmi]

Osaka City [Charco Money]     [Kama]

Suita City [Momo Money]

**Coupon System:** This system uses coupons to make payments for things like donations or voluntary work. The issuers are the operating offices.

**Book System:** This system uses books to make transactions with plus or minus points recorded on both sides. The issuers are individuals.

**Due Bill System:** This system uses due bills to make payments by issuing them with the issuer's name signed on them, or endorsing already-issued bills. Just like drafts, blank due bills have no value. The issuers are individuals.

**Chip System:** Though quite similar to the Coupon System, this system differs in that it uses chips of metal, wood, ceramic, etc. instead of coupons. The issuers are the operating offices.

**Online System:** This system uses computers linked by the Internet to make transactions with plus or minus points recorded on both sides. The issuers are individuals or operating offices.

**IC Card System:** This system uses terminals at public facilities or shops to make transactions. IC cards, owned by individuals, record transaction data as plus or minus points and update it through the terminals. The issuers are usually individuals.

**Time-based System:** This system uses time as the unit to measure the values of transactions: for example, an hour can be counted as one point.

**Yen-based System:** This system uses Yen as the unit to measure the values of transactions: for example, one GREEN is worth about 100 Yen.

**Other Systems:** There are systems using energy, goods, or the number of transactions to measure the values, such as WAT (a unit used by a citizen-owned power plant group, worth 1 kw/h generated electricity), CHARCOAL (a unit worth 1 gram of charcoal), and EKKORO (a unit worth one transaction).

## The Japanese Exception and Its Significance

The two decades long "Japanese crisis," as it is typically described in the Western media, may not be an isolated Japanese economic problem. Their ongoing recession may instead be the symptom of a structural world crisis that chronologically happens to have hit Japan first. The arrival of the so-called Information or Knowledge Age represents a major structural shift; it is not only a new beginning but marks an end as well. The last shift of such magnitude occurred when the Industrial Age precipitated the end of the Agrarian Age. Such dramatic shifts are far from painless. One need only look at what happened to the farmers, many of whom lost their livelihood and way of life; or the landed gentry, who saw their values, power, and traditions fade into irrelevancy as the Agrarian Age ended.

If Japan is but the first nation to experience what is inevitably waiting for the industrialized world, then the rest of us had better take notice.

Until recently, the classical European recipe has been to do a little more like the United States and everything will return to normal. In the aftermath of the Great Recession, however, with millions left unemployed, after the bursting of the U.S. high-tech and real-estate bubbles, Europeans are slowly facing up to the realization that what happened in Japan may also happen in the United Kingdom, Italy, France, Greece, and elsewhere. The specter of deflation—a systemic sign of overcapacity across the board—is now considered a serious possibility outside of Japan as well.

A similar path of denial can be expected in the coming years by the United States, repeating a mantra heard by the Japanese for more than a decade: "Next year, the economy will be back to normal." We can also expect similar economic proposals and debates regarding tax cuts, lower interest rates, and public works. But if we are in effect living through a structural shift at the end of the Industrial Age, such recipes will predictably fail, similar to what has transpired in Japan.

It is under this light that what is going on in Japan in the domain of complementary currencies is relevant for the rest of the world. One of the world's leading economies has turned itself into a real-life laboratory for resolving a variety of economic and social problems from the bottom up, thanks to monetary innovations. China and Switzerland are now in the process of implementing Japanese-style Fureai Kippu system experiments for their own elderly and disabled. Can the rest of the world afford not to learn from those experiments?

## THE SABER

The Saber ("sah-BAIR), derived from the Portuguese word for "knowledge," is a Brazilian complementary currency initiative created to address educational needs, designed in collaboration with Professor Gilson Schwarz from the University of Sao Paolo.[10] Unlike LETS and Time Dollars, both of which are mutual credit systems, the Saber currency is backed by conventional fiat money. Though intended specifically for use in education, this particular design also helps to illustrate how limited public funds can be leveraged to provide a much greater return for use in meeting societies' needs.

Brazil's institutions of higher learning are running below capacity; university lecture halls are rarely if ever filled. This is related to the economic realities of the country, with large numbers of poor. As elsewhere, adolescents from poor backgrounds are less likely to pursue higher educations. Though the economics of education is a very complex issue, inadequate subsidies limit the availability of educational tools, resources, and personnel to help students excel, particularly those students from economically depressed areas. Additionally, poorer students, even those who do excel, usually lack sufficient personal financial means to afford higher educations.

When Brazil privatized its mobile telephone industry in 1998, it introduced a special one percent tax that was earmarked for higher education purposes. By 2003, this Education Fund had grown to more than $1 billion. The question on Professor Schwarz's mind was how to get the best bang for the billion? Conventional solutions, such as the American GI Bill, which helps finance education for those veterans who have served in the military, provide student loans directly to individual applicants for their own education alone. Brazil's proposal instead creates a "learning chain" that co-involves a number of students and allows each to benefit from the same initial amount of money.

The original design for the Saber education currency was allocated first to primary schools, particularly in poorer communities where school funding is not sufficiently available. This currency is designed to incentivize students to help both themselves and other students through tutoring. Each Saber is first given to the youngest students in primary schools, who transfer this currency to older students (for instance, 3rd graders) in return for the help they receive with their schoolwork. In compensation for the hours spent mentoring, these older students can make use of the Sabers they earned to get assistance from 4th or 5th graders, and so on.

Through this learning chain, anywhere from five to ten students receive help from advanced students using the Saber. At the end of this cycle, the currency would finally go to senior students who could then use the Saber to pay for part or all of their university tuition.[11]

Universities could exchange Sabers for conventional money with the education fund, but at a discount of up to 50 percent. This approach not only helps students but makes economic sense to universities. The marginal expense incurred by an additional student has little impact on universities as most of their expenditures are fixed. Similar to empty seats on an airplane or in a movie theatre, universities remain open and professors teach whether a lecture hall is full or half empty. Better to get half of a tuition fee for an otherwise vacant seat than none at all.

The benefits of the Saber not only include economic savings but extend to other important social returns as well.

## A Learning Multiplier

Several decades of research have shed new light on *learning retention,* that is, how much of what is being taught is remembered. Retention depends less on the person who is learning or on the particular topics of study, but is instead more directly related to the kind of delivery mechanism involved—the process by which the learning takes place. Research shows that average learning retention rates are dramatically higher when learning occurs actively rather than passively, as illustrated in the learning pyramid, next page.[12]

What is striking is that traditional education systems commonly use the two *least effective* methods available: lecturing and reading, by means of which only 5-10 percent of what is being taught will be remembered. In stark contrast, an impressive 90 percent retention rate applies to what one teaches others. There is therefore, a ninefold to eighteenfold increase in learning retention rates.

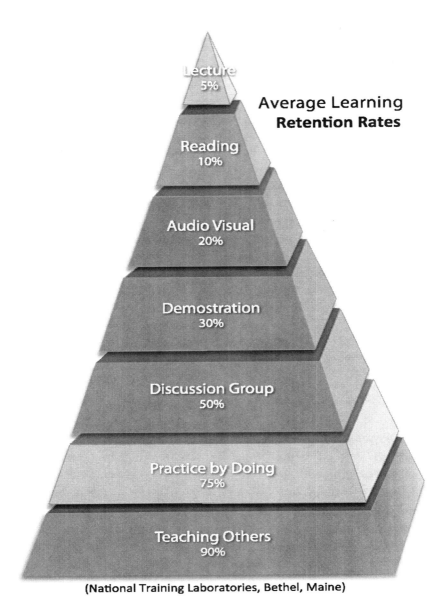

*Figure 15.1 - Learning Pyramid*

Factoring in retention rate gains and other benefits derived by using Sabers amounts to a very significant bang for the educational buck:

- o a fivefold minimum leverage increase via the learning multiplier (the number of students making use of each Saber), which allows educational funds to be used for many more than one student;

- o a tenfold average leverage increase in learning retention via active tutoring (actually from ninefold to eighteenfold increase, but averaged out to its near lowest estimate);

- o a twofold leverage increase as a result of the 50 percent discount applied to redemption of Saber complementary currencies by the Education Fund.

*The overall multiplier effect of using Sabers is at least a hundredfold* $(5 \times 10 \times 2 = 100)$.

This rough estimate of $100 billion in education benefits by use of the Saber compared to $1 billion obtained through conventional scholarships, though significant, still does not tell the whole story. Other benefits, though less-readily quantifiable, include: maximization of university facilities; the hope, opportunity, and stronger bonds generated among students; and the related benefits to family members and society as a whole of increased educational opportunities.

The Saber program could also be expanded beyond the conventional classroom. Students could, for example, teach their newly learned reading and writing skills to illiterate parents or grandparents, or help the elderly and handicapped by reading or recording oral histories of a region. These types of programs would encourage intergenerational relationships and further learning, provide extra-needed assistance for the elderly without burdening government coffers, and offer students the opportunity to experience the sense of accomplishment that comes with active citizenship through rendering service to others.

## The Saber and the Brain Shift

One of the few certainties we have about our collective future is that it will require a massive amount of learning by just about everybody, everywhere. As noted by a background paper for the OECD Innovation Strategy, improvements in learning could very well become a key leverage point for successfully meeting the challenges of the 21st century:

"Only countries that implement policies to reform their education to promote adaptability and creativity in adults and children are likely to remain at the forefront of human development and technology."[13] Other recent reports from different countries have come to a similar conclusion.

The problem is that most educational systems today are not designed with 21st century understandings or objectives, and do not promote adaptability and creativity. Current education and training systems instead tend to develop conformity and alignment instead of creativity, competition instead of collaboration, and knowledge reproduction instead of knowledge creation![14] The public educational systems in the United States and many other countries today are actually based on a very narrowly-focused set of industrial-age assumptions and objectives that, like our monetary system, date back centuries (see insert).

### The Origins of today's Public Education

Today's education system is based on a model to create a society of dutiful, obedient foot soldiers. As Thom Hartmann points out in his book, *Beyond ADD,* our system of learning dates back to early 19th century Prussia (now Germany), a country renowned for its merciless and efficient army—until it suffered a staggering military defeat at the hands of Napoleon. Prussia's shocked leaders were determined to find out why their soldiers had gotten so soft. Philosopher Johann G. Fichte, in his "Address to the German Nation," indicted the country's school system, citing its failure to produce compliant pupils. Brash, undisciplined students, he asserted, went on to become disobedient and rebellious soldiers.

In 1819, Prussia established a universal compulsory school system with the goal of producing dutiful children who would follow orders and become winning soldiers. This strategy worked, at least for a time. Over the next five or six decades, Prussia became a leading industrial and military power due largely to an efficient, though uninspired workforce and army.

Governments from other nations sent representatives to Prussia to discover its secrets of success. Horace Mann, an influential educational figure from America, was among those summoned. Duly impressed, Mann raved about how the disciplined Prussian school system could be useful in America to cure social ills, tame the Wild West, and provide quality workers.

Not surprisingly, U.S. industrial leaders embraced the concept of a system that would provide colonies of compliant workers to labor in factories and on railroads. In the words of Hartmann, "so began the dumbing down of America."[15]

Like our monetary paradigm, the education system that came into being in the 19th and 20th centuries confined itself to a very narrow set of industrial-age objectives and suffered from the limited understandings of the period regarding human intelligence and learning. Moreover, this system of teaching was unaware of and not prepared for the shift that has been taking place in recent decades from left to right brain thinking.

It has been known for some time that there are different forms of intelligence. Project Zero at Harvard has documented eight distinct types, out of which primarily two are developed and measured in the conventional education system: the verbal/linguistic and the logical/mathematical. The other six forms of intelligence tend to be simply ignored.[16] A child who is gifted primarily in one of the other modes of learning—musical, spatial, bodily/kinesthetic, intrapersonal, interpersonal, and pattern recognition—is likely to end up being considered as mediocre and become an educational failure.

Different forms of intelligence are, however, only part of the story. What has also been pretty much ignored are the different ways in which we process information and learn.

In their book, *Right Brain Children in a Left Brain World*, authors Jeffrey Freed and Laurie Parsons-Cantillo, point out that the two halves of our brain each process information, but in different ways. A significant and growing percentage of our population are not internally "wired" to learn by traditional left-brain teaching methods such as passive listening and memorizing facts.[17] As educator and pyshologist Linda Kreger Silverman explains, "the left hemisphere is analytical, sequential, and time-oriented. The right hemisphere perceives the whole, synthesizes, and apprehends movement in space."[18] More students today respond to right-brain dominant methods that are more experiential, kinesthetic, and emphasize an explorative dialogue among students and with teachers.

According to Freed:

> Why are we facing such a crisis in education? I would argue that our left-brained schools have rarely placed an emphasis on creative, critical thinking. Our schools have historically churned out graduates who, while strong on regurgitating information, lack problem-solving skills. Children are taught to conform rather than challenge authority; the result is they often lack the ability to make connections and think in fresh, inventive ways. The traditional American school, with its emphasis on order, drill, and repetition, probably did a respectable job educating children at a time when kids were left-brained, less hyperactive, and not so stimulated. The problem is that students today are fundamentally different. Our classrooms are being flooded by a new generation of right-brained, visual kids. While our school system plods along using the same teaching methods that were in vogue decades ago, students are finding it more and more difficult to learn that way. As our culture becomes more visual and brain dominance shifts to the right, the chasm widens between teacher and pupil. Our schools are no longer congruent with the way many children think.[19]

The magnitude of this brain-hemispheric shift is significant, with more than half of today's school age children believed to be right brain learners. Dr. Silverman estimates that one third of today's student population are strongly right-brained; another 30 percent rely on both hemispheres but tend to favor the right.[20] This is a substantial increase from 1997, at which time approximately 40 percent of children were right brain learners. This shift in how we access information is in no small measure related to technological advancements in recent decades, including the internet, calculators, smart phones, video gamming, and other forms of interactive media.

Freed and Parsons-Cantillo see in the Saber not only an economic instrument to enhance educational opportunities, but also as a means to help develop collaborative skills among students, to cater to the individual forms of intelligence of each child, and to enhance learning among right-brainers.

## Saber and Demurrage

Demurrage can be used to help manage the balance between the numbers of students wanting university seats each year and availability. A demurrage fee would be applied to encourage students to use Sabers in accord with the year printed on the Saber. If they were not used to pay for tuition before or during that year, they could be exchanged for Sabers of the following year but with a penalty of, say, 20 percent, when a new expiration date is stamped on the paper currency. This gives a strong incentive to use the Sabers on or before the deadline.

## Saber and Inflation

Three factors make the noninflationary dynamics of the Saber fundamentally different from those of regular money. They are:

o  Sabers are only redeemable into conventional money by universities or third-level educational institutions within the system, and only for educational purposes;

o  the quantity of Sabers issued would be equal to the universities' capacities to increase their number of students, thereby avoiding the inflation problem generated by a currency that is created in excess of the goods or services available. Extra students would be using seats that would otherwise be empty;

o  the demurrage fee of 20 percent ensures that the Sabers circulate only for a limited and controlled time period, further reducing the possibility of excess currency.

## Support for the Saber

A variation of the original Saber project is being developed by Professor Schwarz, with funding by Brazil's Ministry of Science and Technology, Brazil's Ministry of Culture, and the Brazilian Development Bank (Banco Nacional de Desenvolvimento Economico e Social, or BNDES). It should also be noted that the Saber also enjoys support from the central bank of Brazil, which has formally acknowledged that "social currencies" not only do not pose a threat to conventional monetary management, but instead provide a significant positive contribution to the social fabric and the economy in general.

The legal counsel of Brazil's central bank has recently concluded that, *"social currencies should be regarded as public policy instruments for local development compatible with monetary policy."*[21] This is the first central bank to make such an acknowledgment. Other countries have expressed interest in this concept.

## CLOSING THOUGHTS

Many of our most pressing social concerns are treatable. Improvements can be made without the need to increase taxes, redistribute wealth, borrow, or otherwise increase burdens on already limited public resources and overtaxed economies. Communities around the world are instead finding relief in the form of complementary currencies, such as the Fureai Kippu and the Saber. These monetary initiatives can be designed specifically to address particular concerns by ways and means that do not hurt anyone and instead promote the general good. Many different monetary designs and improvements are now readily available, made possible by the revolution now taking hold in our understanding and use of money.

Society functions in a manner consistent with the systems that are in place. Until and unless there is amendment to the operating systems that govern society, the desired changes and improvements sought by growing numbers of concerned citizens will simply not take hold. But by rethinking money, many new options and opportunities do become readily available.

## CHAPTER SIXTEEN

# Commercial-Purpose Currencies

*Sure, money's all wrong, and the devil decreed it;*

*It doesn't belong to the people who need it.*

~PIET HEIN

While many communities around the world are turning to complementary currencies to help address an ever-expanding range of social issues, new monetary innovations are also being applied increasingly to business-related concerns and objectives. As noted, complementary currencies have been employed for commercial purposes down through history and are finding increasing use again today in business.

One of the most extensive uses of complementary currencies is the familiar loyalty mechanism used by airlines, credit card companies, hotels, and travelers worldwide—frequent flyer miles. Though not customarily thought of as such, frequent flyer miles are a complementary medium of exchange, with ever increasing opportunities offered to earning flight miles, be it with purchases made through branded credit and debit cards, eating at participating restaurants, renting vehicles, and the like. There are many opportunities as well to make use of these earned miles for an expanding array of products and services. These and other commercial-purpose currencies have clearly demonstrated that such systems need not be restricted to small-scale objectives or local applications alone. During the first 20 years of operations, 9.77 trillion frequent flier miles were awarded, and this number is still growing at a rate of 11 percent per annum.[1]

Two of the many vital commercial complementary currency applications are examined next. Each initiative is designed to help enterprises, particularly those that are small to medium-sized, weather the ups and downs of the business cycle, and to help ensure against the loss of jobs during downturns. We begin with the longest surviving commercial-purpose complementary currency in the Western world, the Swiss WIR.

## THE WIR AND THE BUSINESS CYCLE

An insidious feature of economic downturns is the accompanying freeze on credit by banks to businesses. The present money-creation process tends to amplify the fluctuations of the business cycle. When business is good in a particular market, banks tend to be more generous in terms of credit availability, thereby pushing the good times into a potentially inflationary boom period. Conversely, as soon as the horizon looks less promising, access to credit is tightened, contributing to the deterioration of a minor business dip into a full-blown downturn.

With the loss of liquidity, a domino effect ensues. Spending decreases, businesses get stuck with inventory, orders to suppliers for materials and services for new products dry up, and so on. A chain of bankruptcies is started with its impact on unemployment and related social ills. The credit crisis that accompanied the global recession is one case in point. Central banks try to counteract this cycle, but their success is variable, at best.

Several years following the recent global downturn, the economic climate remains uncertain. Many companies struggle to stay afloat, while U.S. unemployment remains stubbornly high—well over 9 percent according to official estimates, with unofficial figures much higher still.[2] The jobless face fierce competition for work, and those with a job are watching their paychecks shrink.[3] While the trillions in bailouts aims at preventing a repeat of the 1930s, these sums could not prevent the massive disruption that has taken place, nor has it restored confidence in the marketplace. According to an Associated Press-GfK poll taken in the first half of 2010, only 20 percent of Americans surveyed believed that the economy was doing well.[4] Given the banking system's inherent aversion to risk, credit availability remains hard to come by and is not likely to return to pre-recession levels any time soon.

All of this begs the question: *What can be done to help businesses weather this and future economic storms?*

Options, though not necessarily of the conventional kind, certainly do exist. One example of what is possible comes to us from Switzerland during the difficult Great Depression period.

Switzerland enjoys one of the most stable economies and highest standards of living in the world. Factors often cited for the economic wellbeing of this nation include tourism, chocolates, precision watches, a world-famous banking system, and political neutrality during and following World War II. While each of these may well play a role, a unique, little-known, but very robust complementary currency has also contributed to the country's economic stability for the past 75 years.

This nation is home to the oldest continuously functioning complementary-currency system in the West. Called the WIR, it is a Swiss acronym for Wirtschaftsring-Genossenschaft, which roughly translates as "Economic Mutual Support Circle." Wir is also the pronoun "we" in German.

In the early 1930s, Switzerland faced economic woes similar to those in neighboring Germany and Austria. By the time of its inception in 1934, WIR's 16 founding members and clients had received notices from their respective banks that credit lines were going to be reduced or eliminated. Bankruptcy was only a matter of time. Unable to count on the banking sector to obtain the necessary capital during this difficult period, these Swiss businessmen decided to create a mutual credit system among themselves, and invited their clients and suppliers to join. Unlike the afore-mentioned Wära and Wörgl systems, the Swiss initiative managed to not only survive the period, but continues quite successfully to this very day.

The WIR provides more than seven decades of experience and demonstrates the degree to which complementary currencies can assist both individual businesses and the economy-at-large.

## How It Works

When business A makes a purchase from business B, A's account is debited and the corresponding amount is credited to B's account. The unit of account is the WIR, with parity between it and the Swiss franc (one WIR equals one Swiss franc). The currency is designed to serve only as a medium of exchange to facilitate business transactions. WIR accounts do not bear interest and do not serve as a practical store of value.

The WIR ("veer") was devised to counteract the business cycle. This internal currency is used to purchase and sell goods and services from business members within the WIR network, especially when national currency is difficult to come by, as occurs during economic downturns. When banks tighten lending practices, members of the WIR network can simply opt to accept or borrow the readily available WIR complementary currency to continue transacting business, thus diminishing the likelihood of more severe supply or demand side disruptions. Once the economy improves and bank credit is again normalized, WIR members can then shift back once again to the national currency. In essence, the issuance of WIR currency expands and contracts countercyclically with the Swiss franc economy.

The countercyclical function of the WIR provides an important macroeconomic advantage not only to WIR members but also to the Swiss economy as a whole. A quantitative study on the WIR's macroeconomic impact was conducted by Dr. James P. Stodder, professor at the Lally School of Management and Technology at Rensselaer Polytechnic Institute. Dr. Stodder's study concluded that, "growth in the number of WIR participants has tracked Swiss unemployment very closely, consistently maintaining a rate of about one-tenth the increase in the number of unemployed."[5]

Simply stated, the study showed that the WIR system contributed significantly to the stability of the Swiss economy and to its low unemployment rates. When the conventional Swiss franc economy slows, more people and firms participate in the WIR economy, thus demanding fewer disruptions to business and far fewer layoffs. The WIR functions as a powerful stabilizing mechanism that limits the severity of the business cycle and the inevitable ups and downs of the economy.

Professor Tobias Studer, from the Center of Economic Studies at Basel University, Switzerland, considers the Stodder research a breakthrough. He reports:

> For the first time, an independent American researcher has arrived at a surprising conclusion: far from representing a factor of disturbance for the national monetary policy, the credits created by WIR constitute a support of the National Bank [the Swiss central bank] in pursuit of its monetary policy objectives.[6]

## History and Scope

It bears noting that the WIR's contributions to both the economy and the banking sector were not always so well appreciated. When operations first began in the 1930s, the WIR was erroneously viewed as a direct threat to the banking system's hegemony, and, prompted a similar response to those taken by the central banks in neighboring Germany and Austria at the time (against the Wära and Wörgl, respectively). The Swiss banks proceeded to mount an aggressive press campaign to stop this complementary currency initiative from occurring. Miraculously, their hostile efforts failed.

In the first three months of operations, the WIR attracted 1,700 participants. Within a year, more than 3,000 businesses made use of this complementary-currency system, and were linked with one another by a catalog of 850 unique categories of goods and services. A cooperative was established to track WIR user accounts, which soon allowed participants to borrow WIR at the low interest rate of 1-1.5 percent. These loans, similar to those issued by a conventional bank, were backed by inventory, real estate, and other hard assets. The system was ultimately credited with saving many of the businesses involved.[7]

The system remains fully operational today, with more than 65,000 members participating in WIR nationally. This represents nearly one quarter of all Swiss businesses. In 2006, trading volume in WIRs was 1.67 billion Swiss francs ($1.4 billion).[8] WIR owns its own bank that operates in both Swiss francs and WIR, with six regional offices that conduct business in four languages.

Benefits to members participating in WIR include:

- o  cost efficiency—commission on sales and payment expenses are limited to 0.6 percent on deals completed in WIR;
- o  cheaper and more readily available credit than is issued in national currency, particularly during downturns;
- o  auxiliary services such as direct mail, publicity among members, publications, and more;
- o  access to a large and prescreened—thus dependable and credit-worthy—client base, which helps engender trust;
- o  ways and means to continue to conduct business during periods of contraction or high interest rates.

Within the context of the recent economic meltdown and the liquidity crunch that accompanied it, a question that begs asking is: *might the WIR's proven ability to facilitate business activity and employment during economic downturns be of use by other communities?* Given that complementary currencies make both business and macroeconomic sense and have become well established in one of the most conservative, hard-nosed capitalist countries on Earth, why should it be any different in the United States and elsewhere?

The case is made below for expanding the WIR model as a means of reducing the impact of the global financial crisis on businesses and governments, both locally and nationally.

## COMMERCIAL CREDIT CIRCUIT (C3)

What began as a financial and banking crisis in 2008 rapidly turned into a major job crisis. The bulk of the global economy and the vast majority of private jobs are provided by small and medium sized enterprises (SMEs). The survival of many such firms was put at risk due to cash flow problems related to the downturn.

### The Problem

Under the current paradigm, SMEs rely upon banks and other finance institutions for credit. When credit lines are tightened, the entire economy is adversely affected, especially SMEs. These firms must overcome unique hurdles to continue operations, particularly during downturns. Unlike large customers who are given 90 days or more to pay for services and goods, SMEs are pressured for prompt payments, often within 30 days. When banks either refuse to provide bridge financing or do so at steep conditions, a deadly cash flow trap ensues for SMEs. This has long been an endemic issue in developing countries, but lately has become more critical in developed countries of late as well.

### The Solution

The Commercial Credit Circuit (C3), like the WIR, provides another option for needed liquidity, and at more reasonable costs than are typically available. This is accomplished by forming a credit circuit among SMEs, their customers, and suppliers, with the addition of an insurer. For a small cost, the insurer underwrites the business deal to guarantee that all parties involved with a business transaction will receive payment.

Unlike the WIR, any transaction using C3 is fully convertible at any time into national money, allowing this currency system to more easily attract business entities that might otherwise shy away from a complementary means of payment.

## How it Works

Let us say that a theatre seat manufacturer receives an order for 100,000 seats from a reputable firm, who will pay for the seats by check on delivery. The manufacturer (business A) has its own workers to produce the seats, and a supplier for the requisite materials (business B). Everything is in place to make the deal happen except for the money needed to pay workers and business B. Normally, business A would have to go to a bank for a bridge loan for this situation, which, depending on factors such as the business climate at the time, may or may not be successful. With C3, the needed financing is available in another way.

The process uses insured invoices or other payment claims as liquid payment instruments within a business-to-business clearing network. Each recipient of the liquid payment instrument has the choice to either convert it into national money (at a cost), or directly pay its own suppliers with the proceeds of the insured invoice. The manner by which C3 works is described below.

### C3 Step by Step

1.  The business that initiates a C3 transaction (business A) starts by securing insurance for an invoice up to a predetermined amount, based on the specific creditworthiness of their own business and that of the claims they obtain on third parties (the clients of A).

2.  Business A opens a checking account in the clearing-network, electronically exchanges the insured invoice for clearing funds, and immediately pays its supplier (business B) with those funds via the network.

3.  To receive its payment, business B only needs to open its own checking account in the network.

4.  Business B now has a positive balance on its account in the network (regardless of when the original invoice comes due from business A).

5.  Business B is thus in position to proceed with one of two options: either cash in the clearing funds for conventional national money (at the cost of paying banking fees plus the interest for the outstanding period (say, 90 days); or paying its own supplier (business C) with the corresponding clearing funds (at no cost).

6.  Business C only needs to open an account in the network. It then has the same two options as business B: cash in the funds for national money, or spend the C3 funds in the network. And so on…

7.  At maturity of the invoice, the network is paid the amount of the invoice in national money, either by the client of business A, or (in case of default by that client) by the insurance company. Whoever owns the C3 funds secured by the insured invoice can cash them in for national money without incurring any interest costs (though any associated banking fees still apply).

## Benefits

The benefits to participating businesses in C3 include:

o   Businesses increase their access to short-term funds as needed to improve their working capital and the use of their productive capacity. The size of this credit can be built up to a stable level between a quarter (covering therefore up to an average of 90 days of invoices) and half of annual sales, at a cost substantially lower than what is otherwise possible.

o   Suppliers are paid immediately, regardless of the payment schedule of the original buyer. Thus, ample liquidity is available at very low cost to the entire SME network. The approach provides a viral spreading of participation to the C3 networks from clients to suppliers.

o   All the necessary technologies are proven; new legislation or government approvals are not required, and the necessary software is available in open source. Only invoices that are 100 percent guaranteed and 100 percent computerized are acceptable in a C3 system. C3 thereby encourages the generalization and more efficient use of IT infrastructure among SMEs, including the opening of new markets and marketing channels through e-commerce.

Government benefits, especially at the regional level, include:

o   Additional income streams are provided for government. An effective way to encourage C3 strategy usage is for governments to accept payment of taxes and fees in C3 currency. This encourages others to accept C3 payment as well, and provides added income to government from transactions that otherwise would not occur. Additional income in national currency becomes available automatically no longer than 90 days after the payment, with no disruption to existing procurement policies. This strategy is now under serious consideration for use by the government of Uruguay.

o   The C3 approach is a dependable way to systemically reduce unemployment. Governments at different levels (federal, state or regional) can contribute to a joint guarantee mechanism, which would be considerably cheaper to fund than subsidies.

o   C3 helps shift economic activities from the black or grey economy into the official economy, because SMEs need to be formally incorporated to participate, and all exchanges are electronic and therefore traceable.

o   C3 systems are best organized at a regional level, so that each network remains at a manageable scale. Businesses with an account in the same regional network have an incentive to spend their balances with each other, and thus further stimulate the regional economy. C3 provides a win-win environment for participants, and promotes other collaborative activities among regional businesses.

o   Each C3 network should use the same insurance standards and compatible software to interconnect as a network of networks to facilitate exchanges internationally.

Benefits to banks and the financial system include the following:

- o C3 significantly streamlines the lending and management for insurance and for loan providers. As the C3 process is entirely computerized, SMEs can become a more profitable sector for banks, as the credit lines are negotiated with the entire clearing network, thus providing the financial sector with automatic risk diversification among participants in the network. In the upcoming surge of new competitors in the market—such as Facebook, Google, or Tesco currencies and banks—this monetary innovation provides an additional window for banks to sell their core activities.

- o Most banks are also involved in providing insurance services. C3 opens up a whole new market for insurances and credit, all the way down to services for microfinance enterprises. As C3 is fully computerized, even such small-scale entities can now be serviced at a very low cost.

- o The C3 mechanism systemically contributes to the stability of employment and of the entire economy, which is helpful for the overall solidity of the banks' portfolios.

## CLOSING THOUGHTS

Owners of small businesses can do something more than hope that the economy gets better, or that someone else will see to their needs. The WIR and the C3 are easily implementable and provide cash flow and other benefits for all those directly involved in these complementary currency programs, as well as to the economy-at-large. Additionally, the software required for C3 is available in open source to encourage start-ups of such systems anytime, anywhere. If Uruguay can achieve this on a national scale, it can be done on any other scale that makes sense to the participants.

## CHAPTER SEVENTEEN

# The Terra, A Trade Reference Currency

*Many have a wait and see attitude to innovate proposals of this nature, but they shouldn't with the Terra. Such a Trade Reference Currency reduces risk, stabilizes the world economy, and is a more cost effective approach for international business.*

~TAKASHI KIUCHI
Chairman, The Future 500
Former CEO, Mitsubishi Electric, America

The world needs a global currency that is nobody's national money. This may at first appear as a surprising idea, but there are several powerful reasons to justify it.

## WHY A NEW GLOBAL CURRENCY?

There are two key reasons why a specialized global currency is required today:

- o Geopolitical: If the dollar should lose its privileged status as a global reserve currency, we can expect a power grab by other currencies for influence in their respective regions, which has historically generated many wars.
- o Practical: A specialized global currency can be designed and administered to resolve several key issues, including economic instability and corporate short-termism.

A few words are warranted on each of these arguments.

## Geopolitical

The dollar's use as a global reserve currency gives the United States a particular advantage as the only country today that can afford a permanent deficit in its trade. This is because central banks are obliged to accept dollars under the current rules of the IMF. Such an advantage, however, should not be considered a permanent status. This same torch was passed from Britain to America after World War II. Some people claim that it may well soon pass, in turn, to China.

Such transitions often incur friction, and fights for monetary zones of influence usually provoke damage. The most dangerous period occurs during the decline of a hegemonic power whereby the old guard no longer commands enough power to impose its own solution, but still retains sufficient influence to block any solution proposed by others. This is the situation we find ourselves in today. If a dollar crisis should erupt, the most likely outcome will be a fragmentation of the global system into three monetary zones: a dollar-dominated zone in the Western hemisphere, a european-dominated zone, and an Asian zone (still under preparation). We might expect high volatility between these monetary zones, even more than what is presently taking place with national currencies. It is also likely that foreign exchange controls will materialize between these zones, which will be costly and otherwise problematic. None of this is advantageous or conducive to peaceful economic and political evolution.

The introduction of the global Terra Trade Reference Currency (TRC) avoids a major potential source of conflict, while solving important problems for all those businesses and other entities that depend on easy and efficient global commercial exchanges.

## Practical

Introducing a special-purpose global currency resolves several other key issues of particular importance today. Contrary to what takes place with conventional money, the Terra would spontaneously operate countercyclically with the business cycle and contribute to the stabilization of the world economy. Perhaps most importantly, the Terra is designed to give multinational corporations a strong incentive for long-term thinking.

Given the stakes that are involved and the current financial instability, we believe this to be a timely and vital proposal.

Even with the detail given here, this chapter should be considered a mere overview. For those interested in a deeper understanding, please consult the White Paper available for download on dedicated web sites.[1]

## CHARACTERISTICS OF THE TERRA

The Terra is based on fundamentally distinct principles from conventional, bank-debt issued money. Key differences include:

o The Terra is 100 percent asset-backed, while conventional money is backed by nothing except the belief that other people will accept it. Therefore, by definition, there can never be fractional reserve Terras, and the supply of Terras does not rise or fall with the expansion or contraction of bank credit.

o The Terra's assets consist of a balanced basket of a dozen of the most representative commodities and services in the world economy. This global reference currency thereby offers a natural inflation hedge.

o The Terra, like the WIR and C3, is naturally countercyclical and therefore helps stablize the economy. Conventional money creation tends to be naturally procyclical, that is, it accentuates the repeated booms and busts that destabilize the economy, even as central banks try to counteract this phenomenon.

o The Terra does not bear interest. It instead has a demurrage charge of 3.5-4 percent per year (to cover the cost of storage of the commodities backing the Terra). The Terra is therefore only a trading and contractual instrument, not a store of value. The Terra therefore encourages trading, while conventional money encourages accumulation.

o The Terra is managed by the Terra Alliance, while conventional money is managed by central banks. The alliance doesn't decide when to create or redeem Terras; member participants make such decisions.

Four types of entities participate in the Terra system: Terra backers, Terra users, commodities/futures markets, and the Terra Alliance itself. In addition, other organizations or individuals may piggyback off the

Terra system, using it simply as a contractual reference unit without participating in the system itself.

## The Terra Mechanism

The Terra Alliance operations are now examined.

### Creation of Terras

A member with excess inventory of one of the commodities comprising the Terra, can sell such inventory to the Alliance. By triggering the issuance of the Terra as an inventory receipt (which is paid for and denominated in Terras), that member is then functioning as a Terra Backer. This is how Terras come into being. They are in a sense, warehouse receipts, which are historically a very old form of money.

### What is a Terra Unit?

A Terra Unit is a claim against a portion of the asset holdings of the Terra Alliance. The Alliance warehouses large quantities of the commodities comprising the Terra. These quantities always equal, in total, the amounts necessary to redeem all of the Terra units in existence.

To use a simplified example, suppose there were 100 Terra units in existence and each unit represented 1 ounce of gold, plus 1 pound of copper and 1 bushel of wheat. In such a case, the Terra Alliance would warehouse 100 ounces of gold, 100 pounds of copper, and 100 bushels of wheat at all times.

Taking a more realistic example, suppose that an oil-producing member decides to sell 1 million barrels of crude oil to the Terra Alliance in exchange for Terras. Given that crude oil is one component of the Terra "basket," the Terra Alliance would use commodities markets to sell enough of the oil and buy enough of the other 11 components such that all 12 components are once again equally represented in the Terra basket.[2]

### Conducting Trade in Terras

Once Terras are brought into existence, they can be bought and sold like any other form of money or commodity. There is, however, a demurrage charge on Terra holdings, at a rate of approximately 3.65 percent per year. Stated differently, a time penalty on keeping Terras is being charged at the rate of about one hundredth of one percent (.01 percent) per day. Due to the electronic nature of the Terra and the power of modern computers, this parking fee can be allocated between the traders precisely based on how long they held onto the Terra units, even down to the minute. This inflation-protected currency therefore offers a permanent incentive to encourage trading with it. Each entity accepting a payment in Terra becomes one of the Terra Users.

*Redemption of Terras*

When members decide for whatever reason to redeem Terras for national currency, they need only present their Terras to the Terra Alliance. They thereby become the "final user." When such a redemption request is made, the Terra Alliance will sell a sufficient portion of its basket to generate the cash needed to cover the redemption, and the final user pays a 2 percent transaction fee. This fee aims at discouraging the cashing of Terras for conventional money. The Alliance will then pay out the proceeds in conventional money through participating banks.

*Piggybackers*

There is a last group of parties who will benefit from the existence of Terras, even though they may never have any dealings with the Alliance, or even may never actually own Terras—piggybackers. Not wishing to be tied to the vagaries of a particular national currency, they could simply use the Terra as a trade reference currency, pricing contracts in it but settling those contracts in an equivalent amount of some other national currency, as agreed upon contractually with the other party.

*Refinements*

More sophisticated implementations of the Terra can include in the "model Terra basket" claims for future services, and even artificial assets such as carbon emission rights. Theoretically, any product or service could be included in the basket at the condition that it can be standardized and that a corresponding futures market can be organized.

## An Example of the Terra Mechanism

Let's consider a series of transactions made possible by an oil producer's decision to accept payment in Terras rather than conventional money (see Figure 17.1).

1.  (a). An oil producer with an excess inventory of 1 million barrels of oil sells that quantity of oil to the Terra alliance instead of selling it for conventional money. (Note that this decision is more likely during a downturn, when demand for oil and other commodities declines and when extra sales on the market would further depress the price).

    (b). and (c). The Terra alliance sells some of that oil to increase its holdings of the other 11 component commodities.

    (d). The alliance credits the Terra account of the producer with a quantity of Terra units equal to the purchasing power of 1 million barrels of oil at that time.

2.  (a). The oil producer uses some of those Terras to buy an oil rig from a company willing to accept the Terras in trade.

    (b). The rig supplier uses some of the Terras to buy components from its own supplier.

    (c). The process continues with the Terras circulating like any other type of money until they are redeemed.

3.  The oil producer, rig supplier, and other Terra users each pay a demurrage charge when using the Terra, based on how long their Terras were held in their accounts.

4.  (a). Whenever Terras are redeemed, the final user will be charged with a 2 percent redemption fee.

    (b). In addition, the Terra Alliance sells that portion of its commodity holdings to which those Terras have rightful claim, and pays the redeeming party in conventional currency.

5.  Piggybackers simply use the Terra as a trade reference currency, pricing contracts in it, but settling those contracts in an equivalent amount of some other national currency, as agreed upon contractually with the other party.

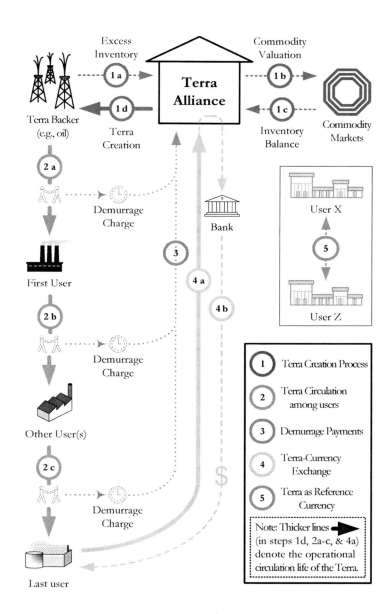

*Figure 17.1 – The Terra Trade Reference Currency Mechanism*

**Benefits of the Terra**

The Terra trade reference currency provides benefits to particular segments of the economy, including: businesses engaged in international trade, governments of both developed countries and less developed countries (LDCs), and the nations that are trading partners.

The benefits, elaborated on further below, include:
1. a more level playing field among nations;
2. lower costs of international business;
3. increased investment in LDCs;
4. improved stability of the global economy;
5. protection against inflation;
6. a shift from short-term to longer term planning.

*1. A level playing field among nations*

About two thirds of the time, management of a national currency is beneficial for both the national economy and world economy. But that still leaves a third of the time in which a policy that is beneficial for the national economy is detrimental to the world, or vice versa.

When, for instance, the British pound was playing the role of a global currency (from the 19th to mid-20th century), there was a tendency to favor the international role of the pound over its role for the domestic economy. That tendency helps explain why Britain was the last country to be able to get rid of war rations after World War II.

When the U.S. dollar started playing the role of a global currency, these priorities were reversed. As Paul Volcker stated when he was Chairman of the Federal Reserve, "Americans are paying my salary, so I am managing the dollar to the benefit of America."[3] We claim that both these outcomes are undesirable.

The Terra solves the quandary between national and global interests by leaving all nations free to manage their currency as they please, without any detrimental effect to their own national economy or to that of the world. By virtue of being privately issued, with all participants enjoying equal benefits of use, participation in the Terra system eliminates the lopsided effects of granting preferred TRC status to any single nation or group of nations.

## 2. Lower costs and risks for doing international business

International business activities typically involve someone—be it the buyer, seller, or even both—taking a currency risk. In theory, with today's 24/7 electronic currency exchanges, trading in currencies, either immediately or at some future date (futures contracts), should be straightforward. In practice, the cumulative costs of such insurance are instead quite high, and efficient markets exist only for half a dozen major national currencies.

The volatility of the Terra would be less than a quarter of what we currently experience between major national currencies, even if only 9 major commodities are included in the basket. Both the risks and the cost of hedging those risks would therefore be significantly lower when using the Terra compared to today's national currencies.

## 3. Increased investment in LDCs

Less developed countries tend to be resource-rich and infrastructure-poor. By making their resources central not just to certain specific kinds of economic activities but to the international financial system itself, powerful incentives will exist for multinational entities and nations to help these LDCs develop their infrastructure and resources.

## 4. Improved stability of the world economic system

Recent decades have seen numerous boom and bust cycles that originated in one nation, but which cascaded contagiously across international borders.

When banks collectively perceive economic activity as slowing, they withdraw credit from borrowers because of the possible increased risk. While this is sound practice for individual banks, it is detrimental for the economies involved, and even for the banking system as a whole. The very act of withdrawing credit makes it harder for the businesses involved to survive. By similar logic, when the economy is good, banks eagerly lend money, thereby potentially driving a healthy economic period into an unsustainable bubble. This amplification of the business cycle is what is meant by procyclical money creation.

The Terra offers three ways by which it actually helps to balance out the boom and bust cycles.

First, it acts as a countercyclical money creation process. The particular time periods when producers of raw materials have excess inventories (that can be sold against Terras) tends to coincide with the downturn of the business cycle.

Second, it offers a complementary monetary system for international trade that is not tied to credit creation or withdrawal but rather to valuable assets.

Finally, it allows resource suppliers to sell those resources for Terras when there may not be enough buyers who can pay in traditional money without significantly depressing the price. This, in turn, generates self-funding buffer stocks. Thes stocks can become critical in the case of crop shortages or failures due to climate change, particularly in the domain of food commodities. Global stocks are already dangerously low.

### 5. Protection against inflation

By structuring the Terra upon the foundation of a representative basket of goods and services that are central to economic activity worldwide, the Terra serves as a kind of proxy for the most significant international inputs of the world economy itself. The value of the Terra would therefore adjust automatically to inflationary pressures due to these inputs.

Using the Terra for contractual agreements, particularly longer term ones, would therefore be an automatic inflation hedge.

### 6. A shift from short-term to longer-term thinking

As has been discussed elsewhere in this book, an overemphasis on short-term thinking has abetted many of our problems today. Stockholders in public companies typically hold management accountable for quarterly results. Long-term threats such as global warming, ocean acidity, and deforestation do not enjoy constituencies willing and able to make long-term investments necessary to rectify them. These are but symptoms of a widespread systemic failure of money.

It is the nature of interest-bearing currencies that a dollar today is worth more than a dollar tomorrow. This encourages a focus on short-term cash flow, and the higher the rate of interest the more short-term becomes the thinking. In contrast, exactly the opposite is true with a demurrage-charged currency. Almost all corporate decisions on investments or allocations of funds are undertaken using the Discounted Cash Flow technique, whereby the interest rate is part of the discount rate.[4] Demurrage is instead a negative interest rate that reduces the discount applied.

The historical record shows that the impact of money on investment timelines isn't just theory. In cultures where demurrage-charged currencies complement interest-bearing currencies, a longer planning horizon develops and more long-term investments are made. Examples of this include the Central Middle Ages and Dynastic Egypt (described in more detail in Part IV).

This difference in planning horizons can be compared to a well-known principle of inventory management. Sophisticated companies strive to have exactly the right amount of each production component (asset) on hand when needed for their production activities. Too little, and they cannot fulfill orders. Too much, and they are wasting money on inventory carrying costs. This concept is called "just-in-time inventory."

Money is also an asset, and can therefore be inventoried. Demurrage-charged money such as the Terra is expensive to hold. Therefore, if you receive it sooner than you need it, you are wasting money. Such a system encourages a mindset of receiving money only when it is actually needed in the future. It encourages a more forward-looking mindset, which balances the immediacy of interest-bearing money.

### Differences from Earlier Proposals

The Terra is a commodity-basket currency. Noted economists have made several proposals of this kind for more than a century. The main reason why these other plans have not been implemented is not due to a technical fault of the concept itself, but rather that they were aiming at replacing the conventional monetary system. Such replacement would have put in jeopardy powerful vested interests. This is not the case with the Terra proposal. The win-win strategy underlying the Terra mechanism includes the financial sector as well. Anything that exists under the current monetary modus operandi would remain in operation after the introduction of the Terra, as it is designed to operate in parallel with the existing system.

The political context for a new international monetary treaty, a new Bretton Woods type agreement, has not been available. The Terra avoids this difficulty by relying on private initiative. From a legal or tax standpoint, it would fit within the existing official framework of international barter (technically called countertrade), and not require any new formal governmental agreements to make it operational.

The final conceptual difference between the Terra and all previous proposals, and perhaps the most important one, is the use of demurrage. The fact that the storage costs of the basket would be covered by the bearer of the Terra resolves the inherent problem that previous commodity proposals faced and couldn't resolve: namely, who will pay for it all?

Growing concern and dissatisfaction with today's monetary situation has led to renewed interest in a return to the gold standard. Some of the advantages and disadvantages are discussed below.

## Advantages of the Gold Standard

The gold standard has indeed some systemic advantages compared to the current system. Specifically, two advantages are worth mentioning. First, the gold standard would reduce inflationary tendencies because gold cannot be created at will by governments or the banking system. And second, the gold standard is more symmetric, in that it provides corrective mechanisms to both those countries with a balance and payment surplus as well as to those with a deficit, so as to correct their balance of payments. Under the gold standard surplus countries would automatically see the value of their currency increase, which would make their products more expensive in the global market and reduce exports over time, thus bringing their trade balance back into equilibrium. Similarly, countries with a deficit would see their currency devalue, automatically making their products more competitive, which would, over time, bring their trade balances back in equilibrium.

The reigning Bretton Woods system is instead not symmetric: deficit countries are penalized, while those with a surplus have no incentive to bring their balances back to zero. The origin of this lack of symmetry can be traced back World War II, and expectations by the United States that it would be the only country whose productive capacity was left intact after the war. This advantageous position turned out to be only temporary, however, and today countries like China and Germany are taking advantage of this asymmetry.

## Disadvantages of the Gold Standard

The gold standard has some limitations as well, especially when compared to the Terra. In reality, the genuine gold standard was formally implemented for only a brief period.[5] By 1910, for instance, the Bank of England covered only about 20 percent of its emissions of Pound sterling with gold. This fact was kept from the public at the time, and illustrates how easy it was for a central bank to abuse the system. The same could easily happen again if the gold standard was reintroduced.

Another limitation is that the price in the gold market today is easily manipulated, given that its volume is so limited.

The Terra, which would include gold as one of the commodities in the Terra basket (at levels that range from 5 to 10 percent of the basket's value), would avoid the pitfalls cited above. Terras would be issued only as inventory receipts and would be audited publicly to ensure that this remains so. Furthermore, it would be far more challenging to manipulate simultaneously all the commodities that are part of the Terra basket.

In short, the Terra would provide benefits similar to those of the gold standard, without having its drawbacks.

## CLOSING THOUGHTS

The Terra Trade Reference Currency is poised to more cost-effectively enhance barter and countertrade, currently a multi-billion dollar industry. Implementation of this currency initiative does not require any new regulations or laws and provides a means to conduct business that otherwise might not take place, creating or saving jobs, and strengthening economies. The Terra TRC would automatically work to counteract the boom and busts of the business cycle and stabilize the economy by providing more cash during downturns, and cooling off inflationary pressures in the peak of an upturn. Most importantly, it will resolve the current conflict between short-term financial interests and long-term sustainability.

Along with creating greater stability and predictability in the financial and business sectors, the Terra TRC provides a robust standard of value for trade. It makes available, for the first time since the gold-standard days, a robust international standard of value that is inflation-resistant.

The Terra and other complementary currency proposals explored in previous chapters give some idea of the scope and diversity of how these applications can be used to resolve critical issues we face.

# CHAPTER EIGHTEEN

# Two Worlds

*Two roads diverged in a yellow wood, and I—*
*I took the one less traveled by,*
*And that has made all the difference.*

~ROBERT FROST

We live in critical times, faced with a series of epic concerns that threaten humanity as never before. In a university commencement address, entrepreneur, environmentalist, and author Paul Hawken stated clearly what is demanded of us:

> Class of 2009: you are going to have to figure out what it means to be a human being on Earth at a time when every living system is declining, and the rate of decline is accelerating. Kind of a mind-boggling situation...but not one peer-reviewed paper published in the last thirty years can refute that statement. Basically, civilization needs a new operating system, you are the programmers, and we need it within a few decades.[1]

Over the course of the last several decades, not one of the major megatrends facing our planet has been adequately addressed. In stark defiance of the growing awareness, concerns, and the many valiant efforts on the part of individuals, communities, non-profit organizations, and nations, each of the world's major concerns have instead only gotten worse. This decline and the persistence of our megatrends is not by accident. It was foretold more than a decade ago in *The Future of Money* (Random House, 1999), during a period of relative economic and political calm, before the dotcom crash, before 9/11, before the wars in Iraq and Afghanistan, and nearly a decade prior to the Great Recession.

In other words, the events and policies that took place over the course of this last decade, though having exacerbated our situation, were *not* in and of themselves the origins of our ongoing concerns. *The root cause of our megatrends is instead directly linked to our centuries-old monetary paradigm.*

The continued lack of monetary rethinking will make the persistence of our major concerns and the continued degeneration of conditions as predictable and irrevocable in the coming decade as in the past. This was a core thesis back in 1999 and remains so today. The key difference between then and now is that the need to act is far more urgent and the time in which to do so is much shorter still.

Our main focus throughout this book is to offer a sense of what is possible by venturing outside the confines of the current paradigm and exploring options available to us by rethinking money. In the pages that follow, we instead explore the approaches being taken within the given framework of the existing bank-debt monetary paradigm and the societal conditions that it portends. It should be understood that what is written below is not theoretical but has already begun to be set in motion. We repeat the claim made back in Chapter One:

*The kind of world we live in is directly linked to the type of monetary paradigm that is operational.*

## DEBT-BASED STRATEGIES

Summarizing the key conclusion of the previous chapters, the prevailing monetary paradigm can be simply stated as follows:

o   all exchanges in every country around the world today take place through a monopoly of a single currency;

o   that one currency takes the form of bank debt.

For more than a generation, debt has been touted as the answer to all economic troubles. This is not only the case for individuals, but applies to corporations, governments, and the financial sector. That supposed *solution* is, however, now becoming less available, or not available at all, principally because excessive debt has itself become a big problem. The consequences of remaining trapped within this conventional monetary box under such circumstances are profound.

**Salvation Through Debt?**

How have we arrived at this outcome in which excessive debt has become such a widespread problem?

At the individual level, getting in debt seems one of the few remaining rites of passage into adulthood. Getting one's first credit card is often perceived as more important than casting one's first vote, and buying a first house invariably means committing to a mortgage that is a substantial multiple of most annual incomes. Even if one doesn't indulge in either of these rites, a substantial slice of one's taxes is earmarked to pay interest on our government's national debt. Over the past half-century, total private debt in America has increased dramatically, from around 50 percent of GDP in the 1950s to a staggering 300 percent today.[2] This level has been reached, ominously, only once before: in 1929, just before the Great Depression.

Accumulating debt has also become fashionable for corporations, a consequence of which has been the steady, continuous deterioration of corporate credit ratings. For instance, Standard & Poor's median corporate rating went from "A" in 1981 to the current "BBB"—just one step better than "junk" status.[3] It should be noted, however that corporate debt is far from uniformly distributed. Many American firms reduced their appetite for debt after 2000, with the end of the dotcom bubble and the spectacular demise of WorldCom and Enron. But the wave of leveraged buy-outs (LBOs) continued a bit longer, and left all companies involved with a lot more debt on their balance sheets.

No industry has become more addicted to debt than finance. In America, while the non-financial sector increased its debt-to-GDP ratio from 58 percent in 1985 to 76 percent in 2009, the financial sector went from 26 percent to 108 percent over the same period.[4] Furthermore, the financial sector steamed ahead longer than all the rest, right up until the day of the financial crash of 2007-8. Leverage is one way to further push the financial efficiency of the system: its capacity to increase throughput for a given capital base. This extra leverage contributed predictably to the fragility of the whole financial system. It is this same debt that led financial institutions to lose trust in some of their own colleagues, which in turn triggered the meltdown and brought down giants such as Bear Stearns and Lehman Brothers.

Other consequences of the 2008 crisis were likely averted by massive governmental support for the financial sector. This was followed by large-scale Keynesian stimuli to avoid a deflationary depression. Both these actions have, however, resulted in huge budgetary deficits and additional public debt. In other words, excessive debt in the financial sector was "solved" by more debt in the public sector. In an ironically compounded next step, the financial sector has now turned against its savior of a year or so earlier, waving the spectre of defaults back at governments.

The threat of debt to an economy is clearly not an unknown one; only the scale has been increased over the centuries. In the 18th century, *Wealth of Nations* author, Adam Smith, warned that, "when national debts have once been accumulated to a certain degree, there is scarce, I believe, a single instance of their being fairly and completely paid."[5] A more ominous caution still comes from noted economist Ludwig von Mises:

> There is no means of avoiding the final collapse of a boom brought about by credit expansion. The alternative is only whether the crisis should come sooner as the result of voluntary abandonment of further credit expansion, or later as a final and total catastrophe of the monetary system involved.[6]

In essence, in continuing as is, a major crash appears unavoidable. The only remaining question regarding the crisis is the time frame.

**Withdrawal Pains?**

A lead editorial by *The Economist* in June 2010 made the claim that, "debt is as powerful a drug as alcohol and nicotine…Weaning rich countries off their debt addiction will cause withdrawal symptoms. Austerity does not appeal to voters, who may work off their frustrations on politicians and (worse) foreigners."[7] If we remain within the box of monetary orthodoxy, this statement will not only certainly prove true, but is in actuality only a very mild assessment of the situation we have created.

As forecast a decade ago, the convergence of global megatrends will oblige us to rethink our monetary system before 2020. The case then was that our monetary system will prove incapable of answering the following money questions:

o   How can we provide the elderly with sufficient money to match their longevity?

o   What can we do when jobs become really scarce?

o   How can we resolve the conflict between financially driven short-term planning and long-term needs?

o   How can we deal with systemic financial and monetary instability?

More than a decade later these questions and the issues they refer to have become more urgent and imperative than ever.

What is now being predictably added to our challenges are massive pressures on governments to reduce their deficits. As of 2011, talks of neo-Keynesian stimuli are over, while deficit reductions are in. This austerity will induce a prolonged period of job scarcity, much longer and painful than most people expected. Among other things, high unemployment is directly linked to housing problems, one of the major triggers of the 2008 crisis. Housing recoveries do not take place unless there is sustainable job growth.

Our view is that we are living through a variation of what took place seven decades ago. Today, we tend to describe the Great Depression as starting with Black Friday in 1929, followed by a continuous period of economic stress that stretched painfully on for most of the 1930s. That was not, however, the way it was perceived at the time by policy makers, the media, or citizens. People who lived through that period experienced it as a long succession of small ups and downs. Short-term improvements and hopes that were triggered by new government or private initiatives were each subsequently dashed by subsequent disappointment.

We are currently on an eerily similar track. Waves of stories about "green shoots," amplified by the media and politicians, are each dispelled by subsequent, unexpected bad news. Big hopes that have been pinned on governmental stimulus programs are now dashed when austerity measures are, by necessity, implemented.

Another important consideration is the psychological, social, and political consequences of this state of affairs, which is not easy to fathom. But one should expect large-scale social unrest in a number of countries, which historically plays into the hands of extremist political parties and populist leaders. History also teaches us that there is a high risk that such scenarios end up being resolved in one way or another through wars. To repeat, President Roosevelt himself admitted that it was only through involvement in World War II that the United States managed to finally extract itself from the Great Depression.

What is the proposed solution by the financial system, working of course within the existing paradigm, for solving excessive governmental deficits? It is privatization.

## THE U.S. PLAN—P3s

The conventional strategy currently proposed by the financial sector involves nothing less than the systematic privatization of most publicly owned infrastructures in the United States. The mechanism, called *Public-Private Partnerships (P3s)*, consists of the sale of most existing publicly owned highways, roads, bridges, tunnels, sewage and water treatment facilities, and more, all occurring through a series of existing and specially created funds. This is not some hypothetical possibility. This supposed "solution" is already being implemented in Illinois, Florida, and California, with 40 other states waiting to follow suit.

Only months after the 2008 downturn, 18 American financial companies including Carlyle, Abertis, Morgan Stanley, Freshfields, and Allen & Overy prepared a document entitled "Benefits of private investment in infrastructure."[8] It contains all the financial and legal details for a systematic privatization strategy to be applied in the United States. The scope of this strategy was summarized in the article in *Euromoney* entitled: "The Road to wiping out the U.S. Deficit" Some quotes follow.

> In 2009, the US government has spent $1.4 trillion more than it received in taxes and raised in debt. There are very few options left. So we will see a gravitation towards new P3s. If one assumes that the federal government will not be selling the navy or the municipalities their schools, there is still an immense amount of assets that can be sold. For instance, the value of all the highways and roads owned by states and municipalities is $2.4 trillion. There are $550 billion of sewerage assets at state and local levels along with a further $400 billion of water assets. Even at the federal level there is $42 billion-worth of amusements and recreation assets. And in the real estate sector, the federal, state and local governments own assets worth $1.09 trillion.[9]

Traditionally, the main obstacle for the sale of public assets came from the political sector, as it alienates voters. More recently, however, the political landscape with regard to P3s has changed (see insert).

### Euromoney P3s Data Points

The following quotes and data offer some illustration of the extent of development of P3s in the United States as of early 2011.[10]

"The moment the political pain from cutting services is more than the votes lost in selling assets, this market will take off...At grass-root level, that political pain threshold has been reached.

"As California lurches through another budget crisis, Governor Arnold Schwarzenegger has put on the block assets including prisons, roads and windfarms.

"Indiana sold the Indiana Toll Road in 2006 to Cintra and Macquarie for $3.8 billion.

"In Chicago, mayor Richard Daley has embraced asset sales with a fervor not matched anywhere else. He sold a 99-year lease to run the Skyway in 2005 for $1.83 billion to a consortium also comprising Macquarie and Cintra. He subsequently tried to sell Chicago's Midway airport for $2.5 billion in 2008, and in 2009 successfully sold the city's parking system in a deal that raised $1.1 billion. The Chicago parking deal was a huge success in every way but one: the transition from public to private ownership caused massive disruptions and a public outcry from residents about a 400 percent increase in the tariffs.

"Transactions are now underway in Hartford, Harrisburg, Indianapolis, Pittsburgh, Las Vegas and Los Angeles."

In essence, politicians realize that the political cost in not doing this is greater than in doing it. The tipping point has been reached.

Another traditional opponent to the sale of public assets are labor unions. But, like the political sector, unions are showing signs of coming around to the idea of privatized infrastructure. The reason for this about face is predictably financial. Financiers are now offering union pension funds access to a share of the deals. "A quarter of the assets of the $4 billion Macquaurie Infrastructure Partners has come from union pension funds...In November 2009, Carlyle closed a deal with co-investment of the Service Employees International Union (SEIU)."[11]

One can also expect that the financial pressures on municipalities, states, and federal governments will continue to build up for as long as needed to implement this plan. The only likely exceptions are with regard to military facilities and locally owned primary and secondary schools. Virtually everything else is being considered for sale. How will people react when the streets on which they live become electronic toll roads? Can one avoid wondering about the price the State Capitols or the White House or will fetch in a fire sale market, or under what conditions state and federal governments will be able to rent their real estate back after the sale?

It is only fair tonote that there are important instances in which privatizations can be successful and beneficial, as has been proven in the case of telecoms and mobile phone businesses. But not all privatizations have proven desirable for citizens. Whatever one's particular viewpoint, should the case for privatizing most of an existing national infrastructure not be worthy of at least some democratic debate? Or will this not even be possible during a sudden financial emergency?

There is no reason to believe that such policies would be limited to the United States. As part of the IMF loan of 2011, Greece had to commit to 50 billion euro worth of privatizations. Another example is Italy where the government of Silvio Berlusconi sold assets that have been in state ownership for centuries.[12] Neither should we expect that such sales of national assets to the financial sector will remain voluntary. After all, transactions of this kind were common practice as part of conditionalities to developing nations seeking IMF support during the 1980s and 1990s. Similar types of conditionalities regarding privatization could be adopted in the future. It bears mentioning that the main function of the IMF is to safeguard the interests of the banking sector. The IMF is therefore an enforcer of the existing paradigm.

### Next Questions

Some questions beg consideration regarding the consequences of this privatization evolution. What, for example, happens after such a strategy has run its course, say over the next decade, and almost everything has been privatized? Why will governments then be more creditworthy when they will have to pay rent on everything they use?

*"Never, ever, think outside the box."*

This coming decade happens to be the very one in which governments will be required to address some very critical issues. One such issue is the need to birth a post-carbon economy, which the world's scientists claim is needed in order to avoid an irreversible global climate change and biodiversity collapse. The trillion-dollar question becomes: *what can the public sector realistically do to meet such an unprecedented challenge, when governments are struggling for financial survival?*

From another perspective, why should anybody bother to vote for a government that has become structurally and financially incapable of significant actions?

Another question, made in the form of a request, came from President Obama when he presented the U.S. budget for 2010: "We simply cannot continue to spend as if deficits don't have consequences. In order to meet this challenge, I welcome any idea."[13]

Unfortunately, there are no new ideas, *nor can there be,* within the context of the given paradigm. Moreover, in a system with no self-correcting device except explosion, a crash such as that predicted by Von Mises is inevitable. The Wära, Wörgl, and the WIR offer lessons from which we have not yet learned.

## CLOSING THOUGHTS

We end Part II of this work by reiterating a few paragraphs presented in Chapter One.

This book recounts the story of two worlds and two paradigms. It offers a brief analysis of current conditions and the logical outcome of attempting to solve existing problems using the same thinking that created many of our concerns in the first place.

The main body of this work, however, considers another prospect for society and the systematic means by which it can be pragmatically realized.

This other world is one in which the long-term interests of humanity and the sustainability of our planet balance the short-term interests of business and industry; where there is meaningful work for all and time for ourselves, our families, and our communities; where the upbringing and education of our children and quality care for our elders are realized and compensated for in equal measure to other forms of employment so vital to society. This other world holds dear the diversity and sanctity of all life and the life-affirming aspects of what it is to be fully human, and consequently, more humane.

The potential for just such a prospect is not only possible but is, as previously noted, actually achievable within the span of a single generation. Many of the elements required for this to happen already exist. Also required is a wide assortment of innovative monetary tools, similar to those used in Curitiba, Brazil, that are made available to us quickly, safely, and inexpensively, by means of a greater understanding of our money.

# THE MYSTERY OF MONEY

*To find the soul of modern man and woman, begin by searching into those irreducibly embarrassing facts of the money complex, that crazy crab scuttling across the floors of silent seas.*

~JAMES HILLMAN

# CHAPTER NINETEEN

# Archetypes

*What lies behind us and what lies before us*

*are small matters compared to what lies within us.*

~RALPH WALDO EMERSON

U p until this juncture in our exploration, we have dealt with money as an exterior reality, something that shapes society "out there." In Part III, we investigate how money connects "in here," within our own psyche, where the engine driving so much of our lives resides. We must become aware of the way monetary systems shape our collective emotions—or perhaps, how collective emotions shape our choices in monetary systems—so that we can make conscious choices in moving forward.

When assessing fundamental change in our monetary system, we need to address some pertinent questions, such as:

o   Why is the peculiar kind of monetary system we have today considered obvious by so many cultures?

o   Where does the dominant power of money emerge from?

o   Are greed and fear of scarcity actually indelible reflections of human nature and material reality, and if not, what is it that engenders and reinforces these specific collective emotions?

o   In short, *what are the origin and mechanism of the emotional dimension of money?*

We wish to caution the reader that the following exploration will put us in touch with one of the foremost taboos of Western society. Inquiries about how much money someone has, or where it comes from, are considered even more inappropiate nowadays than the topic of sexuality.

Talking about a taboo is hazardous. By definition, pointing to a society's shadows risks upsetting some readers. We ask that each of you please take responsibility for the emotions that may arise along the way. We believe, however, that it is by shedding light on the above-cited questions that we can achieve the degrees of freedom necessary to reenvision our money in depth.

## OUR COLLECTIVE INHERITANCE

The recent mapping of the human genome reveals the extraordinary likeness of all human beings. If the DNA of each person were a book of 100 pages, the differences between our individual books would be measured not by chapters or pages, but by little more than a phrase or short sentence. While our covers—our outward appearances—might vary considerably, more than 99.9 percent of our wording would instead be identical. Genetically, at least, it is quite accurate to affirm that the bonds that unite us as a species far exceed any and all things that differentiate us as individuals, whether through our race, nationalities, cultures, or beliefs.[1]

Our commonality is to be found not only in our heritage, biochemistry, and physiology, but in our psyches as well.[2] While much of our identity is unique and influenced by individual circumstance, there also exist many predispositions, behaviors, and values that belong to the human race in general. Just as apes, bees, and cats are each born with certain innate traits common to their species, so do humans enter life with certain emotions, propensities, and behavior patterns that are universally "human." Our psychological common base, the so-called "collective unconscious," contains the vast heritage of humankind's evolution, born anew in every individual.

One of the many things we as modern humans share in common is a collective set of attitudes and assumptions regarding money. Though it is not customarily considered as such, *money is a projection from the collective unconscious.*

As previously noted, money is an *agreement*, a mental construct. Philosopher and author Jacob Needleman observed that, "money is…in the end, a product of the mind."[3] By its very definition, money is also a *collective* affair, in that it can only exist within a community. Additionally, money is not value neutral; different types of money predispose us to feel, think and act in particular ways, mostly in an *unconscious* manner, without our awareness. Moreover, each society considers its own monetary system as self-evident, regardless of whether it uses stones, pieces of metal, colorful paper, or electronic bits as currency. Each of these monetary facets speaks to the collective unconscious nature of our relationship with money.

To have money better serve our needs, it is important that we understand how and why our monetary system leads us to places few of us might consciously choose to go. One means available for our investigation is Archetypal Psychology, a field that provides a lens and language by which to explore the collective unconscious.

Archetypal Psychology was founded by famed Swiss psychologist Carl Gustav Jung (1875-1961). This field of psychology was developed further in the second half of the 20th century by psychologist James Hillman and others.[4] Jung was able to apply his understanding of the collective psyche to events taking place in our world, including his ability to forecast the rise of fascism in Europe as early as the 1920s. In Part III, insights from this field are applied to further our exploration of money.

For our purposes, only two of the key concepts of Archetypal Psychology need to be grasped: *archetypes* and *shadows*. These building blocks help to show how we are predisposed to relate to one another and the world around us, and the role that money plays in our lives.

## ARCHETYPES

A core focus of Archetypal Psychology is the *archai*, the deepest patterns of psychic functioning, "the fundamental fantasies that animate all life." Jung put forward this short definition: "Archetypes are to the soul what instincts are to the body."[5]

Jungian psychologist Bernice Hill offers this explanation:

> Archetypes are primordial, universal energy patterns developed over eons of time and moving throughout the world and human history. They carry a full range of positive and negative possibilities, but they cannot be known completely or directly through the intellect alone. They inform our behavioral patterns and attitudes, and are found in art, dreams, symbols, cultural stories, and myth(s).[6]

For the purposes of this work, archetypes may be defined as: *patterns of emotions and actions that can be observed across time and cultures.* This working definition remains valid even if one is not comfortable with the Jungian approach to psychology.

## Archetypes and Myths

One way to better understand archetypes is through popular myths. Now-popular attitudes might deem a work dedicated to issues such as our monetary system and societal challenges a strange place to employ myths, because many people today consider myths to be only pre-scientific tales about the origin of mankind or about some imaginary heroes or divine beings, and thus of limited value.

Myths are, however, valid descriptions of psychic sequences; they are favorite scenarios that illustrate how specific archetypes manifest, regardless of time or cultural context. Myths are not some unique hero or god's story; they instead reveal shared aspects of who we are. According to mythologist Joseph Campbell, myths represent, "powers that have been common to the human spirit forever, and that represent the wisdom of the species by which man has weathered the millenniums."[7] Scholar Eric Robertson Dodds defined myths as, "the dream-thinking of a whole civilization."[8] They are revelations and expressions about the make-up of our collective being.

Archetypes can be found in hundreds of mythological, classical, and symbolic figures. Joseph Campbell identified and wrote about the *Hero with a Thousand Faces*, as one universal and quintessential story found through the ages that transcends the boundaries of culture. This hero is seen in Sumer as Gilgamesh, in ancient Greece as Hercules, in the Middle Ages as knights in shining armor, or in Japan as the fearless Samurai.

As Jung described:

> These hero myths vary enormously in detail, but the more closely one examines them, the more one sees that structurally they are very similar. They have, that is to say, a universal pattern, even though groups and individuals developed them without any direct cultural contact with one another; for instance, tribes in Africa or the Incas in Peru. Over and over again one hears tales describing a hero's miraculous but humble birth, his early proof of superhuman strength, his rapid rise to prominence or power, his triumphant struggle with the forces of evil, his fallibility to the sin of pride *(hubris)* and his fall through betrayal or a 'heroic' sacrifice that ends with his death.[9]

The Hero is just one archetype among many. Archetypes are features of our collective psyche through which our unconscious interacts with the exterior world. Jung claimed that, "it is a function of consciousness not only to recognize and assimilate the external world through the gateway of the senses, but to translate into visible reality the world within us."[10] He asserted that, "all the most powerful ideas in history go back to archetypes. This is particularly true of religious ideas, but the central concepts of science, philosophy, and ethics are no exception to this rule."[11]

Every aspect of our lives is permeated by archetypes. We visit the archetypal realm in our dreams, though we may be unaware of it. Advertisers, political strategists, and the Hollywood industry use archetypes to prompt us to feel or react in certain ways.

Media stories that capture the imagination of the masses are invariably rich in archetypal content. The fact that more than one billion people around the world, regardless of their cultural affiliations, watched the funeral of Princess Diana, indicates the archetypal nature of the princess' story. She embodied the Cinderella archetype, the supposedly "common" girl whose uncommon grace, beauty, and innate goodness are recognized and rewarded by the prince, who chooses her over all other women. We loved her because she was one of us, and represented what is good in us. Diana also embodied parts of the archetype of the tragic Lover, as seen in Romeo and Juliet.

## A Map of the Human Psyche

There are hundreds of different archetypes that embody the vast array of human characteristics. To capture a broad range of human experiences in a simplified manner, Jungian psychologists Robert Moore and Douglas Gillette have developed a map of the human psyche based upon Jung's Quaternion, consisting of four of the major archetypes found in all cultures.[12] These are the Sovereign, Warrior, Lover, and Magician.

### The Four Major Archetypes

The **Sovereign** energy is the integrating force at the core of the psyche. It activates, accepts, and integrates the forces of all other archetypes, and makes the necessary sacrifices (from *sacer facere*, literally "making sacred") for the good of the whole.

The **Warrior** energy masters discipline, asceticism, and force. The Warrior protects what needs protecting for the common good and destroys what needs to be eliminated, to enable the blossoming of new life.

The **Lover** energy masters sensuous pleasure without guilt. It is the power of empathy and connectedness to other people and all life. The Lover is sensitive to art and beauty.

The **Magician** energy masters knowledge of the material world through science and technologies, as well as that of the immaterial worlds of spiritual, religious, or philosophical teachings. The Magician draws connections between both realms.

Warrior          Sovereign

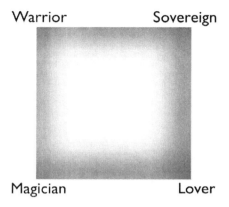

Magician          Lover

*Figure 19.1 - Jung's Quaternion*

Each archetype is active both at the individual and collective levels. Well-established organizations at the collective level embody these archetypal energies. Governments, for example, play the role of the Sovereign. Corporations and armies carry Warrior energy. The arts give expression to the Lover. Science, technology, academia, and religion embody the Magician's role.

It should be noted here that Jung's Quaternion lacks at least one important archetype. The missing archetype is suggested by Joseph Campbell's observation that one dominant myth has shaped most civilizations: each culture may emphasize particular archetypal forces and the hero may be a god or a mortal, young or old, rich or poor, king or commoner, but the hero is *always* a male.

## CLOSING THOUGHTS

Archetypes represent the deepest patterns of our psyches and are, by definition, observable through the ages and across cultures. They influence virtually every aspect of our lives, including our behaviors, philosophies, religions, and mythologies.

There is one essential archetype, however, missing from the Quaternion, which has been repressed for a very long time.

## CHAPTER TWENTY

# The Missing Archetype and Money

*The door to transcendence, to transformation and enlightenment,*

*is a door that leads into a hall of mirrors.*

*Wherever you look, there is only you looking back.*

~L. D. THOMPSON

Clear and mounting evidence demonstrates that for much of human history, a fundamental archetype has been the object of systematic and substantial repression. The missing archetype is the Great Nurturer/Provider, whose most common form is feminine and which is referred to as the Great Mother.

It is this feminine dimension of this archetype that has been the subject of almost continued repression through several millennia. The consequences of this repression run deep and are intimately connected to the subject of money. Our next focus on our exploration of money is therefore the Great Mother archetype.

## ARCHETYPAL EVIDENCE AND SIGNIFICANCE

One very effective way to understand a particular society is to look at its images of the divine. The Great Mother was honored and active over tens of thousands of years and over vast geographic areas. Her presence has been documented from the earliest times of human consciousness. Her image has been carved in mammoth ivory, in reindeer antlers, and on stone at the entrance of sacred caves. Great Mother effigies were the most common figures of the upper-Paleolithic period (30,000-9,000

BCE). Her predominant importance in ancient times is illustrated by the fact that four times more feminine than masculine prehistoric figurines have been uncovered.[1]

The term Great Mother is not meant to imply that an identical, specific image was venerated. Her various images, however, do share unmistakable and important characteristics reflected in nature, in each of us individually, and in the whole of humanity. She holds the mysteries of life and death, reproduction, and fertility. She also embodies all that gives us sustenance, including money.

The first forms of religious expression often found in archaeology and across cultures are images of a mother pregnant with or nurturing her child, identified as the Great Mother or the Fertility Goddess. As Marilyn Yalom, author of *A History of the Breast*, explains:

> At the beginning was the breast. For all but a fraction of human history, there was no substitute for a mother's milk. Until the end of the nineteenth century, when pasteurization purportedly made animal milk safe, a maternal breast meant life or death for every newborn babe. Small wonder that our prehistoric ancestors endowed their female idols with such bosoms...It takes no great stretch of the imagination to picture a distraught Stone Age mother begging one of those buxom idols for an ample supply of milk.[2]

To better appreciate the greater dimensions of this archetype and its vital relevance to humanity and the issues of our day, we must, however, transcend the reductionism that tends to see in Great Mother figures only sexuality, fertility, and nurturing of children. The Great Mother connects the human body and the Earth to the mystery of the sacred. She celebrates the process of time cycles and life itself in all its forms, all renewal, all growth, the paradox of life-death, all change, and all continuity.

Author and educator Starhawk explains:

> She is first of all Earth, the dark, nurturing mother who brings forth all life. She is the power of fertility and generation, the womb, and also the receptive tomb, the power of death. All proceeds from Her, all returns to Her. As Earth, She is also plant life, trees, and the herbs and grains that sustain life. She is the body, and the body is sacred.[3]

Great Mother of Willendorf (30,000-25,000 BCE). This is not the portrait of a specific woman, but rather an emblematic figure of fertility. Seven circles of 'hair locks' hide her face. The vulva is clearly marked. The bosom and the thighs are disproportional compared to the hands, in order to emphasize them.

Archaeologist Marija Gimbutas described the Great Mother as "the symbol of unity of all life in Nature. Her power was in water and stone, in tomb and cave, in animals and birds, snakes and fish, hills, trees and flowers. Hence, the holistic and mythopoetic perception of the sacredness and mystery of all there is on Earth."[4]

## THE ARCHETYPAL HUMAN

Jung's Quaternion can now be expanded to include the missing Great Mother archetype, to provide a more complete map of the archetypal human, as seen in Figure 20.1.

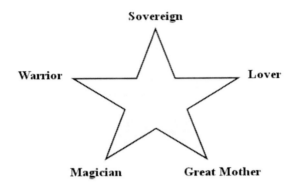

*Figure 20.1 - The (more complete) Archetypal Human*

This archetypal map is not intended to be all-encompassing. Far more comprehensive and complex representations of the human psyche could readily be constructed. The objective here is to use the fewest number of archetypes to portray the most important aspects of the collective human. The five archetypes described above may be considered as primary landmarks that comprise the vast territory of the collective human psyche. As foundational elements, we should understand that any disturbances here would have a profound impact upon individual and collective emotions and behaviors.

## EARLY MONEY AND THE GREAT MOTHER

The intrinsic relationship between money and the Great Mother was self-evident to much of the ancient world. For tens of thousands of years, the Great Mother was the mythical connection to the mysteries of life and to the most fundamental aspects of existence. Similarly, money represents abundance, generosity, sustenance, and is at its deepest level connected to our very survival. Substantial evidence demonstrates that not only was money invented during the extensive period when the Great Mother archetype was honored, but that money's earliest forms were directly related to her.

## Cattle, the First Working Capital Asset[5]

Cattle played a major role as both a medium of exchange and unit of account in much of the ancient world. For instance, the poet Homer (7th century BCE) expressed wealth in heads of cattle. Cattle are still used today in ranching societies as a unit of economic measure, as noted by the colloquialism, "he is worth a thousand head" (see insert).

### Money and Cows

One side effect of the use of cattle for monetary purposes has been that the number of head, rather then the quality or health of the animals, was valued. A contemporary agricultural expert tried to persuade Wakamba tribal chiefs from eastern Kenya not to keep diseased and old cattle, to which he received the following response: "Listen, here are two pound notes. One is old and wrinkled and ready to tear, this one is new. But they are both worth a pound. Well, it's the same with cows."[6]

The roots of popular terms point directly back to cattle. The English word "pecuniary" (financial) comes from the Latin pecus, meaning "cattle." Similarly, the word "capital" is derived from the Latin capus or capitis, meaning "head."[7] The word "fee" evolved from vieh, meaning "cattle" in Old Germanic.[8]

Cattle have been linked to feminine archetypal symbols of fertility and abundance from prehistory onwards. The cow symbolized the Great Mother nearly everywhere in ancient myths. Cows offer literal sustenance by virtue of their milk and they are ferociously protective of their young. Inanna, the Great Mother's representation in ancient Sumer, appears in the late fourth millennium BCE as the patron deity of the city of Uruk's central storehouse. In her name was written, "Heaven is mine, the Earth is mine. I am a splendid wild cow!"[9]

In Egypt, the Great Mother's name was Hathor. She was the Goddess of Beauty and Plenty, whose udder overflowed to the point of creating the Milky Way, the term in use today still for our own galaxy. Hathor gave birth every day to the sun, her "Golden Calf." Her horn was the sacred "Horn of Plenty"—the cornucopia—out of which poured all the fruits of the world.

Hathor capital with a human face and cow ears, in the temple of Hathor, built by Ramesses II in Memphis. Hathor, one of the many forms of Isis, was the goddess of love, joy, fertility, and abundance. Her udder, so overflowing with milk, created the Milky Way.

(Capital from Memphis, XIX[th] dynasty, Middle Kingdom, 1290-1224 BCE).

Many cultures held the cow as sacred. The classical symbol of the Moon Goddess was the white cow, akin to the White Buffalo Woman of some Native American traditions. In Irish mythology the cow was Glas Galven, Goddess of the Sky.[10] In Hinduism, the cow is a representation of Kali, and remains sacred to this day.

## Gold and Amber

The use of gold as currency is also intrinsically linked to the Great Mother archetype, with explicit mythological evidence from many cultures. For instance, Hathor, the Egyptian Cow Goddess, was called the "Golden One." Ancient Nordic legends refer to Gullveid, the "Golden Goddess" who was the owner of treasures of gold. Lakshmi, the Hindu Goddess of Abundance and Wealth, is referred to this day as the "Goddess of Gold".

Amber was another commodity currency used in antiquity and was especially important in international sea trade. In Dynastic Egypt, it was more highly valued than gold. Found in its natural state of fossilized resin, then as now, on the beaches of the Baltic Sea, pieces of amber were considered to be the "tears of the Great Mother."

## The Cowrie

Another form of money related to the Great Mother is the cowrie. Cowries are small, smooth shells usually found in the seas off tropical islands. They were an ancient form of currency used in Africa and elsewhere, and remained in circulation in some countries, such as Nigeria, until quite recently.

In ancient China, the cowrie played such an important monetary role that its pictogram was adopted in written language as the character for money. The first Chinese production of bronze and copper currency took the form of imitation cowries.[11]

Monetary historian Glyn Davies explains the cowrie's enduring choice as a form of money:

> The cowrie shell, of all forms of money, including precious metals, was current over a far greater space and for a far greater length of time than any other...Cowries are durable, easily cleaned and counted, and defy imitation and counterfeiting...For many people over large parts of the world, at one time or other they have appeared as an ideal form of money...They were still officially accepted for payment of taxes until the beginning of the twentieth century in West Africa.[12]

The vulva-like cowrie shell is associated with water, the setting in which the shell is formed. In many cultures, water is traditionally related to the Great Mother through its symbolic elemental connection with fertility, sexuality, prosperity, and fecundity.

The cowrie is also associated with death, in that its utility as currency starts only after the death of the creature that originally inhabited the shell. It has appeared in burial ornaments as far back as Paleolithic times. French archeologist Abbé Breuil explains the cowrie's presence in tombs: "It connects the death with the cosmological principles of water, the moon, the feminine and rebirth in the new world."[13]

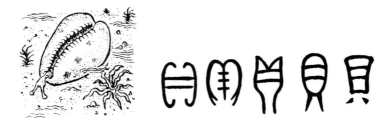

Sequence showing the evolution of the drawing of the cowrie shell into the symbol of money in Chinese ideograms. The ideograms for the words "desire," "treasure," "valueless," and "lending" have all kept the same cowrie shell root.

In Spanish, the feminine name *Concepción* (conception) is still abbreviated as *Conchita* (literally, "little shell," which is also the slang for the female sexual organ). To the Aztecs, the moon Goddess Tecaciztecatl, whose name translates as "the one from the shell," controls the process of birth and generation and is represented by a vulva.[14]

The cowrie shell is also etymologically connected to the Great Mother archetype through cattle. The word "cow" comes from the Sanskrit *gau* and the Egyptian *kau*. It is also the origin of the words *gaurie* or *kaurie*, from which the English term "cowrie shell" derived. The words cow and cowrie shell thus literally share common ancient roots.

**The Shekel**

In addition to her generic association with money, the Great Mother was linked to many of the earliest coins. The ancient Sumerians called their first coin-like object the *shekel,* derived from the words *she* (meaning "wheat") and *kel* (a measurement similar to a bushel). Hence, this coin was a symbol of the value of one bushel of wheat.

The shekel was originally used as proof that wheat taxes had been paid to the temple of Inanna, the Sumerian goddess who ruled over life, death, sexuality, fertility, and wealth. Her temple, as well as being a ritual center, was also the storage place for reserves of cereals, which supported the priestesses and the community, particularly in lean times.

On a large alabaster vase dating from 3100-2900 BCE, a naked man brings a large basket filled with food to Inanna. The Goddess is shown standing in front of a twin-doorpost entrance, symbolizing her temple. An ancient repair with copper rivets is visible above the head of the goddess, indicating that the vase was treasured already in antiquity.

(Alabaster vase, Uruk (Level III) height: 3 ft. Iraq Museum. Photograph Hirmer. Fotoarchive, photo 624.3014, Munich).

Farmers brought their contribution of wheat to the temple to fulfill religious obligations to society and to the Goddess. In exchange, they received a shekel, which then entitled them to sacred sexual intercourse with the priestesses at festival time.

Two thousand years later, the Judeo-Christian worldview reinterpreted these rituals quite differently. The Bible describes these priestesses as "temple prostitutes."[15] Such practices and their significance, however, must be understood within the context of their particular culture and time. The priestesses were representatives of the Great Mother, and intercourse with them was considered as a holy rite with the Goddess of Fertility herself— not an act to be taken lightly. At that time, fertility was truly a matter of life and death, as failure of the crops meant starvation. To the Sumerians this ritual was sacred and ensured fertility in crops, animals, and children, each of which were requisites for survival and future prosperity. The word shekel survives in modern-day Hebrew as Israel's monetary unit.

Ancient Roman silver coin with the head of Juno Moneta (inscription "Moneta") from whose name the word "money" originates. On the obverse are represented the key coining tools. The original feminine dimension of money creation is explicitly demonstrated in this coin.

(Roman coin issued around 45 BCE, actual size 18 mm.)

## Juno Moneta

The word money is itself related to the Great Mother, deriving from the Latin *moneta*. The first Roman mint operated out of the basement of the temple of the Goddess Juno Moneta—symbolically, her womb. The choice of that particular location within the temple is a direct reminder of the relationship of money to the essential feminine (see insert).

### The Goddess Juno Moneta

Juno was a very ancient Italic goddess, initially different than the Greek Goddess Hera, with whom she became culturally amalgamated later during the expansion of the Roman Empire to Greece. Both Juno and Hera, however, were essentially Goddesses of Womanhood.

Juno was part of the Capitoline triad, the Trinity that ruled Rome (with Minerva, the Goddess of Wisdom, and Jupiter, the Sky God). As daughter of Saturn, Juno ruled menstrual cycles and was, therefore, worshipped by Roman women every month at the Calends, the first day of the new moon. Juno presided at all key feminine occasions: she was the *Juno Pronuba*, who made marriage abundantly fertile; *Populonia*, the Goddess of Conception; *Ossipago*, who strengthened fetal bones; *Sospita*, who ruled labor; and *Lucina*, the Birth Goddess, who led the child to the light.[16]

To the Romans, just as every man had his *genius*, the essence of his masculinity, every woman had her *juno*, the essence of her femininity. One modern relic of the Great Mother tradition is that many brides still choose to marry in June, because it used to ensure the blessings of the goddess for whom that month is named.[1]

## CLOSING THOUGHTS

The creation of money was inherently and symbolically related for millennia to the Great Mother archetype. Every monetary transaction was seen at that time as a way of honoring the Great Mother and the abundance she represented.

All this happened, of course, when words reflecting feminine characteristics had not yet acquired their pejorative bias. Words like "silly" still meant "blessed by the Moon Goddess Selene," and "hysteria" implied "having a womb," not a mental disturbance.

# CHAPTER TWENTY ONE

# Repression of an Archetype

*We rarely hear the inward music,*

*but we're all dancing to it nevertheless.*

~RUMI

How then, did money come to be divorced from the archetype that had inspired it? The key is the repression of the feminine in general, and the Great Mother archetype in particular.

## CLIMATE CHANGE AND INDO-EUROPEAN INVASIONS

Repression of the feminine traces its origins back to the rise of aggressive warrior energy during the fourth millennium BCE. This followed a period of massive climate change, which led to intense desertification from North Africa through the Middle East all the way to southwestern China. As a result, these lands, which include the Sahara, Arabian, Syro-Iraqi, and Gobi deserts, were no longer able to support farming or wildlife.

According to one hypothesis, Indo-European invasions were a chain reaction of large-scale population dislodgements initially triggered by this climate change. Affected communities could no longer depend upon their own lands to meet their requirements. They thus became pillaging, nomadic, authoritarian-ruled, patriarchal societies that spread their violent behavior over very large distances. The communities that came in contact with these nomads were either exterminated or survived only by "toughening up" and adopting warlike cultures themselves.[1] Data to support this hypothesis includes geological and archeological evidence of increasing desiccation, and the geographical distribution of societies most closely associated with the more extreme forms of feminine repression—still observable today—in and around the big desert areas.

The myth of Wotan, the God of war, incarnates the early
horsemen, who were the highly specialized caste of
warriors among the Indo-Europeans.
(Wotan, Stela of Hornhausen, Halle Museum).

The powerful influence of the Great Mother during the Stone Age
began to wane. Male deities, particularly gods of war and conquest,
replaced images of her. As archeologist Philip van Doren Stern
describes: "Along with ruthless invasions, undeclared warfare, and
appropriation of women as their rightful spoils, they [warrior tribes] were
developing a society in which masculinity was supreme. An insatiable
desire for property and power, together with insensitivity to pain and
suffering, characterized everything they did."[2]

After military conquest, the standard procedure by these warrior
cultures was to kill off all the adult males of the vanquished group, then
rape and enslave the females. In the short span of a few generations, the
genetic and cultural makeup of entire regions was dramatically
transformed. The ancient all-powerful Great Mother was divided into
different goddesses to fill many different functions, each of whom
became attributes or less important partners of dominant male gods.

Repression, control, and subservience of the feminine, particularly the sexuality and fertility aspects of the Great Mother, have been familiar outcomes ever since.

## GREEK CIVILIZATION

The incomparable contributions made by Greek civilization to virtually every aspect of human endeavor—including architecture, drama, governance, modern language, geometry, medicine, and philosophy—are well noted and have profoundly influenced and enriched our world. Greek culture was, however, also strongly patriarchal and played an influential role in the sweeping alteration of so-called archaic matrifocal mythologies into patriarchal ones.[3] The amber "tears of the Great Mother," for instance, became the "tears of Apollo," which *he* shed upon his exile from Olympus to Hyperborea.

The Greek awakening of the so-called "rational mind" provided new arguments for the repression of the feminine, and became the cornerstone of Western thinking for the next 25 centuries. These include Parmenides' purported declaration of the independence and superiority of reason— portrayed as a masculine attribute—as the only legitimate judge of reality. All the senses were believed to mislead. Intellectual reason alone is able to perceive reality.[4]

Socrates and Plato built on this intellectual argument. Reason became associated with the transcendental, spiritual desire, and the absolute. Everything considered to be outside of reason was dismissed as irrational. The inherent imperfections of matter and the senses, together with instinctual desires and the relative, were all ascribed to the feminine.

Aristotelian philosophy subsequently claimed that women are incomplete and damaged human beings of an entirely different order than men: "For the female is, as it were, a mutilated male."[5] Her womb is but a passive receptacle for the holy male sperm. Aristotle's conclusion was, "the male is by nature superior, and the female inferior...the one rules, the other is ruled."[6] Twenty-three centuries later, Sigmund Freud would still refer to this "incompleteness" in women's nature as proof of their "natural inferiority."[7]

For the ancient Greeks the very act of founding a civilized community became symbolized by "cutting the feminine" (see insert).

### "Cutting the Feminine" as a Civilizing Act

Greek priests would found a new city by cutting a large cow-skin with a knife into a single, thin, uninterrupted rope. That rope would then be spread out to create the perimeter of the new city. This ritual was a metaphor for expunging the feminine nature—symbolized by the cow-skin—thereby creating an ordered "civilized" space.

The founding ritual for Roman cities had the same symbolic content. Rome itself and all subsequent cities founded by Romans involved ritually cutting the Earth—the symbol of the feminine—with a plow, replacing the Greeks' knife, pulled by oxen to mark the perimeter of the new town.

## WESTERN RELIGION

The consequences of Great Mother archetypal repression were felt in all major domains of human activity and belief systems, particularly religion. As the roots of our contemporary monetary system emanate almost exclusively from Western civilization, we focus on its predominant religion over the course of the last 1,500 years—Christianity.

Although we draw attention to the excesses and patriarchal attitudes associated with the Church through the centuries, it is important to keep in mind that Christendom was also responsible for Western civilization's honoring of the Lover archetype. This is expressed in such noble ethics as charity, caring for one's neighbor, the concept of loving one's enemy, blessing those who curse you, doing good to those who hate you, and praying for those who would persecute you—values that were nonexistent in Antiquity.[8] The Church also concretized these noble values systematically on a pragmatic level, in the many vital services and support structures for communities, for example, orphanages, hospitals, and charitable foundations. In addition, and as noted earlier, Christianity was also a primary opponent of the practice of usury.

Nevertheless, monotheism—the belief that there is only one God, who is masculine—would over time leave less and less room for the Great Mother and feminine values. The sole male skyward deity, who ruled as absolute monarch from the heavens, would negate the earth-bound divinities, with repression of Great Mother arechetypal energies.

The snake is tempting Adam and Eve to eat the fruit of the Tree of Knowledge, which will precipitate them both "into sin" and out of Paradise. Notice that the snake has a woman's head, and thereby became the symbol of woman's sinful nature. The snake used to be one of the positive symbols of the Great Mother in earlier times, referring to her wisdom, power and sexuality. Its reprogramming as the personification of evil started here with the story of Genesis.

Adam and Eve, the biblical creation story of Western culture, made Eve, "the mother of all living things," responsible for the Fall and for all subsequent suffering of humankind, along with her accomplice the serpent—not surprisingly, one of the oldest symbols of the Great Mother.

Attacks on the remnants of the Great Mother cultures can be further explained by history. Christianity initially spread most successfully in the cities of the fallen Roman Empire. Its foremost opposition came from the pagans (literally, *pagani*, meaning "people of the countryside") or from villagers (those living in rural *villae*, from which derive the words "villain" and "vilify"), who were more closely connected to nature, the land, ancient fertility rituals, and thus to the Great Mother.

Centuries later, repression of the Great Mother archetype would find its most violent expression in the Inquisition, in which an estimated six million women would be burned at the stake or otherwise put to death as witches.[9] This appalling period of history, which spanned more than three centuries, coincided not with the "dark" Middle Ages as is commonly thought, but rather with the Renaissance and the early Modern period (15th to 18th centuries CE).[10] It was during that same period that our present-day monetary system took form.

Western civilization's extraordinary continuity down through the ages with regard to the repression of the feminine can be summarized by the following set of quotations:

*Sin began with a woman and thanks to her we all must die.*
Ecclesiasticus 25:24 (second century BCE)

*Women are the gate of the devil, the patron of wickedness,*
*the sting of the serpent.*
St. Gerome (fifth century CE)

*Men have broad shoulders and large chests and small narrow hips*
*and are more understanding than women,*
*who have but small and narrow chests and broad hips;*
*to the end they should remain at home, sit still,*
*keep house and bear and bring up children.*
Martin Luther (16th century)

*Husband and wife are one person in law; that is, the very being or legal*
*existence of the woman is suspended during the marriage.*
William Blackstone (18th century)

While the closing decades of the 20th century enjoyed palpable strides forward in the reemergence of feminine values, five millennia of repression continue to permeate the beliefs and systems of Western society, particularly our monetary system.

Print showing "three notorious witches" of various ages being hanged in 1589 at Chelmsford, Essex, UK. The animals, a couple of which are copulating in front of them, hint at the "devilish practices" for which they were condemned.

## CLOSING THOUGHTS

The importance of the Great Mother archetype to humanity is clearly noted by the responsibilities entrusted to her symbolic care. This was acknowledged and expressed throughout antiquity by her many representations in money—the tool that provides the means to achieve our sustenance and very survival. The symbolic thread continues to this day, as noted in the etymology of the words capital and money.

# CHAPTER TWENTY TWO

# Shadows

*The Dark is the Light we cannot yet see.*

~V.J. SHAWKAR

The invention of money occurred during the vast period in which much of the world honored the Great Mother archetype. Our system of national currencies came about, instead, at the onset of the Industrial Age, in a culture conditioned by severe repression of this same archetype. The link between our money and this repression has many profound effects.

To provide a deeper understanding of money's impact upon us, another basic concept of Archetypal Psychology relevant to our work is herein introduced—*shadows*. Shadows helps explain how specific actions and attitudes come into being, persist, and spread. Its influence is typically unconscious.

## SHADOWS

When an archetype is repressed, it does not just disappear. By definition, the rejected psychological content instead manifests in a destructive shadow form.

Carl Jung explained:

> The psychic energy that appears to have been lost [by the repression of an archetype]…forms an ever-present and potentially destructive "shadow" to our conscious mind. Even tendencies that might in some circumstances be able to exert a beneficial influence are transformed into demons when they are repressed.[1]

When repressed, an archetype's energy can manifest as one of two shadows. One represents the repressed archetype's characteristics in *excess*; the other, in *deficiency*.² An individual who represses his or her inner Sovereign archetype, for example, tends to behave either as a tyrant or abdicator. The tyrant possesses an excess of the Sovereign's emotional and behavioral attributes, while the abdicator has a deficiency of the same characteristics. Similarly, the repressed Lover becomes either addicted (excess) or impotent (deficient). The two shadows of each archetype are two faces of the same coin.

**Fear—The Common Denominator**

The common denominator that connects the two shadows of a given archetype is always *fear*. Fear is normally a healthy emotion. For example, when a car veers out of control in front of one, fear unleashes an adrenaline rush that prompts one to react more rapidly to protect oneself. Normally, one's emotions stabilize back to neutral after the danger is over.

When a fear gets permanently embodied, or when it freezes up in an individual's personality as an enduring rather than a transient reaction, it is no longer a healthy emotion, but instead becomes pathological. Such pathologies can manifest on an individual or a collective level, thus becoming a characteristic of a society's culture. This embodied fear splits the archetypal energy into two, so that now-repressed archetype manifests in the form of two polar shadows, as illustrated in Figure 22.1 with the splitting of the Sovereign archetype into its two shadows, the *tyrant* and the *weakling*, due to the prevalence of fear.

The same fear also links the two shadows of an archetype. When one scratches below the surface of a tyrant, one invariably discovers a weakling (abdicator). Conversely, when an abdicator is given power over someone else, he or she will start acting as a tyrant. This is brought on by the unresolved fear responsible for the splitting of an archetype in the first place. A tyrant, for instance, is primarily afraid of appearing weak, while an abdicator is fearful of appearing tyrannical.

Additionally, someone who is under the influence of one of the shadows will automatically tend to attract people who embody the opposite shadow. A tyrant will tend to be surrounded by abdicators and vice versa. It is one common way whereby, in Jung's words, we, "translate into visible reality the world within us."

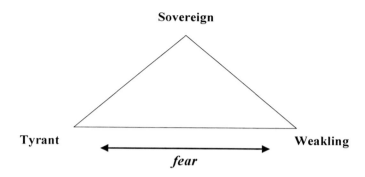

*Figure 22.1 - Shadows of the Sovereign Archetype*

## The Shadow is Not the Enemy

It seems logical to regard the shadow as the enemy. It is the problem we would most like to be rid of, the face we do not want to acknowledge, the aspect of ourselves that elicits the most disapproval from our culture, our family, and ourselves.

The shadow is also our taskmaster, however, relentlessly urging us to grow and evolve. When the ego, the conscious perception of the individual self, narrows our feelings to an acceptable range—the image of what is culturally appropriate—and when personal will is used to maintain that image, the shadows begin to haunt us. Shadows take us to places within ourselves we would rather not explore. Although unpleasant, their role is not to harm but rather, to assist by obliging us to face our own vulnerabilities. Paradoxically, the real enemy is our very reluctance to face the shadows and embrace them in the first place.

In this framework, consciousness can be seen as a personal theater where the ego, individual unconscious, archetypes, and their shadows all play their respective roles. By its very nature, the ego is unaware of these other actors. It is convinced that it alone is in charge, operating under its own free will. Yet, as long as an archetype has not been integrated, the ego will be dominated by the fear-ridden axis between the two shadows, acting out one or the other.

The only way to escape from the influence of the shadows is to overcome our fears and embrace them. By doing so, shadows are no longer in control and the power and wisdom of the repressed archetype can be accessed. This is referred to as *integrating the archetype.*

This process of integration is not easy. But the effort and suffering that often accompanies it are but preludes to the reawakening of the sacred in daily life. The rewards associated with shadow work have been recognized by many respected figures down through the ages, as noted by the following quotes:

*If you bring forth what is within you,*
*what you bring forth will save you.*
*If you don't bring forth what is within you,*
*what you do not bring forth will destroy you.*
Jesus[3]

*"Chaque ombre à son âme reconnait la lumière"*
*(Each shadow in its soul recognizes the light)*
Christian Tzara

*If only it were all so simple!*
*If only there were evil people somewhere*
*insidiously committing evil deeds,*
*and it was necessary only to separate them*
*from the rest of us and destroy them.*
*But the line dividing good and evil*
*cuts through the heart of every human being.*
*And who is willing to destroy a piece of his own heart?*
Aleksandr Solzhenitsyn

## Shadows of the Five Essential Archetypes

Illustrated below is the archetypal human along with the excess and deficit shadows of the five essential archetypes.

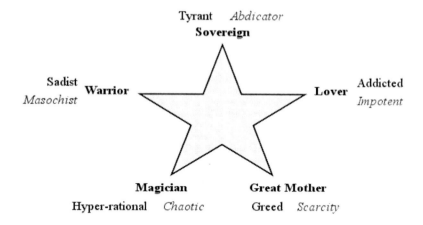

*Figure 22.2 - The Archetypal Human and its Shadows*

The shadows of the Sovereign are again, the *tyrant* and the *abdicator*. The shadows of the Warrior are the *sadist* (excess) and the *masochist* (deficit). The Lover's two shadows are the *addicted* (excess) and the *impotent* (deficit). The two shadows of the Magician are the *hyperrationalist* know-it-all (excess) and the indiscriminate or *chaotic* fool (deficit).

Of particular interest are the shadows of the Great Mother, for, as noted, this archetype is most closely associated with money. Her long and systematic repression has created deeply etched shadows in the collective unconscious and in our monetary system. Many of the most important challenges we face today can trace their origins directly or indirectly to her extensive repression. Her two shadows are *greed* (excess) and *fear of scarcity* (deficit).

To provide us with an adequate language and framework with which to more precisely capture distinctions between archetypes, shadows, and their relationship to money, we turn briefly to Taoism and the concept of yin-yang.

## CLOSING THOUGHTS

Another fundamental concept of Archetypal Psychology is shadows. When an archetype is repressed, it does not just disappear, but instead manifests in a shadow form, either in excess or in deficiency. The common denominator that connects the two shadows of a given archetype is always fear.

Though it seems logical to regard the shadow as the enemy, it is also our taskmaster, relentlessly urging us to grow and evolve. The way to escape from the influence of the shadows is to overcome our fears and embrace them. In so doing, shadows are no longer in control, and the power and wisdom of the repressed archetype can be accessed.

# CHAPTER TWENTY THREE

# Money and the Tao

*The Tao is called Great Mother.*

*Empty yet inexhaustible,*

*It gives birth to infinite worlds.*

~LAO TZU

Another lens on archetypes and money is provided by the philosophy of Taoism. The *Tao*, (pronounced "Dao" or "Dow"), meaning "The Way," explains all forces in nature as complementary pairs, such as Earth-Heaven, water-fire, inhaling-exhaling, pulling-pushing, and so on. These apparent polarities are referred to as "*yin-yang*" pairs. Although such polarities are seemingly separate forces, this ancient Chinese philosophy, like modern physics, which regards action and reaction as inseperable, sees each element as necessary parts of a greater unity.

"Yin" denotes the essential quality of the feminine, which is not to be confused with the biological female. Similarly, "yang" is *not* synonymous with the physical male. According to Taoism, a dynamic equilibrium between these two polarities is required for a healthy expression of the natural order, both in the world about us and in ourselves. For example, a male is not complete without accessing his feminine dimension, just as a female is not complete without embracing the masculine within herself.[1]

The seemingly exotic terminology of yin-yang is used because Western languages and philosophies tend to lack a vocabulary that adequately captures this concept. Jung stated:

Unfortunately, our Western mind, lacking all culture in this respect, has never yet devised a concept, nor even a name, for the "union of opposites through the middle path," that most fundamental item of inward experience, which could respectably be set against the Chinese concept of Tao.[2] This philosophy dates back to prehistory to the teachings of Lao-Tzu (see insert).

### Lao-Tzu and the Tao

The concept of yin-yang in China seems to have originated in prehistoric times. The semimythical Yellow Emperor, estimated to have lived around 2500 BCE, used yin-yang concepts extensively in medical texts. The classical form of Taoism is believed to have been founded sometime in the 6th century BCE by the Chinese scholar Lao-Tzu, curator of the emperor's Imperial Library.

Legend has it that in his old age and disgusted with courtly chicanery, Lao-Tzu resigned from his respected post, left most of his belongings behind, mounted a water buffalo, and headed off to live his remaining years as a recluse. But before doing so, he was stopped by a gate guardian who asked him to first please sum up all he had learned from a life spent with the greatest book collection of the Empire.

On the spot, Lao-Tzu wrote the *Tao Te Ching*. Consisting of only 5,000 ideograms, it is the shortest treatise on good living in existence. It begins with the immortal words: "The Tao that can be spoken is not the real Tao. The Name that can be named is not the Eternal Name." This opening conveys that language and intellect are the first barriers to knowing The Way.

Lao-Tzu stressed the importance of living in a balanced flow, valuing both the feminine and masculine, and the equality between men and women.

Some traits associated with yin-yang are summarized in Figure 23.1. This figure can be read top-down to identify internal yin and yang coherences—the logical connection whereby these concepts reinforce each other in a consistent worldview. The same figure can also be read horizontally, focusing on the polarities between yin and yang manifestations listed in each half of the diagram.

It should be emphasized that the prime importance is an appropriate *balance* between yin and yang. Taoists warn against falling into the trap of believing that *either* yin *or* yang, or any one of the values represented in each of these polarities, is right or wrong, good or bad.

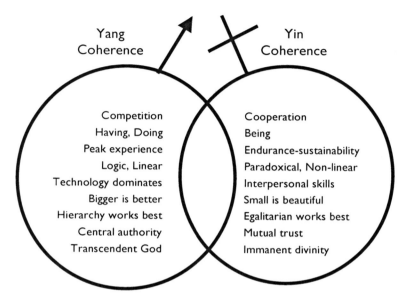

*Figure 23.1 - Yin-Yang Coherences and Contrasts*

The key point is that *both* yin and yang are necessary in life. Without this balance, dangerous pathologies can develop, as displayed by the shadows.

## YIN AND YANG SHADOW AXES

As discussed earlier, when an archetype is repressed its essential energies are expressed as two shadows, each of which manifest deficit and excess aspects of that particular archetype. Employing Taoist concepts, deficit aspects can be understood as *yin shadows*, while excess aspects can be labeled *yang shadows*.

With respect to the five major human archetypes—the Sovereign, Warrior, Lover, Magician, and Great Mother—the yin (deficit) shadows are, respectively: abdication, masochism, impotence, inability to discern, and fear of scarcity. Together they form a collection of shadows referred to as the *yin shadow axis*.

The *yang shadow axis* consists of the yang (excess) shadows of each major archetype, namely: tyranny, sadism, addiction, hyperrationalism, and greed.

Today in our society, a broad spectrum of patriarchal influence, together with the specific repression of the Great Mother archetype, has led to the dominance of the yang shadow axis in our society. For example, we are vulnerable to *tyrannical* leaders who abuse their office, ruling over rather than serving the good of their constituencies. From the ancient Assyrians, who flayed and impaled men alive for sport, to the atrocities and genocides of World War II, Bosnia, Rwanda, and Darfur, the *sadist* shadow has been with us for a gruesomely long time. *Addictions* of all varieties have become endemic in our society, and include illegal addictions such as heroin or cocaine; legal habits such as caffeine, alcohol, and tobacco; and other compulsive behaviors condoned in mainstream culture, such as workaholism; addiction to control; obsession with escapist entertainment; and codependency. Ironically and irrationally, reason is exalted to the exclusion of all other ways of knowing, resulting in a *hyperrationality* that narrows and even perverts our thinking. Finally, we feel constantly driven by *greed* to accumulate more money, goods and possessions, and to act in such ways despite our deeper desires and better judgment.

The pervasiveness of greed and other yang-shadow emotions and behaviors in many races, cultures, and religions down through history lends support to the illusion that they are normal expressions that simply reflect who we truly are.

Our archetypal framework, however, tells a very different story. Though commonly present and very persistent, many of our feelings and actions are inconsistent with a healthy yin-yang balance and point instead to a widespread and long-standing pathology. The prevalance in our society of tyranny, sadism, addiction, hyperrationalism, and greed are each expressions of the yang shadow axis. Together with the Great Mother's yin shadow—fear of scarcity—these aberrant, unhealthy behaviors lead us directly back to our monetary paradigm.

## "YIN" AND "YANG" CURRENCIES

The distinction between yin and yang can be applied to currency designs based upon their underlying agreements, along with the behaviors and emotions they engender. The agreements with regard to our current official monetary system includes a strong hierarchical control via central banks.[3] The embedded interest feature creates competition, as well as the need for perpetual growth and the concentration of wealth, and it rewards the accumulation of money. It is on the basis of these inherent patterns that our conventional money can be understood as a *yang-type currency*. Given that every single one of its features is yang, this money can even be described as "extreme yang."

Other types of monetary systems, like Time Dollars, LETS, and some of the local currencies used in the Central Middle Ages, promote entirely different types of behavior. Some of these currencies were available in sufficiency, provided incentives for circulation and distribution, and promoted cooperation and community building. Money designs with such characteristics reflect yin energy and can therefore be referred to as *yin-type currencies*.

It should now be clearer why we describe differently designed national and local currencies as "complementary." Yin-yang pairs, by their very definition, complement each other. And as Lao Tzu pointed out: "When yang and yin combine, all things achieve harmony."[4]

Central to our issues is that in the currently dominant monetary paradigm there is a lack of yin currency to balance the monopoly of yang-type national currency. This lack is directly related to the fact that in our culture the Great Mother archetype has been systematically devalued and repressed.

### Shadow Money

Money, as noted, is a key attribute of the Great Mother. Repression of this archetype led to the development of monetary systems that embodied her two shadows. On a historical level we can understand how and when these shadows were programmed into the monetary system. After all, this system was developed during the pre-Victorian era, a time of intense rejection of the feminine in almost every way, as reflected in religion, philosophy, ways of knowing, and the treatment of women themselves after three centuries of witch hunts. Since our monetary system developed in the midst of this archetype's repression, it encapsulated the Great Mother's shadows rather than her wisdom.

Not only are greed, and fear of scarcity, embedded in money, but *the fear that links them* is also perpetuated in an endless, vicious cycle by our monetary system. A well-known cliché on Wall Street goes: "Financial markets know only two emotions: greed and fear." Fear customarily characterizes many people's relationship to money and drives our financial decisions and markets, while scarcity is built directly into our bank-debt monetary system. It is scarcity that maintains the value of our national currencies.

We depend on this scarce type of money for nearly everything we need, do, and aspire to. Yet, this built-in scarcity leaves many of us without sufficient means to meet even the basic requirements for survival. This lack perpetuates fear, regardless of our own particular financial situation. Even those who have sufficient money are aware of the fortunes won and lost every day in the fluctuating marketplace. The poor, disenfranchised, and homeless serve as constant reminders of the fate that awaits the rest of us should we happen to become the next losers in the current paradigm. Our sense of financial security is tenuous at best. This causes many to experience the world as a place in which we must struggle to survive.

These shadows and the behaviors they engender can be found in all societies that live with a monopoly of yang money. These emotions and behaviors persist, not because they represent who we *really* are, but rather because of the unnatural state in which we are forced to live. This state of affairs is perpetuated by the monopoly of our national currencies, and amplified by a particular capacity of money to replicate information.

## Money as an Information Replicator

Chilean biologists Humberto Maturana and Francisco Varela describe how systems form and maintain themselves through replication: "This process occurs at all levels: molecular, biological, and social. For every system has its own characteristic replication that forms, expands, and holds systems together."[5]

Replicators of ideas and collective emotions are instruments that maintain particular social systems. These collective ideas and emotions are sometimes called "memes," analogous to the "genes" in biological systems. These memes are the building blocks of a society's constituent parts, including its structures and dominant beliefs.

*Money is a key information replicator*

Money is part and parcel of our oldest information system. Writing itself seems to have been initially invented by the Sumerian civilization to record financial transactions, as confirmed by the earliest tablets found in Uruk. Our monetary system now functions as a key information replicator, a vital linchpin that drives particular and consistent behavior patterns. Every dollar created and spent reinforces—replicates—the values that are deeply embedded in the basic design of our currency systems.

Money shapes our beliefs and social structures and tells us what is and is not possible. This explains how, with the best intentions, even with totally different personal values or perspectives, regardless of gender, race, or socio-cultural biases and affiliations, most of us behave in a manner consistent with the yang shadow axis to obtain money. One expression of this is the emphasis on competition over cooperation. Without it, Western civilization would look and act very differently. Our money is one of the key information replicators that ensures that competition is emphasized throughout society.

Fear of scarcity and the axis of excessive yang shadows are continually reinforced by our yang-type national currencies. This is reflected in many of our cultural stereotypes, such as the tyrannical, greedy scrooges who sadistically enjoy their power over others. A more recent stereotype is the workaholic executive, addicted to accumulating money, power, and glory, often at the price of any ultimate satisfaction. He ends up lonely in a meaningless world.

In professional life, many feel the need to ignore their own and other people's emotions in the performance of their jobs. In the domains of media, medicine, and finance, "professionalism" is equated with taking a hyperrational distance from other people, and is oftentimes seen by others as cynicism and emotional disengagement.

As things stand now, our true natures are not necessarily reflected by our collective ways of being and doing. We live in a global matrix, in which many of our collective emotions and patterns of behavior are instead conditioned by a monopoly of yang-type currencies that reinforce a very particular, limited set of values on the whole of society and each of us individually. Some of the consequences of this conditioning are examined next.

## CLOSING THOUGHTS

Our financial markets know only the two emotions of greed and fear, because all financial markets have one common denominator: the type of money that is used to value nearly everything. Financial markets simply mirror our collective archetypal wounding.

It must be remembered that it is not money itself that is at fault here. Rather, it is the *monopoly* of yang-type currencies that, like hammers, are imbued with only a limited set of functionalities. When *only* hammers are available, we start treating everything as nails.

Despite the many services rendered and achievements made possible by our monetary system, it is the monopoly of national currencies in our world that continually reinforces imbalance. Unlike Hammerville, whose use of only one tool came about through ignorance alone, our limited monetary toolset—by and large the same once created centuries ago at the beginning of the Industrial Age—was brought about not just by ignorance, but also by a long-standing archetypal repression. We examine the consequences more closely in the following chapter.

## CHAPTER TWENTY FOUR

# Consequences of Repression

*That which we do not bring to consciousness*
*appears in our lives as fate.*
~CARL GUSTAV JUNG

When modern psychology and psychotherapy came into being, much of their focus centered on the *individual* patient—on his or her trauma and personal psychological framework. Many of our challenges and behaviors, however, do not emanate from individual disturbances alone.

Archetypal psychologist James Hillman observed:

> Too many people have been analyzing their pasts, their childhoods, their memories, their parents, and realizing that it doesn't do anything—or that it doesn't do enough. Psychotherapy theory turns it all on you: you are the one who is wrong. [But] If a kid is having trouble or is discouraged, the problem is not just inside the kid; it's also in the system, the society…Problems come from the environment, the cities, the economy, racism. They come from architecture, school systems, capitalism, exploitation.[1]

Problems also derive from money choices. As noted, each type of currency is imbued with specific design features that encourage or discourage particular behaviors and values. Our national currencies were simply not structured to address social, economic, or ethical concerns. Rather, they are international trading currencies designed to promote specific business needs, and to this restricted end they have performed admirably.

Though money is not inherently good or bad, and certainly not the root of all evil, the particular design of our national currencies does promote greed, as well as fear of scarcity.[2] Given money's innate capacity to replicate information, and lacking any significant yin-currency system to provide a counterbalance, the skewed yang shadow axis dominates unchallenged, the consequences of which are profound.

## MONEY AND UNDERDEVELOPMENT

Geopolitical power considerations were the main influence that determined the monetary order. Under today's monetary rules, less-developed countries must borrow "hard" currencies from the richest countries to keep their economies running. These countries require more and more money just to pay back the interest on previous loans, the payments for which currently amount to about $300 million per day.

Activist and rock star Bono notes:

Africa (alone) spends $200 million every week repaying its debts to the West. That made no sense to me. It means that for every £1 western governments give to the poorest nations, the poor nations pay back £3 to the west! Is that not barbaric? Is it not barbaric that Tanzania spends more on repaying its loans than it does on health care and education combined?[3]

After the G8 summit in Okinawa in 2000, former President Obasanjo of Nigeria made this comment on Nigeria's debt:

All that we had borrowed up to 1985 or 1986 was around $5 billion. So far we have paid back about $16 billion. Yet we are being told that we still owe about $28 billion. That $28 billion came about because of the foreign creditors' interest rates. If you ask me what is the worst thing in the world, I will say it is compound interest.[4]

When President Obasanjo spoke out a decade ago, the developing world was spending $13 on debt repayment for every dollar it received in grant aid.[5] A mere decade later, the repayment cost has nearly doubled to over $25 for every dollar borrowed.

The monetary rules that have been applied by the IMF to developing nations through its "structural adjustment programs" have been widely criticized. Such adjustment programs, in play since the 1980s, include prioritizing the payback of interest on foreign loans, even if it means dismantling the recipient nation's educational systems and other long-term social investment programs. It has been claimed that if these same rules were applied to the United States, this superpower would itself regress to Third World status in as little as one or two generations. Would not everybody, including the First World and its financial institutions, be better off if all countries were truly able to develop themselves, free of these draconian constraints?

Some efforts have been made to counteract the consequences of excessive Third World debt. For instance, the Millennium Movement successfully promoted the cancellation of at least part of the debt of the poorest countries, although the debt was not actually cancelled. Rather, the otherwise unpayable debt was transferred to U.S. and European governments that, in turn, passed it onto their own taxpayers, who ended up paying banks on behalf of the developing countries. With such debts written off, these poorest countries are in a position to start going into debt all over again. This approach leaves fundamental questions unaddressed. What, for instance, prompts us to create an international monetary system and to maintain rules that make this debt necessary in the first place? Is it not time to address systemic issues with systemic solutions?

Though assistance programs and loans to developing nations in the form of national currencies may have noble objectives, the very act of introducing a monopoly of a yang-type currency into a culture can have disastrous effects. We should remember that our national currencies were never designed to promote values such as cooperation or equality, or address the vast majority of our social needs. They were specifically designed to promote industrialization, competition, and nationalism. This very same currency that we are now using—unsuccessfully—to assist developing nations was instead actually used quite effectively to *colonize, not liberate*, many of those same nations, as seen in Ghana (see insert).

## The Ghana Hut Tax

The British faced an interesting problem in the 19th century, when they colonized what would later become the nation of Ghana. At the time, Ghana consisted of several hundred more or less sustainable communities, each contained within their own traditional region. They traded, but only with one another in closed circuits established by tradition among the different tribes. This trading system permitted Ghanaians to meet their basic requirements. It also provided some measure of independence from the colonial government and the need for British goods. Yet, one goal of having a colony is to procure a secure market within a well-controlled territory. The British, therefore, sought to break up the self-contained, regional patterns in order to create a demand for British goods and to secure colonial control of the area.

The British solution was not to start a big advertising or marketing campaign for their goods. It was not even to try to prohibit the old exchange patterns or use coercion to create new ones. It was a lot cheaper, simpler, and more elegant than that. The colonial government simply created, for the first time, a national Ghanaian currency together with a very modest "hut tax." The tax, (of one shilling per household per year) would be payable only in that national currency. Lo and behold, within a few years, most of the traditional sustainable systems collapsed.

Why?

Every "hut"—every extended family unit in the country—needed to earn some of this new currency to pay their hut tax. This could only be done by trading outside of their traditional framework within a new national system. That alone was sufficient to break up long-standing patterns of regional sustainability.

The lesson should be clear: trying to encourage local or regional development, while simultaneously maintaining a monopoly of a national or supranational currency, is like treating an alcoholic with alcohol prescriptions. The monopoly of bank-debt money affects all of us, in developing and developed nations alike. It coerces virtually all those who come into contact with it to behave in ways that are consistent with the yang shadow axis.

*"We're encouraging people to become involved in their own rescue."*

The entire field of economics has been based on the erroneous assumption that something in human nature and *not* the type of money used is what predetermines our behavior patterns.

**Economics and the Economic Man**

It was at the height of patriarchy in Western society, when the last witches were still being burned in Europe, that Adam Smith wrote his *Theory of Moral Sentiments* (1758) and *Wealth of Nations* (1776). He observed that in all modern societies there existed a universal desire for individuals to accumulate money. This observation heavily influenced the development of Smith's theory—economics—whose purpose it was to allocate scarce resources through the means of individual private accumulation.

The psychological cornerstone of economic theory became the idea of the "economic man." This notion is defined as, "a hypothetical man supposed to be free from altruistic sentiments and motives interfering with a purely selfish pursuit of wealth and its enjoyment."[6] It should be noted that this concept was not introduced nor mentioned by Smith himself.

In traditional economic models, we are all expected to find the economic man within us and empower him to act. That is, we are supposed to act purely rationally and selfishly, and this process will ultimately benefit all. This notion has, however, long begged contention (see insert).

### The Mythical Economic Man

The psychological assumptions behind the mythical "economic man" present substantial problems. The definition itself implies that everyone can and should be totally rational—that is, behave in accord with the hyperrational yang shadow of the Magician. In other words, this definition asks us to push aside any vestige of the various yin aspects of ourselves, including any concerns for our communities.

When the Great Mother is repressed, yin ways and means of knowing are automatically devalued, together with the rest of the yin coherence.

The concept of economic man also assumes that group behavior is of the same nature as individual behavior. No room is left for any group psychology that may differ qualitatively from individual behavior. The hypothetical economic man entails the mistaken "fallacy of composition," which fails to take into account that the whole is greater than the sum of its parts.

Gustave Le Bon, a pioneer of social pyschology, made the following point: "Individual members, however like or unlike their model of life, occupations or intelligence, find themselves overruled by a collective mind set. This way of feeling, thinking and acting directs the individual to behave quite differently from what he would do alone."[7]

Le Bon's definition of group psychology is quite consistent with the findings of his contemporary Jung, regarding the collective unconscious.

## Economics and the Yang Perspective

In all fairness, most economists have long been aware of the oversimplifications built into economic man and do not take its assumptions literally. Economist Wesley Clair Mitchell pointed out, "Economics without input from psychology is similar to doing mechanics while ignoring the laws of physics."[8] Even so, the economic man hypothesis persists as an implicit and necessary condition to make the equations of conventional economics work.

Money's value-nonneutrality and other more recent findings all point to the very important links between the type of money used and economic behaviors. Instead of being a passive facilitator of exchanges, as traditional economic theory posits, the monopoly of a yang-type currency deeply affects the relationships between, and the collective psychology of, the people who use it. Yet, as great as this impact is, it is only the first consequence of archetypal repression and the yang shadow axis.

## THE DOMINATOR PARADIGM

Some of the better-known social pathologies of modern-day society include narcissism, consumerism, and fundamentalism. Though they may not appear to be related to our monetary system or to the repression of the Great Mother archetype, our conventional currencies nonetheless feed and activate these pathologies continuously in a catalytic manner. This activation occurs by means of the "dominator paradigm."

Dominance is the need to control or maintain authority over others to attain a sense of security or identity for oneself. The desire to dominate justifies the need for a repressive social order, and is deeply linked to our historical patriarchy. Recall here the tyrant, the excessive yang shadow of the Sovereign archetype. Intrinsic within this dominance paradigm, and connected to the patriarchal ideology, is a belief in total control over others. This is expressed as an imagined sense of security founded on power by whatever means necessary, whether military, political, economic, religious, or psychological.

Other processes that relate to the dominator paradigm in our society today include the glamorization of violence, vicious forms of sport and play, and the fascination with war and aggressive technologies. While we are all subjected culturally to the yang shadow axis, some are more prone to it than others. Someone who is stuck in this shadow axis tends to create a separate and superior identity, and automatically casts as "others" those entities or people that he or she fears, cannot control, or does not understand. These "others" tend to include any group associated with yin characteristics, such as women and Nature, different cultures and races, and so-called primitive societies. This helps explain the long history of the portrayal and the dismissal by mainstream Western society (which is itself caught in a yang shadow axis) of any such others as weak, impotent, irrational, masochistic (each of which are yin shadows), and thus deserving to live in scarcity.

### Narcissism and Consumerism

The dominator paradigm has a significant cost, not only for those who are dominated, but also for the dominators themselves.[9] It is at the origin of what psychologists have called the narcissism of Western culture.

Psychologist Ondine Norman describes the key components of this narcissism:

> One of the most relevant and important diagnostic characteristics of narcissism is the lack of empathy for others. This is a key feature of the dominator paradigm. One cannot even imagine partnership or the capacity for mutual relationships if one is not able to experience some level of empathy for another's experience.[10]

Such a lack of empathy leads directly to a sense of meaninglessness. Meaning always arises out of relationship, whether with loved ones, God, nature, or one's country. The inability to connect with others, therefore, predictably accentuates a sense of meaninglessness, creating what has been referred to as the feeling of an "empty self."

Psychologist Christopher Lasch points out that narcissism does have some features that are useful in our society: "The management of personal impressions comes naturally to [the narcissist], and the mastery of its intricacies serves him well in political and business organizations."[11] The same narcissist, however, also demonstrates traits that are at the origin of many of society's difficulties, from the incapacity to establish long-term partner relationships to the adoption of what Jungian analyst Mario Jacoby describes as "super materialistic and environmentally unsustainable consumerist lifestyles."[12]

The empty self is also the hook by which consumer advertising works. As B. Earl Puckett, president of Allied Stores Corporation, a large U.S. department store chain, explained: "It is our job to make women unhappy with what they have."[13] A key aim of advertising is to make people feel empty, incomplete, and dissatisfied. The ad's message to our subconscious is: if only you were to wear this brand of sneakers, drive this car, have the next updated technology, or use this perfume, you would finally be whole and no longer feel your emptiness.

### Fundamentalism

The dominator paradigm is also linked to fundamentalism, which is not about what one believes in, but rather about *how one holds* those beliefs. Fundamentalism arises when one regards his or her own beliefs as the absolute Truth and deems all other opinions or faiths to be illegitimate. One extreme manifestation of fundamentalism is terrorism.

Fundamentalism is another way that people deal with the fear of meaninglessness and the empty self. Mario Jacoby writes:

> Whenever archaic rage combines with the search for high ideals and the necessity to find meaning in one's life, rage with all its consequences may flare up in the name of whatever the ideal. Any horror, rage, and vengefulness can then be justified on the basis of the 'ideal' one is apparently serving.[14]

## AND THE WINNER IS?

Who truly benefits in a society that is skewed toward patriarchy and lacks archetypal balance? Who wins with a monetary system that promotes this imbalance, which imposes scarcity on the many, and concentrates wealth in the hands of a very few? Clearly the majority of the billions of poor in our world suffer disproportionately. But though it might seem that men and the wealthy are the likely beneficiaries of such a paradigm, the reality is somewhat more complex.

### Effects on Men

If we understand Western culture as a patriarchy, we might logically tend to place men at its helm. This was the assumption of Pulitzer Prize-winning journalist and feminist Susan Faludi, as she began research for her book *Stiffed: The Betrayal of the American Man*. Her findings, however, surprised even her.

Faludi reports that in our patriarchal society, men are asked to need nothing and no one, and to support their families with total confidence. They are told to go out into the world, into the market, to win, and win big. They should know what they want out of life and how to get it. And throughout, they are to remain unstressed, detached, and ready to do whatever is necessary to protect their families and country.

While the term patriarchy implies that men are in control of everything, they are in actual fact often denied the ability to determine their own lives. They are not given the space or tools to express and work with their full range of emotion or to better know themselves. Some men, particularly in light of today's increasing unemployment, feel so lost and out of touch that they lash out.

Faludi began her research by attending a men's domestic violence group. She reported:

> The men I got to know in the group had without exception lost their compass in the world. They had lost or were losing jobs, homes, cars, families. They had been labeled outlaws but felt like castoffs. Their strongest desire was to be dutiful and to belong, to adhere with precision to the roles society had set out for them as men.[15]

Faludi's research reveals something important about the patriarchy in which we live. "Men feel the contours of a box...but they are told that box is of their own manufacture, designed to their specifications."[16] That box—the patriarchy—gives the illusion of power but instead causes immense suffering for men as well as women.

The wealthy—the other supposed class of winners in our society—like many men, have their own issues.

## The Wounds of Wealth

The psychological issues resulting from this imbalanced monetary situation can be understood as "wounds" because they run deep and touch our most vulnerable nerves, and they are almost impossible to avoid. These wounds can undermine our relationships and make us doubt our own self-worth. Most of us have empathy for the plight of those who suffer from the scarcity that arises from living with insufficient money. The wounds created by poverty are indeed pervasive, devastating, and easily understood. But the monopoly of yang money affects all economic classes—the rich as well as the poor. Less appreciated are the formidable issues of having too much money.

Jungian psychologist Bernice Hill has identified four wounds of wealth, which appear at successive levels of intimate interaction, including: burdens of expectation, isolation, unhealthy family dynamics, and crisis of identity (see insert).[17]

## Four Wounds of Wealth

*1. Burdens of Expectation.* The wealthy are often the targets of the fears, needs, and expectations of others who lack money. Societal expectations permeate many aspects of life, including that of supporting charities and generally "doing the right thing," which often translates into writing check after check. When asked to attend an affair or participate in an event, social or otherwise, the affluent are left to ask themselves: "Am I or my checkbook being invited?"

*2. Isolation.* The wealthy must also question whether their personal relationships are based on money or status rather than true feelings of friendship. As a consequence, the rich tend to socialize only with those from similar financial and social backgrounds, and experience a deep sense of isolation. The painful question lingers: "If I didn't have any money, how many of my friends would still be my friends, and how might I find out?" Love, popularity, and camaraderie can be as paper-thin as money itself.

This lack of trust is reflected in the security measures that are taken: the higher walls built around their homes, possessions, and lives, literally and psychologically. In effect, the affluent tend to seek refuge in "golden ghettos."

*3. Unhealthy Family Dynamics.* How often do we hear of rich-family feuds, the nagging fears and general angst regarding inheritances, wills, and the pressures brought to bear on siblings regarding proper behavior? Even the most intimate relationships— choosing the "right" mate in marriage—are subject to all-important pre-nuptial agreements, becoming yet another business contract. Unhealthy family dynamics is another wound associated with wealth.

*4. Crisis of Identity.* Most importantly perhaps, particularly for those who have inherited wealth, are the questions of identity and self-worth. "Who am I?" can be a painful question when your main public identity is that you have money. Philosopher Jacob Needleman observes that, "the only thing that money will not buy is meaning."[18] Wealthy people too often find that their money has brought them guilt, anxiety, and a sense of meaninglessness.

In an environment where so much is shaped by our financial worth, the scarce commodity is trust. Each of these four wounds has in common a loss of trust: in society, in friends, in family, and finally, in oneself. An all-too-common response to the issues faced by the wealthy is, "I wish I had that problem." This denies, however, the depth of the pain experienced by some.

Clearly, rich and poor suffer within this current monetary paradigm. Individuals within each economic group face their own wounds associated with money. These wounds point to the fact that nobody wins with a one-size-fits-all monetary system, which encourages only some aspects of human nature and replicates greed and fear of scarcity.

## CLOSING THOUGHTS

We live in a world that uses predominately one type of money, which came into being centuries ago and is embedded with industrial-age values. Few can escape the imbalances and struggles that result from the limitations imposed by this medium of exchange.

Yang shadows are the hidden roots of many of our most serious contemporary societal ailments. Rather than a simple cause-and-effect situation, there is instead what chemists refer to as a catalytic effect: an ingredient that does not appear to be involved in the reaction nonetheless powerfully activates it. The social ailments listed are not necessarily mechanical results of the monetary system alone, but rather are the results of an axis in which our money is a decisive information replicator.

The modern monetary system provides rewards for those who accumulate money, by means of earned interest, prestige, and material comfort. This same system also ruthlessly punishes those who do not or cannot participate, through bankruptcy and poverty. The game continues without end, and the results are devastating: tens of thousands of people, the majority of them children, die from starvation each day. That is not a game. It is a holocaust.

To become individually and collectively "whole," integration of all archetypal energies and both yin and yang coherences are required. Repression of the feminine cannot continue, not just because it is inherently wrong, but also because it is destroying us.

Reintegrating Great Mother energy does *not* mean, however, switching from a patriarchal society to a matriarchal one. It cannot be emphasized enough that the sought-after outcome is to find a new *balance* between the masculine and feminine, an equilibrium that honors the specific contributions of each. But such a balance requires an integrated monetary system with both yin and yang currencies working alongside one another in complementary fashion to meet our many needs and aspirations, and which allow for a full expression of our archetypal energies.

## PART IV

# MONEY, ARCHETYPES, AND PAST AGES

*Money ranks as one of the primary materials with which*
*Mankind builds the architecture of civilization.*

~LEWIS LAPHAM

## CHAPTER TWENTY FIVE

# The Central Middle Ages Revisited

*History is a guide to navigation in perilous times.*
*History is who we are and why we are the way we are.*

~DAVID C. McCULLOUGH

I t is our contention that archetypal repression is linked to our monetary system and to the virtual monopoly of yang-type national currencies. Our monetary paradigm acts as a relentless information replicator of skewed patriarchal values, which include the two shadows of the Great Mother archetype: greed and fear of scarcity. It is therefore not with idle curiosity that we examine societies with dual-currency systems that honored feminine as well as masculine values.

We therefore turn our focus once again back to a more distant epoch in which dual-currency systems and a different archetypal framework were in operation.

The purpose of our exploration extends beyond obscure monetary issues in past civilizations. As we have seen, the current paradigm is linked to and may be triggering any number of negative consequences for society, including depletion of precious resources and long-term damage to our ecosystems. Insights from the past that could help point the way to a more balanced future are of vital importance to us today.

## THE MEDIEVAL ARCHETYPAL FRAMEWORK

As noted previously back in Chapter Six, the Central Middle Ages distinguished itself from other periods of Western history by a unique form of prosperity that benefitted all classes of society. Unusual investment patterns in productive assets were commonplace as well. Evidence of the long-term thinking and superior craftsmenship of this age endure to this very day in the form of such public works as the cathedrals of Western Europe.

Another hallmark of this medieval epoch was their dual-currency monetary system. Long-distance currencies, similar in function to today's national currencies, were complemented by local means of exhange, some of which were demurrage-charged and accessible to all social classes. These complementary currencies likely played a significant role in the accomplishments of this age. Moreover, the elimination of the local currencies coincides with the sudden and dramatic demise of this epoch in the waning years of the 1200s.

The distinctive elements thus far noted, however, tell only part of the story. Another dimension of this remarkable age is revealed to us through the lens of Archetypal Psychology.

We begin by examining the status of women during the period.

## A Half-Renaissance for Women

It will be recalled that the study of bodily remains revealed that the women of Central medieval London were the tallest in all recorded history. These findings not only suggest the high standard of living enjoyed at that time, but may also reflect another important dimension of this age.

Historian Erika Uitz writes that, "in the 12th century a window of freedom began to open for town-dwelling European women, only to close again before the end of the 15th century."[1] While conditions were not idyllic, women were unquestionably much freer than either before or after this period. The "official" Renaissance that came into being later, was comparitively speaking of far lesser equality or enlightenment for women, despite being full of progress in the arts and other domains.[2] It is not until the last half of the 20th century that women began to reclaim many of the rights and opportunities that were the norm in the Central Middle Ages.

Work was broadly available for women. Of the 312 professions formally registered as *métiers* (occupations) in France at the end of the 13th century, women were officially employed in 108. The Parisian tax registers of 1292 paint an even rosier picture: women worked in 172 different occupations, including barrel making, soap boiling, candle making, bookbinding, and doll painting. Though rarely, women also worked as butchers and, according to Uitz, "were involved even in mining, sword and scythes making."[3]

Women were typically more literate than men among the lay population. While boys and men of aristocratic lineage were trained primarily in the subjects of weapons and warfare, women were routinely trained in reading, writing, singing, and painting. This training was not limited to aristocratic women, but also included daughters of servants and artisans.[4]

Central medieval women also enjoyed an unusually high level of freedom concerning property. In England, "only thirty wills survive today from that late Anglo-Saxon period [10th to 11th centuries] and ten of these are the wills of women, each of whom was a significant property owner, with the same rights of ownership...as any man."[5] Women also had control over large endowments as founders of monasteries and as general benefactors, making them notable figures in their communities.

Women played a surprising role as well in many religious institutions. Many monastic communities were "double houses," having one monastery for nuns and another for monks, with both houses under the same jurisdiction. One study of 50 such double houses reports that all were under the direction of a woman. Everyone answered to an abbess, not an abbot![6]

The arts blossomed during this age and many women played prominent roles. Among the famous mystics and authors, are included the likes of Hildegard von Bingen, Herade von Landsberg, Margery Kempe, Julian of Norwich, Catherine of Siena, and Catherine of Genoa.

Notable women of the period had significant influence on the intellectual life and politics of the age. This included the likes of Queen Anne, Countess Mathilde, and Eleanor of Aquitaine. As Duchess of Aquitaine, Eleanor was wealthy and powerful in her own right. But as queen consort first of France (1137–1152), then of England (1154–1189), following her annulment from King Louis VII and subsequent marriage to Henry II, she became one of the most powerful of all Central medieval figures. She also sired two of England's future kings: Richard the Lionheart and King John. One of Eleanor's lasting contributions was as a patron of "Courtly Love" literature (see insert).

## Courtly Love

Of the many artistic achievements realized during this rich cultural period, the most progressive and enduring expression was the literature of "Courtly Love" *(L'Amour Courtois)*. It marked a significant change in the way Western civilization viewed the concept of love. Courtly Love and its literature have been considered "an essential stage in the emancipation of women."[7]

This literature portrayed a glamorous, new romantic life, which often included secret and forbidden extramarital affairs. These affairs occurred particularly among nobles and aristocrats in the milieu of royal courts (hence, *court*ship, *court*esy, and *court*esan), with the male typically vying for the prized affections of the exalted lady mistress.

Patronage by the likes of the Count of Toulouse and Eleanor of Aquitaine reveals the importance of and support for this literature from the highest levels of power.

Courtly Love originated from the late-11th century region of southern France, called Languedoc. This literature emanated from a worldview referred to as *Gai Saber,* literally the "happy wisdom" or "happy science." Gai Saber and Courtly Love effectively challenged and redefined some of the most traditional Christian ideals, including love, marriage, virtue, and fundamental concepts such as manhood and womanhood.

Historian Régine Pernoud proclaims: "Love was invented in the 12th century."[8] According to Uc de St. Circ, a 13th-century troubadour, Courtly Love for a man is to reach heaven through a woman. It transformed the view of women from that of property to lover and partner.

Noted novelist and scholar C.S. Lewis declared:

> [Courtly Love] effected a change that has left no corner of our ethics, our imagination, or our daily life untouched. It erected impassable barriers between us and the classical past or the Oriental present. Compared with this revolution, the Renaissance is a mere ripple on the surface of literature.[9]

A knight paying homage to his Lady. This is the official Seal of Raymond de Mondragon, and as such, conveys the very image this lord intentionally wanted projected of himself. This image contrasts sharply with those of previous and later knights who would invariably emphasize their Warrior prowess.

(Bronze seal mold of Raymond de Mondragon, France, 12th century).

The profound social impact of Courtly Love is explained not just by the nature of its content, but by its availability to a much broader audience: it was the first poetry written in popular language. Previous literature was written in scholastic Latin and was typically accessible only to church-trained scholars. First appearing in Occitan, or "Langue d'Oc," the language of the southern half of France during that time, this movement spurred the development of poetry in many other nascent vernacular languages, including Catalan, Germanic, English, and Italian.[10] Literary historian Meg Bogin explains that, "for the very first time, common folk actually had something to read!"[11]

The freedom, quality of expression, and values embodied by this literature would vanish with the end of this medieval period. Courtly Love would, however, come to influence Europe yet again, after its rediscovery in the 18th century, during which time it was instrumental in spawning the Romantic Movement.[12]

Some historians have tried to explain the unusually active role of women during the epoch as due to simple "labor scarcity." Yet, if working opportunities were in short supply, why were there six-hour workdays, 90 or more holidays, and Blue Mondays? Why would people invest so much time in chiseling ornate sculptures in remote corners of gigantic cathedrals? More puzzling still, why would anybody build cathedrals with the capacity to house three or four times the entire town's population, whose completion would never be seen by its originators during their own lifetimes?

The particular dedication of the cathedrals offers testimony that something more significant was afoot. Nearly all of the French cathedrals built during this time were dedicated not to Jesus, whose religion they were supposed to be about, but rather to *Notre Dame* (Our Lady). More peculiar still was the form in which Mary was widely represented—in the powerful archetypal image of the Black Madonna.

## The Black Madonna

During this unique age, the Black Madonna manifested as the period's most original and preeminent religious icon. The most venerated statues, important pilgrimages—including the famed Santiago de Compostela— and many religious centers all honored her. Well over 500 Romanesque statues of the Black Madonna have been identified as originating during the Central Middle Ages.[13] In France alone, no less than 80 cathedrals, more than 250 churches, and 302 dedicated sanctuaries were built specifically to venerate her.

The Black Madonna was also a major theme in the poetry of Courtly Love. While Black Madonna icons certainly existed before Courtly Love verse, the explosive proliferation of statues around much of Europe coincided with the spreading of that literature. Courtly Love troubadours wrote about *Notre Dame de la Nuit*, and honored her as "the Madonna of Transformation," and as the "Queen" of their spiritual quest.[14]

Scholar Petra von Cronenburg concludes: "The literature of Courtly Love, the mystical love for the Black Madonna...all had one common purpose: the internal experience of the *Hieros Gamos* (sacred marriage) with androgynous qualities, the integration of the masculine and feminine within, the merging of the human and the divine."[15]

The relevance of the Black Madonna figure becomes clearer when we realize that she represented the power of the feminine in her own terms. This is in marked contrast with the later "white Madonna" with her blue and white gown, who was only an intercessor, an intermediary to the divine. In other words, the Black Madonna represented not only the Great Mother archetype, but archetypal balance as well. References that parallel this are found in the esoteric traditions.

*Esotericism versus Exotericism*

All major religions have had exoteric, as well as esoteric traditions.[16] Exotericism refers to the official, publicly available teachings; esotericism pertains instead to "hidden" knowledge, customarily available only to initiates. The esoteric traditions include the *Kabbalah* in Judaism, *Sufism* in Islam, and *Tantra* in both Hinduism and Tibetan Buddhism. In Christianity, the transmitters of such esoteric traditions included the Augustinian, Benedictine, Cistercian, and Templar orders. All of these Christian esoteric traditions had a different relationship with the feminine than that conveyed by the official exoteric message.

In the esoteric text of Gnostic origin, the *Gospel According to the Hebrews*, for instance, Jesus explicitly called the Holy Spirit his Mother. Various mystical Christian traditions, including those of Jakob Boehme, Meister Eckhart, Hildegard von Bingen, Mechtild of Magdeburg, Julian of Norwich, and the Portuguese cult of the Holy Ghost, all make reference to the Motherhood of God.[17] The Hebrew tradition talks about the feminine *Shekinah*, the "Indwelling of God." In Hinduism there are many manifestations of the divine in feminine form. In the Sufi traditions she is called *Laïla* (the night) and is honored as the highest goal of the mystical quest.[18]

Author Jacques Bonvin notes that, "only the Black Madonna was able to crystallize all the beliefs of Pagan traditions within the Christian faith, without falsifying any of these beliefs. In this, the Black Madonna is unique."[19]

Among the most prominent figures in Christendom to promote esoteric Christian teachings was Saint Bernard (see insert).

## Saint Bernard, Lover of the Black Madonna

Bernard of Clairvaux was a leading personality of the 12th century. He was born in Fontaines, near Dijon, France, where the chapel had a Black Madonna. According to a 14th century legend, Bernard, while still a young boy, was initiated into his vocation by "three drops of the milk of the Black Madonna." In esoteric tradition, "three drops of virgin milk" refer to the mysterious *materia prima*, the "raw material" of the alchemists.

St. Bernard is credited with transforming the troubled Cistercian order—then reduced to a handful of monks in a single monastery at Citeaux, France—into "a vast multinational enterprise of civilization."[20] This involved hundreds of monasteries from Russia to the Iberian Peninsula, every one of which was dedicated to "Our Lady."

The Cistercian order became deeply involved in esoteric research, with specialized scribes translating Hebraic and Islamic alchemical texts, which Rome would certainly not have considered as "Catholic."[21] St. Bernard himself wrote an astounding 200 sermons on Solomon's "Song of Songs," the very poem that Jewish Kabbalists considered one of their most important texts. It begins: "I am black, but I am beautiful, O ye daughters of Jerusalem."[22]

St. Bernard also encouraged the pilgrimage to Santiago de Compostela in northern Spain, which is replete with Cistercian and Templar sites.[23] This pilgrimage was known as the path of the Black Madonnas, as it connected the majority of the Black Madonna sanctuaries.

The founding charter for the famed Order of the Templars was authored by St. Bernard as well. This charter, and all other official Templar documents, placed the name of Our Lady ahead of the name of Christ, in stark contrast with contemporary Christian practice.

St. Bernard was not the only influential personality to have used the Black Madonna as his life's inspiration. St. Ignatius of Loyola, for example, gave his sword to the Black Madonna of Montserrat when he founded the Jesuit order. Joan of Arc prayed to the Black Madonna, and her mother prayed to the Black Madonna at Le Puy for her imprisoned daughter. Goethe used the Black Màdonna as the model for his "eternal feminine" in Faust.[24]

Political tension and occasional violence are not uncommon between the exoteric and esoteric traditions within a particular religion. Such conflicts develop in part because esoteric knowledge tends to extend beyond the confines of the traditional customs and doctrine of its own faith, embracing instead the broader body of aligned teachings from other religions. The medieval boom of the Black Madonna and the upsurge of rich, esoteric Christian traditions in Europe, coincided with the interrelated blossoming of the Sufi traditions of Islam,[25] the Kabbalah of Judaism,[26] and a burgeoning interest in the practice of alchemy.

## Alchemy and the "Blackness" of the Madonna

What is the esoteric message of the Black Madonna and, in particular, her intentionally black color?

At the most literal level, the Black Madonna symbolizes Mother Earth, and, like the Earth, she is dark in color. The child she holds in her arms represents humanity—every one of us. She refers back, therefore, directly to the age-old worship of the Great Mother and to her nurturing relationship to humanity.

At the more subtle level, the pitch-black color of the Black Madonna connects with alchemy. A linguistic clue of that connection is revealed in the etymology of the word "alchemy" itself, which derives from two Arabic words: *Al,* the general Arab particle; and *Khemit,* the "Black Earth," the traditional name for Egypt, the place where the alchemical art was reputed to have originated. The strikingly abnormal color of the Black Madonna specified that She was not just representing Mother Earth, but the black Earth of alchemy itself.[27]

Alchemy has become confused with its literal symbolism of transmuting the vilest metal (lead) into the noblest one (gold). As is made clear in the warnings of alchemists of all ages, however, this is primarily a "philosophic" or symbolic transmutation, a metaphor for a fundamental personal transformation. True initiates of alchemy had only contempt for those who would mistakenly interpret alchemical textbooks literally as some sort of technology to get rich materially. The true essence of alchemy as a guide for personal evolution was encoded metaphorically. The riches that were sought after were not worldly goods or gold, but rather the wealth of spiritual knowledge and wisdom.

The reason for disguising its transformative nature so elaborately was to protect the alchemist from being labeled a heretic or worse, branded a sorcerer, an offense punishable by death at the stake. The metallic transmutation was merely a ruse, a symbolic guise, a coded language. It was used by practitioners, some of whom were well-known Benedictine monks, to protect that knowledge from being misused by non-initiates.[28] Such deception allowed true alchemists to continue their research and extensive writings about that sulfurous topic, without inviting attention and disapproval from the Church.

Alchemy was, in fact, one of the main traditional Western esoteric paths for personal spiritual evolution. Sir Isaac Newton attached more importance and wrote more pages about his research on alchemy than on physics and optics combined. Another of alchemy's many notable practitioners was Carl Jung.[29]

Alchemy is a path towards spiritual evolution, through which one's consciousness transforms into metaphysical gold, shining brightly like an inner sun. The mysterious *materia prima*—the so-called lead that gets transformed into gold—is none other than the alchemist himself or herself. Jung referred to this process as "individuation," which comes as a result of the integration of the *animus* (the masculine aspect, which is conscious in men and unconscious in women) with the *anima* (the feminine aspect, which is unconscious in men and conscious in women).

The very first step in the alchemical process is known as the *nigredo*, literally the "work in *black*," described by Jung as the death of the ego, the "*dark* night of the soul," or the "garment of *darkness*."[30] Medieval and renaissance scholars also referred to this process as melancholy (literally, "*black* humors"). "Saturnine melancholy" was the difficult, unpleasant, but indispensable initial step required in order to attain true inspiration and wholeness (see insert).[31]

### Alchemy as a Symbolic Individuation Code[32]

Three key elements are involved in the alchemical process: *sulfur*, the yang or masculine principle, associated symbolically with the sun, and fire; *mercury*, the yin or feminine principle, associated with the moon, silver, and water; and *salt*, the symbol of the material body.

The Black Madonna of Montserrat, Catalonia, was the most famous Madonna of Spain. Her features, though similar to "white" Madonnas, along with those of the child on her lap, are pointedly painted pitch-black.

Alchemy aims at creating the legendary "Philosopher's Stone," (the integrated self, or Jung's individuated human). This integration is realized by a mystical marriage of both the masculine and the feminine dimension of the alchemist him or herself. As the alchemical handbook, *Aurofontina Chymica,* states, "this blackness doth manifest a Conjunction of the Male and Female."[33]

In his book *Mammon and the Black Goddess*, Robert Graves writes: "The Black Goddess is so far hardly more than a word of hope...She promises a new pacific bond between man and woman...She will lead man back to that sure instinct of love which he long ago forfeited by intellectual pride."[34]

## ᴍᴇᴅɪᴇᴠAL ARCHETYPAL REPRESSION

A move toward ever-stronger authoritarian rule was established from the first half of the 13th century onwards. Local autonomy was replaced by the centralization of power. This power shift preceded an economic succession of events.

In 1265, a monopoly of yang royal coinage was instituted. The gradual elimination of local yin currencies followed. The resulting monetary contraction was aggravated further by the debasement of royal coinage by King Philip IV, around 1295. A powerful economic collapse then followed around 1300.

The downturn led to widespread epidemics and famines that continued to weaken the population for several generations, and culminated in the outbreak of the deadly plague in 1347. The depression and misery would persist for more than a century, until about 1470.

The power shift and economic events, though unquestionably destabilizing in their own right, should nevertheless be understood as part of a more comprehensive breakdown that took hold. The archetypal values that had been honored during the previous three centuries were systematically reversed. The parting shot came by way of a brutal campaign unleashed by the increasingly powerful papal authority in Rome.

The target of this papal campaign was the unorthodox Christians of southern France, collectively referred to as the Albigensians (derived from *Albigi*, the ancient name of the southern French province of Languedoc, where the sects were centered, and the region from which the literature of Courtly Love originated). The Albigensian Crusade led to the first Inquisition by the Church (see insert).

### The Cathars and the Albigensian Crusade

Conventional recounting tells of a specific Christian sect, the *Cathars,* whose heretical practices, notably including gender equality, provoked Rome's reaction during the 13th century. Recent findings suggest a more complex account.

The Cathars were but one of many popular sects of the time, which included the *Vaudois, Béguins, Bogomils,* and others. Particular teachings aside, these various sects harbored common concerns regarding the mounting authoritarianism and materialism of Rome.

Until this period, the Pope was considered the Bishop of Rome; the first among bishops, but ultimately only one of many important voices in the Christian community.[35] Over the course of the 12th to 14th centuries, however, papal authority became enforced more and more in the context of new doctrinal issues, such as clerical celibacy, the idea of purgatory, fixing the number of sacraments, and other details of liturgy.[36] This growing centralization of power within the Church, combined with the increasingly lavish lifestyles of the upper clergy, provided the ferment against Roman ascendancy.

Some of the Christian dissidents of the period came to be referred to as *Cathars*. This term was first used in 1163 by the German monk, Eckbert of Schönau, as a derogatory play on two words: the Greek *katharos* (the pure), and the more popular *catier* ("sorcerers who adore cats," from the Latin *catus*, "cat").[37] So-called Cathar sect members instead referred to themselves as *les bonhommes* (the good people).

In 1209, Pope Innocent III ordered the Albigensian Crusade to counteract the rejection of Rome's authority. An agreement with the ruler of northern France, King Louis IX (later sanctified as Saint Louis), recognized the King's authority over the lands previously held by southern Languedoc nobility.[38] In turn, the King supported papal religous control.[39] This alliance between the Pope and King brought an end to the once brilliant Languedoc civilization.

One infamous episode that took place in the town of Béziers reveals the brutality of the Albigensian Crusade. Only part of the town's population was considered to be heretical. But when asked how soldiers could distinguish the Cathars from others, Arnaud Amaury, the official papal emissary sent to oversee the attack, replied: *"Tuez les tous. Dieu reconnaitra les siens."* ("Kill them all. God will recognize his own.")[40]

In spite of wholesale massacres, opposition to Roman authority persisted, prompting Pope Gregory IX to institute the Dominican Order in 1231, assigning it the duty to carry out inquistions for the apprehension and trial of heretics.

The Albigensian massacres and Inquisition were accompanied by a gradual erosion of women's rights, both within the Church and throughout society. As Petra von Cronenburg explains:

> The leadership role of women abbots in double
> monasteries was curtailed. Sacraments became
> deliverable exclusively by male priests...Women, who
> earlier were relatively free and could become poets,
> medical doctors or heads of guilds, became gradually
> constrained to the role of object of exchange in marriage,
> despised as demonic temptresses, and appreciated only
> for their capacity to produce heirs.[41]

The Church condemned all Courtly Love literature, deeming it
inspired by the devil. This triggered strong resistance at first, even
among the clergy. According to von Cronenburg:

> When education for women was cut back, and when
> finally even nuns were restrained from teaching, the
> movement of the "Beguines" took form, which refused
> to take religious vows so as to permit them to continue
> educating women and girls. But in 1312, their properties
> were confiscated and their rights curtailed, as the
> Inquisition moved against them as well.[42]

By the end of the 14th century, the once flourishing expression of
feminine values in much of Western Europe during the Central Middle
Ages was practically eradicated.

The ensuing power shift is examined below from several viewpoints.

## An Archetypal Ending

An archetypal perspective interprets the events that led to the demise of
this age as part of an underlying shift in consciousness, from a period of
more or less balanced masculine and feminine values to that of patriarchy.
This included the formation of imperialist monarchies and the strong
repression of the Great Mother archetype and feminine roles in general.

The concept of an unquestionable hierarchical authority, embodied by
a king or emperor, was directly reinforced on the religious front by
centralized papal authority and monotheism. This is exemplified by the
drawing below, in which the King of Sicily is crowned by the archetypal
king, Christ himself.

The king being crowned by Christ himself. The text on the open book says:
*"I am the light of the world. Follow me."*

(This drawing by Moreno Tomasetig is taken from a mosaic representing
the coronation of King William II of Sicily, in the Cathedral of Monreale, Italy).

A strictly monetary perspective does not mention, much less attempt to understand, other significant changes that occurred at the time of this economic collapse. It does, for instance, take into account the stunning reversal of women's roles in the workplace, and their renewed subjugation in society.

An archetypal perspective, in contrast, not only includes an explanation of the monetary changes that occurred, but also provides a more encompassing context by which to understand other shifts and reversals that accompanied the economic breakdown. Appreciation of the Great Mother archetype and her repression offers us a framework to account for the simultaneous backlash against women, the end of Courtly Love literature, the official de-emphasis of the Black Madonna movement (replaced from the 14th century onwards by conventional white Madonnas), the Albigensian Crusade, and the centralization of royal and papal power. This archetypal perspective also accounts for the subsequent predominance of other traits associated with the dominant yang coherence.

The patriarchal backlash would only intensify over the next six centuries. The Inquisition by the Church (which endured until 1784), sanctioned many forms of torture and, as previously mentioned, executed an estimated six million women. Many of these women were burned to death as witches.

Paralleling the persecutions and killings, the possibilities of gainful work by women rapidly shrank to the point that, by 1776, the French legislator Turgot would complain that women were being excluded from virtually all commercial activities, "Even those that are most appropriate for their sex, such as embroidery."[43] Until the middle of the 20th century, most women in the West could not even open their own bank account without marital consent, a situation that Eleanor of Aquitaine would have likely found absurd. The widely available local currencies were simply abandoned, and a monopoly of scarce, yang-type, conventional currencies was permanently established, further reinforcing the yang shadow coherence, patriarchy, and women's dependency.

## Zeitgeist of the Central Middle Ages

The monetary perspective offered earlier in this work, though important, does not take into consideration the many changes that occured during the Central Middles Ages.

At the same time, it is also necessary to keep in mind that we do not claim that the archetypal perspective is the product of a linear causality between feminine values, Black Madonna worship, and complementary yin-yang currency systems. Rather, we see a mutual causality, a nonlinear coherence among these phenomena, occurring as a probability wave: all these variables emerged at the same time and then collapsed together as well. The Germans call this a Zeitgeist, a "spirit of the times," when a particular set of cultural values and traits arise simultaneously. The zeitgeist of the Central Middle Ages included honoring the feminine, the appearance of complementary demurrage-charged yin currencies, and a remarkable prosperity that benefited all people and which lasted for more than two centuries.

## CLOSING THOUGHTS

The uniqueness of the Central Middle Ages and the circumstances related to the demise of this golden age cannot be sufficiently explained solely by the monetary perspective offered earlier in this work. The complementary currencies very likely contributed to the high standard of conditions of this epoch; their elimination also helps shed light on the dramatic reversal that occurred in the late 1200s and 1300s. But the monetary framework does not by itself adequately explain the coherence that was operational in Western Europe at that time. Yin-yang currency systems were part of a constellation of phenomena that took hold that also included reintegration of Great Mother archetypal energies, feminine values, Courtly Love literature, Black Madonna worship and the like. The rise of each of these elements offers a more thorough understanding of the zeitgeist of this age, which culminated in a remarkable prosperity that benefited all levels of society, long-term thinking, community projects, and the advancements of women during this period. In similar fashion, archetypal repression helps explain the simultaneous elimination of the complemementary currencies, the reversals for women, rising authoritarianism, the Inquisition, and other phenomena that occurred during the waning years of this golden epoch.

## CHAPTER TWENTY SIX

# Dynastic Egypt

*The past has revealed to me the structure of the future.*

~PIERRE TEILHARD DE CHARDIN

nother exceptional epoch marked by notable prosperity, long-term thinking, and other features found in the Central Middle Ages, including a dual-currency system, occurred much earlier in history in Dynastic Egypt. A major distinction with respect to its latter medieval counterpart is that Egypt's golden age lasted markedly longer, extending from as far back as the 2nd millenium BCE to as late as 30 BCE (see insert).

### Egyptian Millennia[1]

Ancient Egypt's civilization extends from at least the Old Kingdom (2575 BCE) to the Roman period (30 BCE). To give some sense of the time expanse under consideration, consider that when Alexander the Great conquered Egypt in 332 BCE, this

civilization was as ancient to Alexander as he is to us today. The timeframes given below are categorized according to governance.

**Late Predynastic Period** (3100–2950 BCE)—begins with the unification of Upper and Lower Egypt. Earliest known hieroglyphic writings date to this period.

**Dynastic Egypt** (2950–332 BCE)—so named to denote the 31 hereditary lines (dynasties) of Egyptian-born rulers. This vast epoch is subdivided into Early Dynastic Period (2950–2575 BCE), Old Kingdom (2575–2150 BCE), Middle Kingdom (1975–1640 BCE), New Kingdom (1539–1075 BCE), the Late Period (715–332 BCE), and three intermediate periods. The first pyramids are believed to have appeared during the Early Dynastic Period.

**Macedonian/Ptolemaic Period** (332–30 BCE)—begins with Alexander the Great's arrival from Macedonia. He and his descendants (which included Ptolemy I-XII) ruled over Egypt for the next three centuries. This period ends in dramatic fashion with the famed suicide of Cleopatra VII (herself a direct descendant of Alexander).

**Roman Period** (30 BCE–395 CE)—begins with the defeat of Antony and Cleopatra by Octavian, which culminatied in Roman control over Egypt (30 BCE). Roman rule brought an end to the Egyptian dual-currency system. In 395 CE, Egypt became part of the Byzantine Empire.

## THE EGYPTIAN ECONOMY

As in the case of medieval Europe, no systematic statistical analyses were performed during these ancient times. The economic landscape can, however, be inferred from a number of indirect indicators, such as diets, working conditions, education, and archeological findings.

*Food.* Egypt has long and universally been considered the breadbasket of the ancient world. No less than 15 different words were commonly used during the Old Kingdom to distinguish different types of bread, which speak to a prosperous society. More than 40 words existed at the time of the New Kingdom for bread and cakes.[2] The advice offered by a scribe to his disciples suggests an affluent and fair-minded society: "Do not eat bread while another stands by, without offering your portion to him. Food is always there. It is man who does not last."[3]

Besides bread, cheese, onions, melons, beans, and many vegetables, there was also a plentiful supply of meat and fish. The famed Greek historian Diodorus Siculus reports that, "the Nile contains every variety of fish and in numbers beyond belief; for it supplies all the natives not only with abundant subsistence from the fish freshly caught, but it also yields an unfailing multitude of fish for salting."[4]

Egypt's fertility in grain was the highest in the ancient world; average yield estimates ran as high as ten times the norm. One sign that something special was taking place in food production was the fact that Dynastic Egypt initiated the first historically documented foreign aid program. Written records denote that Egypt gave grains free of charge to the Athenian citizens when they suffered a famine in 445 BCE.[5] The bountiful food supply was matched by this society's taste and selection of beverages.

*Drink.* Both beer and wine were abundant and commonly consumed at all levels of society. The Greek-Egyptian Athenaeus, one of the earliest-known wine critics, described Egyptian wines with a sophistication that would rival today's connoisseurs:

> Wine of the Mareotic region is excellent, white, pleasant, fragrant, easily assimilated, thin, not likely to go to the head, and diuretic. The Taeniotic wine is better than the Mareotic, somewhat paler; it has an oily quality, pleasant, aromatic, mildly astringent. And the wine of the Antylla province surpasses all others.[6]

The substantial quantity of consumption led a Middle Kingdom Wisdom Text to advise to lend a hand to an elder who drank too much beer, and to respect him as his children should.

*Education.* Formal instruction was not uncommon, particularly from the Middle Kingdom onwards. Official day schools, known as "Houses of Instruction," were established in association with the royal residences and many temples. "Quite simply, anyone who was anyone in Dynastic Egypt could read and write."[7] Not everybody knew the hieroglyphic form of writing, reserved as it was for sacred texts or inscriptions on public monuments. Laundry lists, however, as well as dressmaking advice and other household trivia indicate that even ordinary housekeepers and servants were able to read and write in the common demotic script.

*Workdays.* Workdays were eight hours long and there were many holidays. According to records of the time, only 18 of 50 consecutive days were working days for the entire labor crew.[8]

*Archeological Confirmation.* In addition to written accounts, there is mounting archeological evidence of the generally high standards of conditions of the age. According to Mark Lehner, lead archaeologist of the University of Chicago/Harvard University Giza Plateau Mapping Project:

> Bones in the area [Giza] suggest that workers enjoyed quite a lot of prime beef. Previous excavations have discovered that they also ate bread and fish, and drank beer. Analysis of human remains suggests that workers apparently had access to medical treatment. Evidence has been found of healed broken bones, amputated limbs, and even brain surgeries.[9]

For the sake of accuracy, it should be pointed out that though the majority of findings lend support to the overall affluence of Egyptian society, archeological evidence is not uniformly consistent. One exception is noted in the study of the skeletal remains in the Tell el-Amarna area (see insert).

### The Exception of Tell el-Amarna

Tell el-Amarna was briefly the capital of ancient Egypt during the short reign of the pharaoh Akhenaten 1379–1362 BCE. Recent excavations at this site show that, "anemia ran at 74 percent among children and teenagers, and at 44 percent among adults. The average height of men was 159 cm [5 feet 2 inches] and 153 cm [just over 5 feet] among women." According to researcher Jerome Rose, professor of anthropology at the University of Arkansas, "adult heights are used as a proxy for overall standard of living. Short statures reflect a diet deficient in protein. People were not growing to their full potential."[10]

The discrepancy between the archeological findings at Tell el-Amarna and others is partially explained by some of the specifics of this period and site. The reigning pharaoh Akhenaten was considered an unpopular heretic, and the conditions related to his experimental new city built in the middle of the dessert does not reflect conditions in and around the Nile basin or the overall economic reality of the millennia in question.[11] In short, Tell el-Amarna can be considered an exception to the general rule of Egyptian economic wellbeing, due to unusual times and place.

What then was the source of this ancient civilization's success? Though the fertile black soil of Egypt was indeed exceptional, this "gift of the Nile" accounts for only part of this society's abundance. Productive assets, such as their irrigation systems, which were maintained at a quality envied by the rest of the ancient world, obviously contributed as well, as did their apparent industriousness and the unique economic incentives that were then operational in Egypt. But these and other elements, though distinctive and important, were themselves likely the by-product of yet another ancient Egyptian peculiarity—their monetary system.

Egyptian estate dating back to 18th dynasty with grape harvesting and wine making in the upper register; and fowl trapping and preparation in the lower register. Notice the emphasis on storage vases repeated in both registers.

(TT 52 Nakht. Metropolitan Museum of Art 15,19c).

## THE EGYPTIAN DUAL-CURRENCY SYSTEM

Two currencies operated in parallel in ancient Egypt.

Long-distance currencies, in the form of standardized gold rings and silver bars, were used in international exchanges with nations such as Mesopotamia and Nubia. These currencies were used for the purchase of important items such as real estate, luxury items, and marriage contracts. They functioned as both a medium of exchange and as a store of value.

Another type of currency was widely in use as well. It was demurrage-charged and linked to the storage of food.

### Egyptian Demurrage and Food Storage

The Egyptian demurrage-charged local currencies, like their medieval counterparts, appeared to function purely as a medium of exchange for daily trade among Egyptians. A key distinction was that the demurrage fee in Egypt was based on the actual cost of the storage of food.[12] Food storage was by no means a unique feature of Egyptian society. Storing for a bad season and next year's seedlings was an essential practice common to all agricultural societies dating back to the beginning of the agricultural revolution (10,000 BCE), and still in use to this day. The Egyptians, however, also used food storage as the basis for their monetary system, which provided great benefits not just to the wealthy but to all Egyptians, thus setting this society apart from others of its time.

The food-storage currency likely worked as follows: Imagine yourself as an ancient Egyptian farmer who, after the harvest, has a surplus of ten bags of wheat. You bring these bags to your local storage site and the scribe gives you a receipt specifying that he "received ten bags of wheat," followed by the official's name and the date of this transaction. Depending on the period and locale, these wheat receipts were written on either *papyri*, a thick paper-like material, or, we contend, on an *ostrakon* (plural: ostraka), a broken piece of pottery shard, millions of which have been found throughout Egypt.[13]

The key to the wheat-currency system becomes clear when you return, perhaps a year later, to cash in your ten-bag ostrakon. The scribe looks at your pottery-shard receipt and orders only nine bags returned to you. The conversation might go as follows:

*"I brought you ten bags; why do you return to me only nine now?"*

Somewhat irritated, the scribe replies, *"Don't you see that was a year ago?"*

*"So?"*

*"Do you see that guard standing in front of the storage building? He eats, you know! So do I, for that matter. Notwithstanding all our precautions, we also lose some wheat to rats and mice."*

*"Yes, but what has that to do with my tenth bag?"*

This tenth bag is a demurrage charge equivalent to the cost of storing the wheat for one year. The redemption value of these Egyptian ostraka receipts would age. For instance, had you returned six months instead of one year later to recover your bags, you would have received 9.5 bags in return (a 0.5 bag demurrage charge, or one half of an annual demurrage fee for storage). In essence, the longer the food was held in storage, the greater the cost that was incurred, similar to the fees of a parking meter. For this reason, people would tend not to hoard such currencies, but would use them instead as a pure medium of exchange; in as timely a manner as was practical and possible.

These wheat receipts served as a local currency, circulating in parallel with the long-distance money of silver bars and gold rings.

## Egyptian versus Medieval Demurrage

Though far more ancient, the Egyptian demurrage system was patently more sophisticated than its medieval counterpart. This approach was not only fine-tuned to the month and even the day, but was also tied to the "real world" of spoilage and costs of storage. The analogous medieval *Renovatio Monetae* was instead a stop-and-go process performed every five or six years, or after the death of a lord.

The arbitrariness of both the frequency and level of taxation in the medieval demurrage resulted in abuses. For instance, Duke Johann II of Saxony had his money reminted 86 times during his 18-year reign (from 1350 to 1368). One ruler in Poland changed his coins systematically four times per year. Such misuse ended up discrediting the entire practice.

The Egyptians seemed quite content with a system that permitted even the most modest farmer's production to become money at the farmer's choice. Often teased by the Greeks for their mundane-looking local money, Egyptians in turn considered the Greek passion for gold and silver coins a rather odd obsession, and viewed such precious-metal coins as "a piece of local vanity, patriotism or advertisement with no far-reaching importance."[14] The Egyptians accepted foreign coins only for their bullion content—as a simple raw material—as confirmed by Greek coins found in Egypt that had been cut open just to verify their metal content.

The particulars of how or when this food-storage, demurrage-charged money was first implemented are unknown. What is known is that during the Ptolemaic period (332–30 BCE), the Egyptians considered the demurrage-charged currency as the *old money.*

One intriguing hypothesis regarding this currency's origin is offered in the Bible (see insert).

Silver Stater from Acanthus (Northern Greece, 500 BCE) found in a hoard of Greek coins in the Nile Delta. This coin has been cut open to check the purity and quality of the metal. Its intricate design represents a lion attacking a bull, but the Egyptians considered the coin only as silver commodity.

## Joseph and Demurrage

The biblical story of Joseph (ca. 1900-1600 BCE) may offer a clue to the origins of the demurrage currency in Egypt. It is not, however, only what is written in the Bible but also what is left unexplained that is of interest.

Betrayed by his jealous brothers, Joseph was "sold to the Ishmaelites for twenty pieces of silver, and they brought him to Egypt," (Genesis 37:28). Once there, Joseph managed to interpret the Pharaoh's premonitory dream of seven fat and seven lean cows. Joseph recommended that food reserves be stored during the seven fat years, to make them available for lean times. The Bible claims that the pharaoh and others were so impressed with this solution that Joseph was named General Superintendent, the second most powerful position in all of Egypt.

We know, however, that food storage was a typical component of ancient economies and dream interpretation seems a flimsy reason for Joseph's dramatic rise in power. Another explanation is tempting.

Would it not be possible that Joseph may have helped either promote or invent a demurrage currency system backed by food storage and was, thus, credited with saving the Egyptian economy?

These ostraka appear to have served as common currency for ordinary daily exchanges for at least sixteen centuries and perhaps much longer still. The demurrage charge was built into all transactions using the "wheat standard" and standards based on other similar storable food items (such as grains, barley, and wine) as currencies. This monetary system may help explain some of the as yet unanswered mysteries regarding the economic strength of Dynastic Egypt, unique in its time.

**The Case for Ostraka**

Millions of ostraka wheat receipts have been found in various places in Egypt dating to the time periods in question. Despite this fact, it must be stated here that the generalized use of these pottery shards as fully-fledged demurrage-charged monetary system has yet to be directly confirmed.

The main study on demurrage currencies was conducted in 1910 by the German Greek-classics scholar, Friedrich Preisigke, who focused exclusively on the Ptolemaic period from 332 BCE onwards.[15] His research was also limited to those paper-like currencies in the form of *papyri* found in the Imperial Collection of Greek-language papyri from Egypt. Almost completely ignored in this research was the abundant and more ancient ostraka.[16] No less than 1.6 million ostraka were found in one single dynastic village (at Medinet), a relatively well-preserved and ancient region in the Egyptian desert.[17]

Preisigke himself certainly does not make the claim that the food-receipt system was invented or was new during the period he describes. There were some additional banking functions added during the Ptolemaic period, but receipts for food deposits with temples are abundant much earlier. Nor does he state that money was used only in the form of papyri. Preisigke instead implicitly inferred that the papyri and ostraka played the same function. He points out, for example, that he found papyri used in some areas of the Delta, but in Memphis ostraka were used.[18]

Preisigke also observed that taxes were payable in ostraka, which lends itself to the argument that food receipts were commonly used as money. Preisigke noted that, "particularly in villages, some taxes were payable in nature. A landlord would request to have the renter of a farm pay for him the taxes in wheat owed by the landlord to that location, and that amount would be deducted from the renter's dues."[19]

The wheat receipt written on an *ostrakon* was the most common currency used among ordinary Egyptians. The particular receipt above is relatively "small change." Its translation reads: "Second year of the reign of Ramses II, second day of third month of Shamu. On this day three *hin* (a quantity of about 1.5 quarts) of wheat were received by the undersigned officer of the West." The value of such receipts would slowly diminish over time to reflect storage costs. Such cost represented a modest demurrage fee.

(Kestner Museum inventory # 4633, Hannover).

Preisigke makes additional astute points regarding the use of wheat in Egyptian accounting mechanisms:

> There seems even to exist a clearing system between long-distance deposits through a state-run accounting system. One could therefore receive a cheque drawn in wheat that was deposited in one place, and withdraw that amount in another place, for a fee. Netting between transactions seem to have taken place (if one needed 100 units of wheat transported from A to B; and 90 units from B to A; they would only have to transport 10 units from A to B).[20]

Because of the limited time focus of Preisigke's work, some may conclude incorrectly that demurrage currencies first appeared during the Ptolemaic period. It must be emphasized here that no study other than Preisigke's has ever been undertaken regarding such "unconventional" currencies. To our knowledge there has not been much interest in yin-type currencies, be it of ancient Egypt or of the Central Middle Ages. The zeitgeist of academia during the 19th and much of the 20th centuries simply did not lend themselves to such investigations.

Though direct, irrefutable evidence in support of our monetary claims is still lacking, there is, however a strong convergence of many indirect circumstantial claims that we believe support our claims that the ostraka may be considered to be like modern day paper with many different uses, from informal notes to formal contracts and the like. We claim that this would include their use as common money, similar to the use of modern-day checks or paper money. What is an established fact is that countless numbers of ostraka have been found all over Egypt with information indicating that they were receipts for storable food, specifying the amount in weight of the commodity exchanged and its dates.

Again, further study on the yin-currencies of dynastic Egypt along with many other ancient societes is certainly warranted.

## A GRECO-ROMAN ENDING

That the monetary system may have been linked to the prosperity of Dynastic Egypt is also suggested by the fact that the end of the good millennia in Egypt coincided with the demise of the dual-currency system by the conquering Romans. The net results of the replacement of the demurrage-charged ostraka by a monopoly of "modern" Roman currency with positive interest rates—with the interest tending to accrue to Rome—were significant and enduring. The Egyptian economy, which had enjoyed a distinctive prosperity for well over 2000 years and was once the envy of the ancient world, eroded after only a few generations under the new monetary regime. Egypt ended up degenerating to the status of a developing country, a condition it retains to this very day.

General opinion, dating back to the Greek historian Plutarch in the first century CE, claims that ancient Egypt's abundance was merely a gift of the Nile. But an economy that functioned quite successfully for millennia came to an end at the same time as the demise of the dual-currency system. The Nile, ever-present and ever-flowing, was there when the economy flourished and remained there after the economy declined. We submit the hypothesis that at least some of the credit for the proverbial "breadbasket of the ancient world" should be attributed to those funny-looking, demurrage-charged ostraka.

## CLOSING THOUGHTS

The converging evidence from Dynastic Egypt offers testimony that using a dual-currency system provided solutions and new possibilities that otherwise could not have existed. The Central Middle Ages and Dynastic Egypt were two civilizations that enjoyed economies that were exceptionally prosperous and stable, encouraging a more active participation of all social classes.

CHAPTER TWENTY SEVEN

# Dynastic Egypt Revisited

*The basic discovery about any people is the discovery*

*of the relationship between its men and its women.*

~PEARL S. BUCK

Archetypes do not belong to any one culture or period of history; they are fundamental psychological patters that belong to humanity, and transcend race, nationality, society, and time itself. What does significantly differentiate one individual, community, culture, civilization, and epoch from another is the degree to which archetypes are integrated or repressed and the type of money that is operational.

We repeat our claim that archetypal repression is inexorably linked to today's major issues and that the lack of integration of the Great Mother archetype in particular has profoundly influenced our monetary paradigm and its spread of skewed patriarchal values. With our own present-day interests in mind, we continue our reexamination of another past society that used a dual-currency system and that honored feminine as well as masculine values.

## DYNASTIC EGYPTIAN ARCHETYPAL INTEGRATION

As previously noted, among the many important similarities between the Central Middle Ages and Dynastic Egypt are: dual-currency systems, prosperous economies, and long-term thinking. Additionally, a similar archetypal coherence was in play. In Dynastic Egypt, veneration of the Great Mother archetype took the symbolic form of Isis.

Seti I from the 19th dynasty is shown suckling the breast of Isis. The milk of Isis is the source of the Pharaoh's wisdom and authority to rule.

(Wall-painting,Temple of Seti I, Abydos, approx.1300 BCE).

## The Isis Cult

Most of today's commonly held beliefs about Dynastic Egypt emanate from Western research dating back to the 19th century and first half of the 20th century. Egyptologists of the period, likely influenced by their own cultural biases, held that Egyptian culture was inherently patriarchal, with an all-powerful male pharaoh at the top. More recent findings, however, paint a very different picture, with religious, legislative, and social traditions that were clearly and predominantly matrifocal. At the center of this tradition was "the great Isis," the supreme goddess in Egypt, the almighty Great Mother, worshipped uninterruptedly for more than three millennia, from well before 3200 BCE to at least 200 CE.

The relationship between Isis and temporal power is illustrated by the many representations of a pharaoh suckling the breast of Isis to receive the divine nourishment of wisdom from her, thus giving the pharaoh his right to rule. She was also the Seat of Wisdom, identified by her hieroglyph in the form of a high-backed throne that rested on her head. This *cathedra* chair was her key distinguishing feature.[1] "The throne maketh the king," as many texts have said since the first dynasty.[2] The lap of the Goddess Isis became the royal throne of Egypt.

Isis was also the indispensable "bridge" between the land of the living and the realm of the departed. Mythology holds her as the originator of the important ritual of mummification, and all the magical rituals necessary for the transition to the hereafter.

The apparent Egyptian fixation with death centered on the belief that though mortality was inevitable, it was not necessarily the end. By taking all the correct precautions it was possible to enjoy an afterlife in the "Field of Reeds," a land of pleasure and plenty.[3] The elaborate mummifications and burial arrangements were considered pragmatic undertakings necessary to ensure the continuation of the "good life," even after death. The Egyptians believed they could take their material possessions with them to the afterlife, which is why they were buried with their most precious belongings.

Initially reserved for the pharaohs and their family members, such arrangements became accessible to any men and women who could afford them, starting from the Middle Empire onwards. These customs revealed an acceptance of death and preparation for it as a fact of life, an outlook quite consistent with Great Mother cultures, which encompassed her key attributes of sex, death, and money.

The Isis myth provides abundant clues of the Egyptian reverence for the Great Mother archetype. In contrast with Greek and other Indo-European mythologies, the feminine principle was not only honored, but also systematically empowered. Osiris, the male God of the Afterlife and the God of the Nile (including floodwaters and vegetation), is, comparatively speaking, almost a sidekick. He is the hapless one whom Isis rescues time and again out of love (see insert).

## Isis: the Feminine Savior

Isis was the first daughter of Nut, the overarching night sky "who bore all the gods," and the little Earth-God, Geb. Her Egyptian name was Au Set (Exalted Queen), which was later modified during the Ptolemaic Period to the now familiar Isis by the colonizing Greeks.

According to popular legend, Isis lived with her brother and lover, Osiris, God of the Nile. Their brother Seth, jealous and evil, killed Osiris, dismembering him into 13 parts. Thus began the long saga whereby Isis recovered Osiris' body parts, one by one, marking each location where a part was found with a temple and sacred city. All parts were found but one, his sexual organ, which Isis replaced with a golden phallus. She then invented the art of embalming and returned Osiris to life. Impregnated by his golden phallus, Isis bore a child, Horus, the Golden Sun God.

In stark contrast to contemporary and subsequent patriarchal religions, it is the feminine principle that embraces the heavenly, solar, male god. As Jungian psychologist Erich Neumann explains, "the daytime sky is the realm where the sun is born and dies, not, as later, the realm over which it rules."[4]

Initially the Goddess of the Hearth and Home, the powers of Isis became universal. She became known as "the Lady of the Innumerable Names" (myrionymos) and as "Isis the All-Goddess," (Isis Panthea).[5] "I am the Mother of All that is, Mistress of all elements, origin of all time, first among all gods and goddesses...I govern everything."[6] She was the Queen of Heaven, the Mother of the Sun, the Maker of Sunrise and Maker of Kings. She was the mourning wife, tender sister, and the originator of all the arts and of all that makes life civilized. She was the Lady of Joy and Abundance, Sochit (the grain field), and Hathor (the generous source of food). As "Destiny," she overcame Fate and caused righteousness to prevail. As Isis Medica, she was the healer of all ills. Finally, "She was in the fullest sense Love."[7] Isis was indeed Almighty.

From the beginning, Isis turned a kind eye to humans, teaching women to grind corn, spin flax, weave cloth, and to calm men enough to live with them. Each living being was considered to be a drop of her blood; and feminine values were as important as masculine values as revealed in the conditions of women.

## The Status of Women in Egyptian Society

Egyptology confirms that women were remarkably privileged in Egyptian society, especially when compared to the relative conditions of women from other cultures of the time and down through history.

### Legal Status

Historian Max Mueller claims that, "no people ancient or modern has given women so high a legal status as did the inhabitants of the Nile Valley."[8] The legal status of Dynastic Egyptian women not only surpassed other societies of the period, but compares favorably to the status in many nations today.

Egyptologist Janet H. Johnson writes:

> From our earliest preserved records (Old Kingdom) the formal legal status of women (no matter if they were unmarried, married, divorced, or widowed) was identical to that of Egyptian men. Egyptian women, like Egyptian men, were legally responsible for their own actions and personally accountable to both civil and criminal law. They were able to acquire, own and dispose of both real estate and other personal property. They could enter into contracts in their own names; they could initiate court cases and likewise be sued; they could serve as witnesses in court cases, they could sit on juries; and they could witness legal documents…Women had legal rights and were willing to fight for them.[9]

### Marriage

Marriage contracts dealt predominantly with financial matters and were, "extremely advantageous to the wife…Either party could divorce the other on any grounds, but the economic consequences of the annuity contract made this a serious step for the husband."[10] In the event of divorce, women also tended to have custody rights of children. This was in stark contrast with, "patriarchal Rome, where a pregnant widow was obliged by law to offer her newborn baby to her dead husband's family; only if they had no use for the child was she given the chance to raise her baby herself."[11]

Egyptian women could also choose who they wanted to marry independently of social class—even slaves or foreigners. This too differed significant from the customary practices of other societies of the time. During their rule over Egypt, the Romans would introduce complex inheritance regulations to pressure Egyptians to marry only within their own social class.[12]

As in many of the comparatively favorable conditions enjoyed by Egyptian women, Isis played a pivotal role, in this case, as the "upholder of the marriage covenant." During a wedding, it was in Isis' name that the husband made a "solemn contract to be obedient to his wife."[13]

### Women and Poetry

Another parallel with the Central Middle Ages was the unusual appearance of love poetry in Egypt, comparable in some respects to Courtly Love literature. Egyptians were, in fact, the people known to write love poetry.[14] Much to the amazement of contemporary Greeks, Egyptian women often took the initiative in courtship, addressing the man or proposing marriage in love poems and letters.[15]

### Women's Work

Regarding careers and work, women were excluded from a number of positions, for example, city mayors and royal scribes, and from certain crafts, such as sculptors, carpenters, and public gardeners.[16] Then again, men were similarly excluded from certain activities. For instance, women were the key producers in the two principal industries in Egypt: food and textiles.[17]

The foremost industrial craft in Egypt was the manufacture of linen textiles. It was critical for both the living and the dead—a single mummification could require as much as 1,000 square yards of linen cloth.[18] As in the medieval period, women participated in all aspects of linen manufacturing: harvesting the flax, hackling, roving, spinning the fibers into threads, and the weaving process. Weaving frequently included mass-production "factories" with many workers supervised by an overseer, who was usually a woman. Women also reportedly accepted payment for finished cloth and bore the title "Overseer of the House of Weavers." It was only in the later part of the New Kingdom that some men were allowed to enter the weaving industry.[19]

Hatshepsut, the best-known female Egyptian pharaoh, and the greatest builder of her dynasty. This statue captures her self-confidence and femininity.

(Granite statue at the National Museum of Antiquities in Leiden, Netherland, including a cast of the original head, located at the Metropolitan Museum of New York).

Many women held high positions in public administration and courtly functions. This included female stewards for kings, queens, and princesses, "seal bearers" (treasurers), and chiefs of funerary priesthood. This is well documented in the Old Kingdom.

*Women Rulers*

While women appeared equal or may even have been favored in some legal and private matters, the most powerful position of all—the pharaoh—was almost always, but not exclusively, held by men. Not infrequently there existed female regents, i.e., a pharaoh's who mother ruled on her son's behalf until he matured. More significant still, between 3000 and 1000 BCE, four women officially assumed the throne.[20] It was during the regency of Ny-netjer of the Second Dynasty (2770–2649 BCE) that, "it was decided that women might hold the kingly office."[21]

While rarely actualized, the mere fact that there was no ideological or theological barrier for women to rule in Egypt was a remarkable situation and indication of the ancient Egyptian mindset. Even today, many nations, including such world-leading countries as the United States, China, Russia, France, and Japan, have yet to elect a female president or prime minister.

Seen from a modern perspective, and in light of recent advancements in women's rights, Egypt was still primarily a man's world. Women's unique status in Dynastic Egypt is more readily appreciated by comparison with conditions in other societies of that period (see insert).

### Women's Status in Other Ancient Civilizations

A basis of comparison for women's status is offered by two civilizations with which Egypt had extensive commercial and cultural contact: Mesopotamia and Greece. A small sampling of their characteristic laws and customs are synthesized here.

Mesopotamia's Hammurabic law (ca. 1750 BCE) considered it normal practice for a man unable to repay his debts to give away his wife or children as slaves in compensation. The father, without the involvement of either the mother or daughter herself, customarily arranged all marriages.[22] A common position in the ancient Middle East it was that, "adultery is possible only on the side of the wife, because she is the property of the husband."[23]

Historian and author Gerda Lerner writes:

> Divorce was easily obtained for men, who merely had to make a public declaration of intent. It was difficult for a wife to obtain a divorce and only those without blemish might attempt it because the law states that: 'If [the woman] has not kept herself chaste but is given to going about out [of the house], and so belittle her husband, they shall cast that woman into the water.'[24]

Athens and other Greek city-states did not recognize a woman's independent existence. Women had no political rights and did not participate in any decision-making. Fathers or male relatives arranged a woman's marriage. Women could not own or inherit any property, nor enter into any transaction involving more than the value of one bushel of grain.[25]

Greek women were also excluded from public life. Women were kept in seclusion in the *gyneceum,* an isolated area in the back of the house, where no man could enter except close relatives. Greek historian Xenophon (428–354 BCE) proposed that, "it is better for a woman to stay inside the house, and not show herself at the door."[26] The Greek playwright Menander (342–292 BCE) wrote that, "a decent woman must stay at home; the streets are for low women." The only women accepted in public or permitted to be educated into literacy and the finer social arts, were *hetaira* (prostitutes).[27]

Egyptologist Joyce Tyldesley states:

> Egypt was undoubtedly the best place to have been born a woman in the whole of the Ancient World. During the dynastic period, as the Greek historian Herodotus observed, Egyptian women enjoyed a legal, social and sexual independence unrivaled by their Greek or Roman sisters…They could own and trade property, work outside the home, marry foreigners and even live alone without the protection of a male guardian.[28]

It is again Isis who is officially credited with having made, "the power of women equal to that of men."[29]

## EGYPTIAN ARCHETYPAL REPRESSION

Both the medieval and dynastic ages ended when a centralizing power took over. In Europe it took the form of kings ruling by "divine right." In Egypt it occurred by the loss of sovereignty to ancient Rome. But unlike the abrupt medieval demise, the Egyptian end came gradually with cultural erosion by foreign patriarchal influences, namely: Mesopotamian, Hittite, Persian, Hyksos, Greek and Roman, followed by Christianization.

As in Europe, Egypt's decline coincided with replacement of its yin currency by a yang monetary system imposed by Rome. This change was accompanied by increased concentration of wealth, characteristic of the Roman Empire. In Kerkereosiris, a Fayum village typical of the period, some 1,500 families farmed 3,000 acres—a mere two acres per family. In stark contrast, one privileged family, the Apions, who had twice achieved the position of praetorian prefect in public administration during the 6th century CE, controlled a whopping 75,000-acre estate.[30]

In Egypt as in medieval Europe, the constellation of yang shadows became increasingly dominant: a monopoly of yang-type currencies prevailed, patriarchy was affirmed, and the repression of the Great Mother archetype ensued. This repression increasingly activated the collective emotions of greed and fear of scarcity, which became embedded in the culture through the monetary system.

## Commonalities

Honoring the Great Mother archetype, demurrage-charged currencies, and widespread prosperity can each be understood as imprints of the same archetypal coherence. The great epochs in both Egypt and medieval Europe coincided with honoring both yin and yang values. The end of each period coincided with renewed archetypal repression.

Again, we do not claim a "magical," direct causal effect between Great Mother veneration and the choice of monetary systems. In each age when the Great Mother was honored, however, a yin demurrage-charged currency was also adopted, which very likely contributed to the unusual abundance and exceptional economic conditions.

These two societies also had in common an archetypal coherence that differed markedly from the rest of the world. And not only did each culture honor the Great Mother, but in many respects, the medieval Black Madonna was none other than Isis herself—her titles and emblematic chair were merely transferred. More surprising still, some of the Black Madonnas venerated in France were actually original Egyptian statues of Isis (see insert).

### The Black Madonna—Egyptian Connection

There are numerous connections between the medieval Black Madonna and the Egyptian Isis. Both icons are seated in the same straight chair—the Cathedra—the symbol of her power and, not coincidentally, the origin of the word "cathedral." Other connections include the "oriental" anecdotes in many Black Madonna legends, the esoteric Egyptian "alchemical" link, and the identical and particular kinds of miracles performed in their legends. A few of the many other associations are listed below.

Several Black Madonna statues—namely, the Black Virgin of Boulogne in France and at the Sablon in Brussels, Belgium—are reported to have arrived by river, standing on a boat with no sails or crew, with a copy of the Gospels in an oriental script.[31] This is an exact transposition of the ritual along the Nile by which Isis arrived by boat in her sacred cities. Isis was traditionally invoked as "Star of the Sea," "Seat of Wisdom," and "Queen of Heaven," three titles by which St. Bernard referred specifically to the Black Madonna a millennium later.

The literal and symbolic blackness of the Black Madonna also has deep associations with Isis. Plutarch describes the famed "Veil of Isis" as black. Members of Isis' main priestly groups were known as the "wearers of black" because they specialized in mourning her.[32] Isis' brother and lover, Osiris, was also called "the Black One." The spells invoking Isis began with, "thy kingdom resides in that which is utterly black."[33]

The famed pilgrimage to Santiago de Compostela derived its name from *compostus stellae* (literally "compost of stars" in Latin). This pilgrimage was associated with the Black Madonna sanctuaries. It was also called the "Path of the Milky Way," a direct reference to Isis in her Hathor form, and a name by which our own galaxy is known. Some of the Black Madonna statues were popularly referred to as *les Egyptiennes*.[34] Examples include the Black Madonna of Chartres in Northern France, and in Southern France, the Black Madonna of that of Meymac, which dates back to the 12th century.

In a number of cases, the connections are even more explicit. Several medieval statues that were revered as the Black Madonna were actually antique statues of Isis that had been directly imported from Egypt. A chronicle from 1255 mentions that upon the return of Louis IX from the Crusades, "He left in the country of Forez an image of Our Lady carved in black color that he had brought back from the Levant." In actuality, this is an original Egyptian statue of Isis with Horus on her lap.

Another Egyptian "Black Madonna" statue, long preserved and honored in St. Germain des Prés (a suburb of Paris), was removed and destroyed during the 16th century on orders of Bishop Bretonneau, because he did not appreciate its "pagan origins."[35] The famous Black Madonna from Le Puy and other such statues were also destroyed by French revolutionaries in 1793. Fortunately, a scientist named Faujas de Saint-Fons had made three very detailed analyses and a scientific description of that specific statue earlier in 1777. He determined the statue to be "of Isis with Osiris [sic], which had been modified into a Madonna."[36] He even mentions hieroglyphic inscriptions identical to those that he had found on the well-known archeological "Table of Isis."[37]

## CLOSING THOUGHTS

Both the Central Middle Ages and Dynastic Egypt offer testimony to the relationships between types of money and our collective psyches and society. These past civilizations also provide a warning that is relevant today. Medieval economist Guy Bois views the events that culminated in the Plague as "precedent[s] of a systemic crisis."[38] It might be prudent to heed these lessons of the past and expand our understanding of how monetary systems affect all of us, particularly in light of the ongoing instability of our current global money system.

## CHAPTER TWENTY EIGHT

# The Balinese Exception

*Life and livelihood ought not be separated but to flow from the same source, which is spirit. Spirit means life, and both life and livelihood are about living in depth, living with a meaning, purpose, joy, and sense of contributing to the greater community.*

~MATTHEW FOX

The study of matrifocal societies offers insights about how an archetypal and monetary framework different from our own might impact our lives and society. Such an investigation requires us to look to the past as most indigenous peoples and matrifocal societies have by now either been destroyed, adapted beyond recognition to the ways of invaders, or otherwise succumbed to the pressures of the modern world.

Fortunately, there is at least one known exception. One unusual indigenous culture has managed to endure and maintain much of its ancient cultural heritage and monetary system. Present-day Bali offers us at least some sense of what honoring the Great Mother archetype and yin-yang values in society is actually like.

## EXCEPTIONAL BALI

Quilted rice paddies, volcanoes soaring up through the clouds, dense rain forests, blue-green seas, religious statues and an almost endless array of colorful festivals are some of the images that greet the millions of tourists who visit the island of Bali each year. Bali is part of the archipelago of Indonesia, a mostly Islamic nation in which the Balinese are proud of preserving their particular Hindu culture.

Pura Ulun Danu Bratan (The temple on Lake Bratan). This major Hindu-Buddhist temple was founded in the 17th century on the shores of Lake Bratan in the mountains near Bedugul. It is dedicated to Dewi Danu, the goddess of the waters. Pilgrimages and ceremonies are held here to ensure that there is a supply of water for farmers all over Bali. Smaller water temples downstream are specific to each irrigation association (subak).

Like many tropical islands, the Balinese economy derives part of its income from tourism. But Bali differs from most other tourist meccas. A clue to this island's exceptional culture is noted by the literally thousands of cultural and religious activities that take place in Bali annually. The vast majority of these activities are performed not for foreigners, however, but for the Balinese themselves and for their deities.

It is still true today as it was when Swedish artist Tyra de Kleen observed in the 1920s that, "at their temple feasts [the Balinese] combine two good purposes, namely to please their gods and amuse themselves."[1] Out of the 5,000 dance groups listed with the provincial authorities in Bali a decade ago, less than 200 were paid performances staged for tourists, while the other 4,800 performance groups performed only for "temple time."[2]

Temple groups play for foreigners in order to earn income for their instruments, costumes and such. They do not, however, earn an income for their art. In comparison, practically all traditional dance groups on other Pacific Islands today, like Hawaii, Fiji, and Tahiti, perform mainly for tourists.

The Balinese exception begs inquiry. What is the secret of their resilience? Why has this indigenous culture survived when so many others have not? How can a people with a GNP per capita that is about one tenth that of the United States find the money, time, and the resources for such extravaganzas and activities? To answer such questions, we must look at some key features of this unusual society.

## COMMUNITY: THE BANJAR

Community is an essential element of Balinese life and culture. Many important activities, such as rice growing and the elaborate preparations for festivals and religious ceremonies, require the efforts and cooperation of not only family members and friends, but on occasion, the participation of entire communities.

The order and cooperation common to the Balinese society is realized by interrelated, local organizational structures.[3] The most significant of those structures, to which most Balinese still belong, include:

o   *Subak*: for water irrigation cooperatives for rice production;

o   *Pemaksan*: for the coordination of religious rituals;

o   *Banjar*: the most important civic organization, which orders the social aspects of the community.

These organizations form an integrated structural fabric that strengthens each community and the culture as a whole.

The Banjar is the principal civic organization in Bali. It operates in a decentralized, hyper-democratic, and cooperative manner at a grassroots level. Written references to the Banjar date back to 914 CE (a century prior to the advent of the Central Middle Ages).[4] This system's longevity is in no small measure related to its adaptability. Anthropologist and local resident Fred B. Eiseman explains that, "even today, among families who have spent several generations in an urban setting away from the rice fields, the Banjar still plays an important role."[5]

The number of Banjars in an area varies from only one in a small village to several in larger towns. Each Banjar has its own rulebook, the *Awig-awig*, all of which are based on the same general democratic principles. The Banjar leader, the *Klian Banjar*, is elected by a majority vote of members and can be dismissed at any time, though this is rarely done. He or she receives no remuneration for this function. Anthropologists Clifford and Hildred Geertz describe the leader as "more an agent than a ruler."[6]

Each family has one representative in the *krama,* the Banjar council, where every member is considered equal and has one vote. No special status is granted to wealthier or higher caste members. At monthly meetings, new activities are proposed and ongoing projects are discussed. The contributions of time and money for each project are then decided upon, customarily by a majority vote. In short, the Banjar functions as a community-based planning and implementation unit, which budgets all its activities.

Balinese leaders credit the Banjar—a system of mutual cooperation—for the resilience of Balinese culture. Two Klian Banjars describe the benefits this way: "Banjar is what holds the community, each other, together."[7] "Banjar is the most fundamental organization that keeps the Balinese character intact."[8]

But what holds the Banjar together?

## A Complementary Currency System

A key to the Banjar is their dual-currency system.[9] The *rupiah* is the conventional national Indonesian currency. The *Nayahan Banjar*, or "work for the common good of the Banjar," is a time-services currency whose unit of account is a block of time equal to about three hours of work. The availability of both currencies provides unusual flexibility in mobilizing local resources.

On average, a Banjar starts between seven and ten different projects every month, big and small. The expected contributions of each family unit, in rupiah and in Nayahan, are estimated for a project. In poorer Banjars, the rupiah monetary constraint is typically more binding, while in richer ones, the Nayahan time commitment tends to be more challenging. In all cases, a mixture of rupiah and Nayahan currencies is used, although the proportional mix varies widely by project and by Banjar.[10]

Community members consider the Nayahan Banjar money more critical than rupiah for keeping cooperation strong. The importance of the time commitment to these projects is reflected by the main penalty meted out. It is not a rupiah fine, but ostracism, the exclusion from the Banjar of someone who refuses three times in a row to respect community decisions. Such bans can be devastating, as Clifford and Hildred Geertz report: "The Balinese still say today that to leave the *krama* [Banjar council] is to lie down and die."[11] A Klian Banjar explains the impact of such isolation: "When they [ostracized Banjar members] have an important family ceremony, like a cremation, marriages, or coming-of-age rituals, then nobody will give time for helping them in the preparations." The rituals are sacrosanct and each requires a communal effort. Depriving someone of time from the community is thus considered the ultimate retribution.

It should be noted that use of the national rupiah, by both the Banjar and the Balinese people, only dates back to Indonesian independence in the 1940s. Up until that time, the offical conventional currency was the Dutch Guilder. While the Nayahan Banjar has been in use since before written records as a time-backed currency for public works, the principal medium of monetary exchange used by the Banjar was an odd-looking coin, noted for a traditional square hole in its middle, called the *Uang Kepeng*, or "Coin Money."[12] This currency was outlawed in the 1950s and finally went out of circulation in the 1970s. Research by international currency expert, Stephen DeMeulenaere, has brought our attention to this currency (see insert).

### The Balinese Uang Kepeng

The Uang Kepeng has a long history. Its use in Bali can be officially traced back to the formation of decentralized local governance in 914 CE, though its introduction to Bali is likely to have occurred centuries earlier.[13] It is, however, from the time that the Uang Kepeng became the official medium of exchange of the Banjar and could be taxed, spent on public works projects, and circulated as a fully-functioning currency, that its significance to Balinese society was formalized, according to DeMeulenaere.[14]

A Uang Kepeng coin (front side on the left). Cast from bronze or copper alloy, these coins from China date back to the 6th century BCE. They appear in Bali as early as the 7th century CE, and were used in trade and commerce. An inscription uncovered in the village of Sukawana suggests that by the 9th century these coins were already being used in Balinese Hindu rituals.

This coin money was minted in China and used as trading tokens, much in the same manner that trading beads were used in North America with indigenous peoples.[15] Chinese seafaring merchants traded these tokens and other goods, such as ceramic objects, to obtain local Balinese spices.

Though the Balinese came into contact with, and were governed by, other cultures periodically during their long history, the only currency they formed a particular attachment to were these odd-looking coins. Dutch anthropologist De Kat Angelino noted back in 1921 that the Balinese preferred Uang Kepeng as a medium of exchange to Dutch, British, and Mexican money, which they instead often melted to make into silver jewelry.[16]

The use of Uang Kepeng subsided only after the introduction of the Indonesian rupiah in the 1940s, although it continues as a ceremonial currency and for fines in some Banjars to this day.

The Uang Kepeng are closely connected to the Balinese economics and mathematics. The Balinese calculation system, similar to that of the abacus, was developed using these coins. Miguel Covarrubias noted in the 1930s that, "the Balinese do not count in the present Dutch monetary system of guilders and cents...the ringgit, big silver coins (worth two and a half guilders) are normally divided [instead] into 1,200 Kepeng."[17]

The Uang Kepeng were typically strung together and carried in bundles of twenty-five coins each. The Balinese word for 25 is *selae*, derived from *se* (one). The word *ikat* means to tie something together in a bundle. The word for fifty is *sekat*, i.e. two bundles of *selae* that have been tied together. The word for seventy-five, *telung*, means three bundles of *selae* that have been tied together, and so on. When someone is broke, they say "Sing Ada Pis," referring to the other name for the Uang Kepeng, *Pis Bolong* or "Pierced Piece."

## The Uang Kepeng and Current Change

It was only when new national banking and currency laws were put into effect after Indonesia gained its independence, that the Balinese were forced to accept the Indonesian rupiah in replacement of the Guilder and the Uang Kepeng. According to many unofficial accounts however, the Uang Kepeng continued to be used by the local Banjars as a medium of exchange up until the early 1970s.

It should be understood that the Uang Kepeng was the more popular form of currency. This complementary currency and the rupiah were functionally different types of money. The replacement of the local currency by the official legal tender was not a trivial matter; it changed the dynamics of the Balinese monetary system. Though both currencies were interest-bearing, the interest was applied in very different ways. With rupiah, like with all modern national currencies, interest is automatically assigned and exacted. But in the case of the Uang Kepeng, the interest feature was less formal, more flexible, and did not tend to accumulate over time. The interest might be paid back in Uang Kepeng or in goods or services, such as assisting in a harvest or a religious ceremony. Additionally, there was no formal control over the supply of this money; Uang Kepeng were readily available.

According to DeMeulenaere,

> We might think that it would not be possible to manage a currency without being able to control its supply, and that only a scarce currency is a strong currency, and by extension, that a currency lacking scarcity would be weak. The Balinese, however, and other traditional societies that used an abundant currency as a medium

of exchange, developed unique means of keeping the circulating supply low enough in order to maintain its value: they spent it on ceremonies or artistic displays of their savings. In Bali, those with too much Uang Kepeng had statues of a goddess made out of the coins, which were displayed prominently in their homes. The coins were also used in large quantities during the ritual blessing of a new house, or for cremations and other religious and cultural ceremonies. In these ways, demand for the currency and its value was maintained over the centuries.

As a readily available local means of exchange, Uang Kepeng encouraged the circulation of locally-produced goods and services, supporting the agricultural economy, the local marketplace, and the women who managed it all. Until the 1950s, Uang Kepeng protected the Balinese agricultural economy and society from penetration and destruction by foreign money, trade and tourism, market and currency fluctuations, or other adverse situations. Up until that time, the introduction of foreign money did not affect the local economy or the behavior of the people, who could choose to participate in both economies and not be forced to choose between the traditional economy of Uang Kepeng and the new economy of Indonesian rupiah.

The decline of Uang Kepeng as a medium of exchange corresponds with a shift in economic behavior towards earning the Indonesian rupiah. Although many significant elements of traditional life remain vibrant in Bali, the monetary protection blanket they once had with Uang Kepeng has been stripped away, leaving the Balinese people and society increasingly vulnerable to situations beyond their control and subject to the same financial and consumption pressures faced by all of us living in the modern world.[18]

Complementary currencies, especially the Uang Kepeng[19] and Nayahan Banjar, have been a mainstay of the Banjar system for more than a millennium. This dual-currency system keeps community spirit and collective cultural expressions strong by enabling greater options in project choices and a diverse array of activities. Banjars in poorer communities automatically favor projects that require time, such as the great temple dance, the *kecak*, which traditionally involves much manpower. In contrast, more affluent districts that are less concerned about financial costs are, therefore, more inclined to approve projects that can be paid for in rupiah. For example, one single project in a wealthier Banjar had a budget of 1.2 billion Rupiah (equivalent to about $132,000) and proportionally much lower expenditures of time.[20]

The Banjar system extends beyond religious and cultural events to civic activities, such as support for building primary schools or local roads, especially when the central government is unable to provide funding. In short, local resources can be mobilized to support a fuller spectrum of undertakings, whatever the community chooses to focus on.

## The Great Mother Archetype

The repression of the Great Mother archetype has, as noted, cast its shadow upon much of our world. Precious little is left of the once vibrant cultures in which everything was considered sacred, a belief common to many so-called "primitive" societies. Some 5,000 years of an imbalanced patriarchal supremacy has helped shape the modernist view that perpetuates a split between spirit and nature, mind and matter, soul and body.

Bali, however, has managed to preserve key elements of its heritage that predate the Central Middle Ages and endure in part to this day, despite seventeen centuries of invasions, foreign religious influences, European colonization, integration into the predominantly Muslim nation-state of Indonesia, and terrorism. This resilience forms part of a cultural coherence that we refer to as the "Balinese exception."

Daily life in Bali integrates the mundane and the spiritual. This is evidence of the yin coherence, an honoring of the more feminine aspects, such as the community cooperation found in a vast tapestry of offerings, daily rituals, and festivals.

One of the many offerings to deities and spirits made fresh
each day and found all over the island of Bali.

## Offerings

A clue to understanding this culture is provided by the etymology of the word *bali*, meaning "offering" or "gift." It is a fitting name for a culture in which, with but one exception during the year, no day passes without at least some form of offerings.

Authors Francine Brinkreve and David Stuart-Fox write:

> They [the offerings] are found everywhere. Each day the lady of the house places little palm leaf containers with beautiful flowers on a family shrine. A driver places a similar offering on the dashboard of his car or truck. A family member graciously carries towers of fruits and cookies to a temple on its festival day. Whole villages sometimes create enormous offerings several meters

high. And within offerings, such wondrous details as
little rice dough figurines and delicate palm leaf
creations are almost hidden from view. The immense
variety of form and color of the Balinese offering is truly
amazing.[21]

## Festivals

Each of the many thousands of temples in Bali has its own *odalan*
festival, a special feast that celebrates the gods coming to the annual
commemoration of the founding of their temple. "The people renew their
ties with the gods and also reinforce their bonds with each other during
the elaborate preparations and ceremonies."[22] Such festivals are filled
with dances, some masculine and warrior-like, others feminine and
graceful.

There are procession rituals in which each family presents its
offerings to its deities and ancestors. These rituals are accompanied by
prayers with the sprinkling of holy water and blessed rice on the
foreheads of participants, and carnivals, night-long drama dances, and
trance dances in which participants receive visitations from spirits. The
more important festivals can go on for days and even weeks.

## Death

Miguel Covarrubias, who first visited Bali in 1937, described the
particular Balinese ritual response to death:

Strange as it seems, it is in their cremation ceremonies
that the Balinese have their greatest fun. A cremation is
an occasion for gaiety and not for mourning, since it
represents the accomplishment of their most sacred duty:
the ceremonial burning of the corpses of the dead to
liberate their souls, so that they can thus attain the higher
worlds and be free from reincarnation.[23]

Death is a cause for celebration: "The grand send-off of the soul into
heaven, in the form of a rich and complete cremation, is the life-ambition
of every Balinese."[24]

The material body is seen as the container of the soul. Death is but a
passing from one form to another, the beginning of another chapter, a

normal part of life's cycle, like a tree shedding its leaves. Life on this Earth is considered by the Balinese as just an incident in the long process of the soul's evolution. In short, death is most certainly not a taboo in Balinese culture.

Cremations, religious ceremonies, and artistic activities permeate life and hold great meaning to the Balinese, who participate with pride, intention, and craftsmanship. Many hours or even weeks of preparations are required, along with the combined efforts of the entire community.

In every aspect of daily living there is a deep and abiding honoring of what is best described as the yin expression of life, in which the spiritual and the mundane are seamlessly intertwined.

## Balance and Trust

Together with its particular archetypal framework and dual-currency system, another characteristic that is exceptional about Bali, and distinquishes this society from much of the rest of the world today, can be described in a single word—*trust*.

Returning to Dr. Bernice Hill's *Sacred Wounds of Money*, we recall the difficulties often associated with being financially well-off in our society: the burdens of expectation; a deep sense of isolation accompanied by suspicions regarding relationships and friendships; a tendency toward dysfunctional family dynamics; and having one's own sense of self brought into question. We noticed that each of these wounds is characterized by a lack of trust at different levels of interaction. Though their particular objects of concern may differ, lower and middle classes also suffer considerably from a lack of trust, with regard to both fellow citizens and the "abundance of the universe," in a society that uses only conventional national currencies.

When poverty strikes and people are forced to live paycheck-to-paycheck without much in the way of job security or savings, increasing attention is paid to concerns such as individual survival and caring for one's own. In such a paradigm, one is continually confronted with scarcity, competitiveness, and the yang-shadow coherence.

A very different set of dynamics emerges in a society in which a means of exchange is available to all, whether it is in the form of money, time, or whatever each member of that society can contribute. A deeper sense of security, belonging, and identity are reinforced, and the walls of separation are no longer necessary. With a complementary currency system, the basic needs of even those at the lowest end of the financial spectrum can more easily be met. There is, therefore, far less reason for the haves and have-nots to mistrust or to envy.

Trust, pride, contentment, quality of life, and the values of a people are not easily measured from a strictly conventional perspective. These phenomena, which permeate qualitatively different dimensions, do not lend themselves well to quantifiable statistics, linear logic, or sound bites. As a result, the possible implications inherent in Balinese archetypal integration are often overlooked. As we have seen, there is a clear connection between the honoring of the Divine feminine, dual-currency systems, and a more egalitarian society.

The Balinese reaction to recent tragedies offers some comparative sense of how a different perspective and archetypal integration impact upon a culture.

## BALI'S "9/11"

Bali became world news after the terrorist bomb attack in the town of Kuta on the night of October 12, 2002, in which more than 180 people were killed. Bali's "9/11" occurred exactly one year, one month, and one day after the attack on the World Trade Center in New York. Though the terrorist attack itself was widely covered in the global media, the Balinese reaction to this horror was not given much notice.

Two reports follow. The first is by the police in the days immediately after the bombing:

> Lt. Col. I Made Murda of the Bali police told us that, although hundreds of shops had their windows blown out by the blast, not one single looting has been reported. Down in Legian there are all these shops without windows and doors, all their wares there for the taking, but nobody has.
>
> There were also fears that there could be an instant reaction against the Muslim population of Bali, but no such thing has happened. What has happened is that there have been peace vigils and prayer meetings all over the island, and Christians, Muslims, locals and foreigners working hand in hand in the relief effort.[25]

The second report is from the Parum Samigita, the Think Tank for the Banjars located at the ground zero area where the blast occurred (Kuta, Legian and Seminyak). Their spokesperson, Asana Viebeke, delivered the following speech in English on Friday, October 25, 2002:

### Now We Move Forward!

We Balinese have an essential concept of balance. It's the *Tri Hita Karan*, the concept of triple harmonious balance. The balance between god and humanity; humanity with itself; and humanity with the environment. This places us all in a universe of common understanding.

Who did this? This is not such an important question for us to discuss. Why this happened—maybe that is more worthy of thought. What can we do to create beauty from this tragedy and come to an understanding where nobody feels the need to make such a statement again? That is important. That is the basis from which we can embrace everyone as a brother, everyone as a sister.

It is a period of uncertainty, a period of change. It is also an opportunity for us to move together into a better future—a future where we embrace all of humanity, in the knowledge that we all look and smell the same when we are burnt.

The past is not significant. It is the future that is important. This is the time to bring our values, our empathy, to society and the world at large. To care. To love...

Why seek retribution from people who are acting as they see fit? These people are misguided from our point of view. Obviously, from theirs, they feel justified and angry enough to make such a brutal statement.

We would like to send a message to the world: embrace this misunderstanding between our brothers and let's seek a peaceful answer to the problems that bring us to such tragedy. We embrace all the beliefs, hopes and dreams of all the people in the world with love.

Do not bring malice to our world. What has happened has happened. Stop talking about the theories of who did this, and why. It does not serve the spirit of our people. Words of hate will not rebuild our shops and houses. They will not heal damaged skin. They will not bring back our dead. Help us to create beauty out of this tragedy.

Everybody in the world is of one principal brotherhood. *Tat Tvam Asi*—'You are me, and I am you.' These are the concepts by which we, as Balinese, live our lives.

If we hate our brothers and sisters we are lost in Kali Yuga (the Dark Age). If we can love all of our brothers and sisters, we have already begun to move into Kertha Yuga. We have already won 'The War Against Terrorism.'

Thank you for all your compassion and love.

Asana L. Viebeke

Kuta Desa Adat[26]

In October 2005, another wave of terrorist attacks took place in Bali. The response was the same as with the first bombing. Balinese culture, its dynamic balance of yin and yang, its archetypal integration, its commitment to peaceful resolutions, and recognition of the sacred in everything in their world, leaves this culture better prepared than most to deal with such events.[27]

There are, however, signs of change taking place. The nature of this shift and the likely reasons behind it merit our attention.

## RECENT CHANGES

On almost any given morning or late afternoon, the main roads of Bali today fill with traffic. Increasing numbers of Balinese are working in manufacturing plants, import-export firms, hotels, new fast-food chains, malls, and shops that cater to tourists. Street vendors, taxi cab drivers, and massage therapists solicit passersby taking in the sights of Ubud, Kuta, and Sanur.

Balinese culture certainly endures. Religious icons and offerings are quite evident still, as are traditional processions and festivals of one kind or another. But many of the familiar icons of globalization are now commonplace as well and clash more than blend with time-honored customs. The assertion made two decades ago that, "tourism is for Bali, not Bali for tourism," begs review. A more complex reality is emerging.

Informal interviews with several dozen Balinese revealed that some ill-defined shift is occurring. Television, tourism, and globalization are often cited as likely agents of added economic pressures and cultural change. But, most Balinese are unaware of the impact that the supression of the dual-currency system has had on their culture. Fortunately, a few Balinese nevertheless do very much appreciate the impact and importance of a robust dual-currency system. This includes Prince Tjokorda Raka Kerthyasa, head of the Bali Heritage Foundation, who is today working to reinstate the Uang Kepeng.[28]

A particular set of cultural values and traits arose simultaneously in Dynastic Egypt, the Central Middle Ages, and Bali, and included integration of Great Mother archetype and a dual-currency system. Moreover, a similar set of challenges that included changes to the monetary paradigm and repression of yin values coincided with the fall of Dynastic Egypt and the Central Middle Ages and is currently bringing pressures on the Balinese.

In concluding, we wish it understood that our review of past ages and Bali is not intended as a recommendation of any one particular way of life, constellation of values, beliefs, or means of worship. Furthermore, the *specific* measures and directions taken by each of these mostly homogeneous, agrarian-based societies are not necessarily applicable to today's multicultural, complex, global economy.

The relevance of these civilizations to ours today is the greater range of options and possibilities that become available by means of integration of a fuller spectrum of archetypal values and by availing ourselves of the greater potential of money. Given the many distinct advantages we enjoy today in comparison to virtually any other known period of history, including that of a greater understanding than ever before of money, it is reasonable to expect that we can achieve the best of what these former ages were able to achieve, and far more still.

## CLOSING THOUGHTS

The intricate and colorful fabric of Balinese culture bears homage to the often-neglected yin-aspects of society. These are the invariably under-financed yet vitally critical areas of the arts, community-building, and family life. As a direct consequence of a deficit of economic options, these major contributors to a society's wellbeing are often found to be struggling and moribund among vast swaths of populations around the world.

Bali has had a long history of a dual-currency monetary system, which has afforded this rich Hindu culture a capacity to withstand the onslaught of foreign invasion right up to the 1970s, when one of their yin currencies, the Uang Kepeng, was made illegal. Over the past four decades a slow erosion of core Balinese culture and values has taken place. Phenomena such as mass media, massive tourism, and globalization are often cited as the cause of this decline. The attrition of the balanced yin- yang monetary structure, however, contributes to this process.

This monetary equilibrium can be readdressed and, in the case of Bali, is currently under reconstruction, armed with a clear understanding of the functional dynamics of money and its deep psychological and archetypical underpinnings.

## CHAPTER TWENTY NINE

# Invitation To A New World

*Insanity: doing the same thing over and over again*

*and expecting different results.*

~ALBERT EINSTEIN

I n 1901, Georg Simmel observed in his book *Philosophy of Money* that, "the debate about the future of money is not about inflation or deflation, fixed or flexible exchange rates, gold or paper standards; it is about the kind of society in which money is to operate."[1] In these final pages, we offer some parting thoughts on monetary innovations and the kind of society we believe to be possible.

We will close with an invitation to you, the reader, to join us online, where our exploration of money and societal transformation continues.

## WHAT IS TRULY POSSIBLE

Our age is blessed with an epic opportunity. There now exists the real possibility of not only addressing many of our most vital concerns, but ushering in an unparalleled age that can significantly enhance conditions for *all* of humanity and the living systems of our precious planet. To this end, we reaffirm some of the claims made in this book.

We *can* provide meaningful work for all. We *can* deal far more effectively and proactively with the costly booms and busts of the business cycle. We *can* ensure the conditions necessary for free enterprise and economic development to flourish, while simultaneously protecting the collective long-term interests of society and the environment. We *can* bring about a world in which social concerns such as the upbringing and education of our children and quality care for our elders are firmly addressed, and where the diversity and sanctity of all life and the life-affirming aspects of what it is to be fully human are supported and secured. We *can* achieve all this, and more.

These prospects are not only possible but achievable within the span of a *single generation*. Furthermore, this transformation can be realized without conflict or hardship, and without the need to raise taxes, redistribute wealth, or seek assistance from the federal government. The technologies, skills, and means required for such a shift are known and are already being utilized in successful pilot programs around the world, and are ready for widespread deployment.

We reaffirm that these and other claims made throughout this work are not conjecture, but are instead supported by an ever-growing body of scholarship and by real-world experience, past and present. Curitiba, Time Dollars, LETS, social currencies such as the Fureai Kippu and Saber, commercial currencies such as the WIR, C3, and the Terra TRC; hard-earned lessons from the Great Depression; millennia of history, the notable accomplishments of the Central Middle Ages, and so much more...all offer testimony to what is possible, what is *truly* achievable through a greater understanding and utilization of money.

Humanity has the knowledge and the means to bring about the greatest transformation in all of known history. What we do *not* have is the luxury of unlimited time.

## A TIME TO ACT

Many of the arguments offered in this work were, as previously noted, first presented more than a decade ago in *The Future of Money*. Looking back, the year 1999 was perhaps an inconvenient time to make a case for the urgent review and amendment of our centuries-old monopoly of national currencies. It will be recalled that, despite concerns over Y2K, a general mood of optimism characterized the dawn of a new millenium. The U.S. economy then boasted 4.5 percent unemployment and an inflation rate of 2.1 percent; gasoline pump prices averaged $1.17 per gallon, Internet companies enjoyed unprecedented returns, as the Dow-Jones soared to 11,750. Some economists of note, so buoyed by conditions and future prospects, entertained the possibility that even the age-old business cycle had finally been tamed.

Optimism at the turn of the millenium spilled over to other areas, including confidence in our ability to deal with looming issues such as unfunded liabilities and the environment. The baby-boomer generation was, after all, then still more than a decade away from retirement. And though there was already a clear consensus among the majority of the world's leading scientists regarding greenhouse gases and climate change, debate continued, and the twenty years estimated as necessary to birth a post-carbon economy seemed a long time off given the context of our short-term culture.

In essence, there were many apparent indicators in 1999 to counter the call for monetary reform.

But the 999th year of the second millennium and the first decade of this third millennium came and went. And not one of the megatrends cited in this book or its predecessor were addressed. Each of our vital issues and the state of the world has instead only gotten worse.

Baby boomers, who will live longer than previous generations, are now beginning to retire. Yet, the funds required to match their longevity and ensure their golden years are lacking. These and other social issues have been made more problematic still by the global recession and overburdened public coffers.

Though the recession is at least *officially* considered at end, its root causes have not been addressed. The supposed recovery of 2010 has come and gone, and 2011 saw continued economic instability, austerity measures, and ongoing hardships for the SMEs that comprise the bulk of all private jobs. Official unemployment figures in the United States and elsewhere remain stubbornly fixed at nearly double the levels of a decade ago, with unofficial figures much higher still. The concentration of wealth continues to increase as more and more middle-class citizens face uncertain economic futures. The private sector remains locked in a singular pursuit of short-term objectives, while traditional pre-recession neoliberal economic policies and unprecedented neo-Keynesian stimulus packages have each demonstrated their inadequacies. And privatization, the supposed "solution" to allow governments to meet their more-immediate fiscal concerns, will deprive our economies of the resilience needed to ensure future stability and development. More ominous still, the first decade of the new millennium is now officially established as the warmest on record. With precious little of note having been achieved in this regard to date, and with ten of the twenty years estimated to bring about a post-carbon economy now behind us, we must seriously consider the options left us, and fast.

## BACK TO MONEY

We reiterate that our ineffectiveness in the face of contemporary global challenges is *not* an expression of the intractability of climate change, job losses, or other pressing concerns. The persistence of such issues is instead related to our continued inability to identify and address the systemic root causes of these concerns and, more specifically, to grasp their link to our industrial-age monetary paradigm.

No matter how sincere the desire or how determined our efforts, we simply cannot and must not expect our difficulties to disappear until and unless we understand the functional dynamics of the current monetary system and enact monetary amendments. To continue to think and act otherwise while expecting revitalization to somehow magically take hold, is truly *insane*.

In contemplating what kind of world is possible, we are reminded of the etymological roots of the words "money" and "currency." The term *money,* as noted, derives from Juno Moneta and is linked to a constellation of perennial values vital to humanity and society. The term *currency* is linked to the "condition of flowing." (from Latin, currens, prp. of currere "to run)." As civilizations such as medieval Western Europe and Dynastic Egypt reveal, some currencies are needed to function like a healthy circulatory system; to flow and nurture each and every member of society to the betterment of all. The restricted use of any one type of money, no matter how well designed, impedes the full expression of who we are and what is *truly* possible.

We are in the midst of Great Change. It can either take the form of a breakdown on an unprecedented scale, or a significant breakthrough for civilization. A positive shift will, however, not just happen on its own accord. The kind of transformation that enhances life and allows us to overcome many present-day concerns will require review and amendment of those very same systems that, notwithstanding their contributions to the many remarkable accomplishments of our time, also fueled the myriad crises that are now converging upon us. This is particularly true of the key information replicator of the Industrial Age—our centuries-old monopoly of national currencies.

The time for the democratization of money is now. With so much to gain and so little to lose, why delay any longer?

## AN INVITIATION

Our journey in pursuit of monetary innovations and societal transformation continues online at our companion websites:

http://www. newmoneyforanewworld.com

and

http://www.lietaer.com

CHAPTER THIRTY

# The Dynamics of
# Transformation and Money

This chapter, regarding the changes now taking place to our economies and society at large, and the vital role of monetary enhnacements, will be posted online on our companion websites:

http://www.newmoneyforanewworld.com

and

http://www.lietaer.com

# ENDNOTES

## ENDNOTES—PART I

### CHAPTER ONE

1. Information regarding Curitiba results from a field trip to the area in the late 1990s by Bernard Lietaer and by a follow-up interview in June 2007.
2. The Hammerville metaphor was developed by the authors during the four years that preceded the publication of this book, and was presented on numerous occasions during that period of time.

### CHAPTER TWO

1. John Maynard Keynes, *A Treatise on Money* (London, 1930), 13.
2. Richard Wagner, interview by the authors (22 June 2004).
3. Jacques Rueff, *The Age of Inflation,* translation by A. H. Meeus and F.G. Clarke (Chicago: Henry Regnery Co., 1964).
4. See: Peter Sloterdijk, *Aus Herbstschrift I* (Steierischer Herbst, 1990).

### CHAPTER THREE

1. Ken Dychtwald, from a speech addressing the Academy of Criminal Justice Sciences Meeting (San Francisco, 3 April 1999).
2. Ibid.
3. Ibid.
4. Jonathan Sacks, *The Dignity of Difference: How to Avoid the Clash of Civilizations* (London, New York: Continuum International Publishing Group, 2003), 106. The Organization for Economic Cooperation and Development (OECD), based in Paris, is an association of the most developed countries in the world.
5. Peter G. Peterson, "Gray Dawn: The Global Aging Crisis," *Foreign Affairs* (January-February 1999).
6. Ibid.
7. See: http://www.nchc.org/facts/cost.shtml.
8. See: http://www.nchc.org/facts/cost.shtml.
   See also: Fidelity Investments, Press Release (6 March 2006).
9. Paul Eccleston, "Ecological credit crunch potentially more damaging than financial crisis, says WWF" *The Daily Telegraph* (London, 29 October 2008), quoting WWF's International Director, James Leape, and the *WWF Living Planet Report.*
10. Ibid.

11. Sigmar Garbriel, "Biodiversity 'fundamental' to Economics," *German Federal Environment Minister* (9 March 2007). http://www.bbc.co.uk.

12. "Deforestation continues at an alarming rate," *Press Release, Food and Agriculture Organization of the United Nations* (FAO), (Rome, 14 November 2005).

13. As announced at the UN Climate Change Conference in Bali, Indonesia, by the United Nations Framework Convention on Climate Change (December 2007). http://unfccc.int/meetings/cop_13/items/4094.php.

14. NASA GISS Surface Temperature (GISTEMP) Analysis, which "provides a measure of the changing global surface temperature with monthly resolution for the period since 1880," as reported by the Carbon Dioxide Information Analysis Center (CDIAC). http://www.cdiac.esd.ornl.gov.

15. Remarks by Sigmar Gabriel, German Federal Minister for the Environment, Nature Conservation and Nuclear Safety, based on "The Economics of Ecosystems and Biodiversity" report by The European Union and German environment ministry-led research, and presented at the UN Convention of Biological Diversity (Bonn, 19 May 2008).

16. "Economic Sector and Climate Change" report by Munich Re (21 May 2008). http://www.munichre.com.

17. Munich Re, press release (29 December 2005). http://www.munichre.com.

18. Jim Coleman, "Cap and Trade - The Booster Shot Our Economy Needs," *Terra Rossa* (20 February 2008). http://www.terrarossa.com.

19. "Summary for Policymakers," *Climate Change 2007: The Physical Science Basis.* Contribution of Working Group I to the Fourth Assessment Report of the Intergovernmental Panel on Climate Change, Intergovernmental Panel on Climate Change (2007).
http://www.ipcc.ch/pdf/assessmentreport/ar4/wg1/ar4-wg1-spm.pdf.

20. The 2001 joint statement was signed by the scientific academies of Australia, Belgium, Brazil, Canada, the Caribbean, China, France, Germany, India, Indonesia, Ireland, Italy, Malaysia, New Zealand, Sweden, and the United Kingdom. The 2005 statement added Japan, Russia, and the United States. The 2007 statement added Mexico and South Africa. Professional societies include: American Meteorological Society, American Geophysical Union, American Institute of Physics, American Astronomical Society, American Association for the Advancement of Science, Stratigraphy Commission of the Geological Society of London, Geological Society of America, American Chemical Society, and Engineers Australia. "The Science Of Climate Change" (Royal Society, May 2001); "Joint science academies' statement: Global response to climate change" (Royal Society, June 2005) http://royalsociety.org/displaypagedoc.asp?id=13619.
"Joint science academies' statement on growth and responsibility: sustainability, energy efficiency and climate protection."
http://royalsociety.org/displaypagedoc.asp?id=20742.

Potsdam Institute for Climate Impact Research, (May 2007)
http://www.pik-potsdam.de/news/press-releases.

21. John Thornhill, "Income Inequality seen as the Great Divide," *The Financial Times* (London, 19 May 2008).

22. Sacks, *The Dignity of Difference*, 107.

23. Edward N. Wolff, "Recent Trends in Wealth Ownership," a paper for the conference: Benefits and Mechanisms for Spreading Asset Ownership in the United States (New York University, 10-12 December 1998).

24. "Executive Pay Special Report," *Business Week* (9 April 2001).

25. Center on Budget and Policy Priorities and the Economic Policy Institute (April 2008).

26. David Boyle, "The New Alchemists," *Resurgence Magazine* (January 1999).

27. Sacks, *The Dignity of Difference,* 107.

28. Stijn Claessens, Larry H.P. Lang, and Simeon Djankov, "Who Controls East Asian Corporations," *Policy Research Working Papers,* no. 2054 (Washington, D.C.: The World Bank 1999).

29. Ibid.

30. "State of the World Population 2002: Useful Facts," *Planetwire.* http://www.planetwire.org.

31. Anup Shah, "Causes of Hunger are Related to Poverty" (19 November 2005). http://www.globalissues.org.

32. Department of Labor Commissioner's Statement on the Employment Situation News Release: unemployment rose by 1.8 million in the last four months of 2008.

33. Tomoko A. Hosaka, "Japan's exports tumble on global spending freeze," *The Associated Press*, as reported by MSNBC (25 March 2009).

34. Sharon LaFraniere, "20 million migrant workers in China can't find jobs," *The International Herald Tribune* (2 February 2009).

35. "World economy may lose 51 million jobs," International Labour Organization (ILO), as reported by United Nations Radio (28 January 2009).

36. Former UN Secretary General Kofi Annan addressing UN Economic and Social Council (ECOSOC) annual session (3 July 2006).

37. Paul Craig Roberts, "Forget Iran, Americans Should be Hysterical About This: Nuking the Economy," *Counterpunch* (11-12 February 2006). Paul Craig Roberts presents his argument as follows: "The U.S. economy came up more than 7 million jobs short of keeping up with population growth. U.S. manufacturing lost 2.9 million jobs, almost 17 percent of the manufacturing work force. The knowledge jobs that were supposed to take the place of lost manufacturing jobs in the globalized "new economy" never appeared. The information sector lost 17 percent of its jobs, with the telecommunications work force declining by 25 percent. Today there are 209,000 fewer managerial and supervisory jobs than 5 years ago." http://www.counterpunch.org.

38. Floyd Norris, "Off The Charts," *New York Times* (8 August 2009). For the decade, there was a net gain of 121,000 private sector jobs, according to the survey of employers conducted each month by the Bureau of Labor Statistics. In an economy with 109 million such jobs, that indicated an annual growth rate for the 10 years of 0.01 percent.

39. The U.S. Labor Department reported in February 2008 that average hourly earnings increased 3.7 percent in 2007. As prices increased even more during that time, the real earnings in terms of purchasing power actually *decreased* 0.8 percent. Average earnings were $596, or $30,992 per year. (Note: This is the total earnings of all private sector, non-farm, non-supervisory employees, full and part-time, divided by total number of hours worked.) Source: Bureau of Labor Statistics, *Real Earnings Report.*

40. Employees Put In More Hours, CNN.com (31 August 2001) http://www.cnn.com.

41. Barbara Killinger, *Workaholics: The Respectable Addict* (Toronto: Key Porter Books, 1991), 7.

42. Jacob Hacker, *The Great Risk Shift* (Oxford: Oxford University Press, 2006).

43. James Surowiecki, "The Financial Page: Lifers," *The New Yorker* (16 January 2006), 29: "The percentage of companies that offer health benefits has dropped thirteen percent over the past five years, and even employees that are covered now generally pay more of their own costs. With pensions the shift has been fundamental: defined-benefit plans, in which companies guarantee a set payout to employees, have been gradually replaced with defined-contributions plans like 401(k)s. With a defined-benefit plan, the company assumes the risk of investing assets, absorbing the impact of market downturns, but with a 401(k) it is entirely up to the employee to prosper or plummet...Meanwhile, the risk of exposure of anybody unfortunate enough to lose a job has soared. People who are unemployed stay unemployed, on average, about fifty percent longer than they did so in the seventies, and only about half as many receive unemployment insurance as did in 1947. The explosion of health-care costs means that the consequences of forfeiting company health insurance are graver than ever...So, economists estimate that income volatility is about twice what it was in the early seventies."

44. United Nations Population Division, "World Population Prospects: The 2004 Revision Population Database." http://esa.un.org.

45. William Greider, *One World, Ready or Not: The Manic Logic of Global Capitalism* (New York: Simon and Schuster, 1997).

46. Wassily Leontieff as quoted in Jeremy Rifkin, "After Work," *Utne Reader* (May-June 1995), 54.

47. These numbers of monetary and banking crises are extracted from Gerard Caprio, Jr. and Daniela Klingelbiel, "Bank Insolvencies: Cross Country Experience," *Policy Research Working Papers,* no.1620 (Washington D.C.: World Bank, Policy and Research Department, 1996). Since then, an additional series of crises should be added, including the Asian, Russian and

Argentinian crises. See also: Jeffrey Frankel and Andrew Rose, "Currency Crashes in Emerging Markets: an Empirical Treatment," *Journal of International Economics 4* (1996), 351-66; Graciela Kaminsk and Carmen Reinhart, "The Twin Crisis: the Causes of Banking and Balance of Payment Problems," *American Economic Review* 89, no. 3 (1999), 473-500; Carl-Johan Lindgren, Gillian Garcia, and Matthew Saal, *Bank Soundness and Macro-economic Policy* (Washington D.C.: IMF, 1996).

48. Joseph Stiglitz, "How to Reform the Global Financial System," *Harvard Relations Council International Review* 25, no. 1 (Spring 2003), 54-9.

49. *Triennial Central Bank Survey of Foreign Exchange and Derivatives Market Activity in 2010 – Final results* (December 2010). http://www.bis.org/publ/rpfxf07t.htm.

50. This number originates from the survey performed every three years by the Bank of International Settlements (BIS). In addition to these "traditional" foreign exchange transactions, the BIS counted in April 2004 "a *daily volume of $2.4 trillion* in monetary derivatives in foreign exchange and interest rate related products, including outright forwards and foreign exchange swaps... Gross market values more than doubled, from $3.0 trillion to $6.4 trillion, in the three years to end-June 2004." Bank of International Settlements (BIS), *Triennial Central Bank Survey of Foreign Exchange and Derivatives Market Activity 2004—Final Results* (Basel, Switzerland, 17 March 2005), 1.

51. These statistics are derived from the total daily foreign exchange transactions as reported every three years by the BIS, and compared to Global Annual Trade divided by the number of days.

52. "Russia blames U.S. for Global Financial Crisis," *Reuters* (7 June 2008). http://www.reuters.com/article/ousiv/idUSL0749277620080607?sp=true.

53. Catherine Clifford, "Household net worth sinks $11.2 trillion," *CNNMoney* (12 March 2009).

54. Tami Luhby, "Americans $1.7 trillion poorer," *CNNMoney* (5 June 2008).

## CHAPTER FOUR

1. Geoffrey K. Ingham, Concepts Of Money: Interdisciplinary Perspectives From Economics, Sociology, xi.

2. The Forum on Magic, held in Aaron Burr Hall, Princeton University (May 30, 2008). http://www.princeton.edu/prok/issues/3-2/forum.xml.

3. William Greider, *The Secrets of the Temple* (New York: Touchstone Books, 1987), 240.

4. Binyamin Appelbaum, "Fed to Take a Step Out From Behind the Veil,"*New York Times* (25 March 2011).

5. Edmund L. Andrews, "Greenspan Concedes Error on Regulation," *New York Times* (23 October 2008).

6. Glyn Davies, *A History of Money from Ancient Times to the Present Day* (Cardiff: University of Wales Press, 1994), 27.

7.  This definition has also been explored by Rabbi Nilton Bonder in his book, *The Kabbalah of Money: Jewish Insights on Giving, Owning, and Receiving* (Boston: Shambhala Books, 1996).

8.  *Money Facts* by the Subcommittee of Domestic Finance, Committee on Banking and Currency, House of Representatives 88th Congress, 2nd Session (21 September 1964): "Money is anything that people will accept in exchange for goods or services, in the belief that they may, in turn, exchange it, now or later, for other goods or services."

9.  Charles F. Durban, "The Bank of Venice," *Quarterly Journal of Economics* 6, no. 3 (April 1892).

10. *Money Facts* by the Subcommittee of Domestic Finance, Committee on Banking and Currency, House of Representatives 88th Congress, 2nd Session (21 September 1964): "Legal tender is any form of money that the U.S. Government declares good for payment of taxes and both public and private debts...This note is legal tender for all debts public and private" is written on every U.S. dollar bill. What this means in practice is the following: if you owe someone money and he/she refuses your offer to pay with dollar bills, you can walk away and simply declare the debt void. If needed, the courts will back you in such a declaration.

11. To be more accurate, while the Charter of the Bank of England dates from 1688, the monopoly of emission of paper money was assigned by 1694, when an additional 1.2 million pounds were urgently needed to fight a war against the French. In the case of Sweden, the power of emission had to be similarly transferred to the Bank of the Estates of the Realm when the crown needed urgent money to fund a war against Denmark. While the introduction of paper money made the transfer of the power of emission of money from sovereigns to banks possible, the proximate cause of that process was war.

12. John Kenneth Galbraith, *Money: Whence it Came, Where it Went* (London: Andre Deutsch, 1975).

13. Regulations specify that only 10 percent of a deposit need to be kept as a reserve in case the customer withdraws the funds. Therefore, up to 90 percent is available to make new loans. Changing that percentage is one of the techniques whereby the Federal Reserve controls the quantities of credit money the banks will be able to create. The exact percentages also vary with the kind of deposit made: the longer the term of the deposit, the lower the percentage of "reserves" required. The 90 percent rule of this example, enabling a "multiplier" of about nine to one, is an illustrative average.

## CHAPTER FIVE

1.  Charles Handy, *The Empty Raincoat* (London: Arrow Business Books, 1995), 108.

2.  A detailed description of this process is provided in Bernard Lietaer and Stefan Brunnhuber, *Money and Sustainability – The Missing Link* (2008).

3.  John Jackson and Campbell R. McConnell, *Economics* (Sydney: McGraw Hill, 1988).
4.  Marc van de Mieroop, "The Invention of Interest" in William N. Goetzman and K. Geert Rouwenhorst, *The Origins of Value: The Financial Innovations that Created Modern Capital Markets* (Oxford: Oxford University Press, 2005), 24.
5.  Source: http://www.appropriate-economics.org/materials /Brief_History_of_interest.html.
6.  In Islam, for example see: Gillian Tett, "Banks Create Muslim 'Windows' as Islamic Banking Expands its Niche," *The Financial Times* (2 June 2006), 6: "The central religious precept driving the Islamic finance industry is the idea that riba (a word that can be translated either as "interest" or "usury") is haram ("forbidden" or "sinful")…At first glance, this appears to rule out most aspects of modern finance. But although the Koran bans the creation of money, by money, it does allow money to be used for trading tangible assets and businesses—that can generate a profit…Ironically, some of [the] structures and techniques [of modern Islamic banking] echo those that flourished in Christendom in Europe between the 12th and 15th centuries. The Christian Council of Nicea (325 CE) banned the practice of usury among the clergy and in 1140 this principle was extended to church members."
7.  http://www.sacred-texts.com/chr/ecf/002/0020342.htm.
8.  http://www.newadvent.org. "The 12th canon of the First Council of Carthage (345) and the 36th canon of the Council of Aix (789) have declared it to be reprehensible even for laymen to make money by lending at interest. The canonical laws of the Middle Ages absolutely forbade the practice. This prohibition is contained in the Decree of Gratian and orders that the profit so obtained to be restored; also the Third of the Lateran (1179) and the Second of Lyons (1274) condemn usurers. In the Council of Vienne (1311) it was declared that if any person obstinately maintained that there was no sin in the practice of demanding interest, he should be punished as a heretic. It is a curious fact that for a long time impunity in such matters was granted to Jews. The Fourth Council of the Lateran (1215), canon 27, only forbids them to exact excessive interest."
9.  Estelle and Mario Carota, "The Ignored Doctrine on Money" (1986) in John H. Hotson, *The Comer Papers* (Ontario, Canada: 1987), 1.
10. Andrew Lowd, in his thesis, "Alternative Currencies in Theory and Practice."
11. Pierre Thuillier, "Darwin Chez les Samourai," *La Recherche,* no. 181 (1986), 1276-80.
12. Elisabet Sahtouris, *Earth Dance: Living Systems in Evolution* (Alameda: Metalog Books, 1996).
13. David Loye, personal email to Stephen Belgin (2005).
14. Ibid.

15. Ibid.
16. Margrit Kennedy, et.al., *Interest and Inflation Free Money: Creating an Exchange Medium that Works for Everybody and Protects the Earth* (Okemos: Sava International, 1995), 26.
17. Ian Dew-Becker and Robert J. Gordon, "Where Did the Productivity Growth Go? Inflation Dynamics and the Distribution of Income," paper presented at the 81st meeting of the Brookings Panel on Economic Activity (Washington, D.C. 8-9 September 2005). http://www.brookings.edu.

## CHAPTER SIX

1. All three labels describing this period are quoted from Guy Bois, *La Grande Dépression Médiévale – le XIV–XVeme siècle: le Précédent d'une crise systémique* (Paris: PUF, 2000), 11.
2. Eva Matthews Sanford, "The Twelfth Century—Renaissance or Proto-Renaissance?" *Speculum 26* (1951), 635-42. See also: Warren Hollister, ed., *The Twelfth Century Renaissance* (New York: John Wiley & Sons, 1969); Charles Young, ed., *The Twelfth Century Renaissance* (Melbourne, FL: Krieger Publishing Company, 1977); Chris Ferguson, *Europe in Transition: A Select, Annotated Bibliography of the Twelfth-Century Renaissance* (New York, London: Taylor & Francis, 1987); Jacques Verger, *La Renaissance du XIIe Siècle* (Paris: Editions du Cerf, 1996).
3. Robert Delort, *La Vie au Moyen Age* (Lausanne: Editta, 1982), 45.
4. Bois, *La Grande Dépression*, 16.
5. Marcel Bloch quoted in Bois, *La Grande Dépression*, 15.
6. Guy Fourquin, *Histoire Economique de l'Occident Medieval* (Paris: Armand Collin, 1969), 215.
7. Francois Icher, *Les Oeuvriers des Cathédrales* (Paris: Editions de la Martinière, 1998), 20.
8. Bois, *La Grande Dépression*, 21.
9. Bayard, *La Tradition Cachee*, 42.
10. Robert L. Reynolds, *Europe Emerges: Transition Toward an Industrial Worldwide Society, 600-1750* (Madison: University of Wisconsin Press, 1967), 185-6.
11. R. Philippe, *L'Énergie au Moyen Age: L'Exemple des Pays d'Entre Seine et Loire de la fin du XIeme Siècle a la fin du XVeme Siècle* (Paris: 1982).
12. Frances and Joseph Gies, *Cathedral, Forges and Waterwheel: Technology and Invention in the Middle Ages* (New York: Harper Perennial, 1995), 107.
13. Robert Lacey and Danny Danzinger, *The Year 1000: What life was like at the turn of the first Millennium* (London: Little Brown & Co., 1999), 87.
14. Bois, *La Grande Dépression*, 52.
15. Alex Werner, ed., *London Bodies: The Changing Shape of Londoners from Prehistoric Times to the Present Day* (London: Museum of London, 1998), 108. The sizes of the bodies are based on bone lengths and are therefore

subject to error. "But where large samples are involved as here, the error is a constant that can be ignored for the purposes of comparison."

16. See for instance, Georges Duby, *Europe des Cathédrales: 1140-1290* (Geneva: Skira, 1966).

17. Sacheverell Sitwell, *The Gothick North: A Study of Medieval Life, Art, and Thought* (Boston: Houghton Mifflin, 1929).

18. Delort, *La vie au Moyen Age*, 211-2.

19. H. Kraus, *A Prix d'Or: le Financement des Cathédrales* (Paris: Cerf, 1991). It should be noted that abbeys do not fit into this general rule: they were built and owned by the order that lived there. The bulk of the financing for the abbeys came from donations of land or other endowments by nobility.

20. Barbara Schock-Werner, "Le Chantier de la Cathédrale de Strasbourg," *Chantiers Médiévaux* (Editions du Zodiaque, DDB, 1995). The funding for each cathedral was by a special legal and financially-independent institution, called "la Maison de l'Oeuvre Notre Dame." One of the most complete records relates to the cathedral of Strasbourg in Alsace, France. In 1206, the Oeuvre Notre Dame at Strasbourg consisted of a committee of citizens, including the local Bishop. However, from 1230 onwards the role of the Bishop and clergy dropped to the point that after 1262, the Bishop was completely excluded from the committee. In 1290, "L'Oeuvre Notre Dame" became an official municipal function and remains so to this day, with a brief exception after the French Revolution (1789 to 1803), when it was controlled by the French State ("Régie des Domaines").

21. Bois, *La Grande Dépression*, 11.

22. Fourquin, *Histoire Économique de l'Occident Médiéval*, 192.

23. Henry S. Lucas, "The Great European Famine of 1315-1316," *Speculum 5*, no. 4 (1930), 343-77.

24. Chronicle of Gilles Le Muisit, abbot of Saint-Martin de Tournai (1272-1352) in *Textes et documents d'histoire du Moyen Age, XIVe-XVe siècles*, tome 1, S.E.D.E.S. (Paris: 1970), 8-9. See also: R. Fossier, *Le Moyen Age, le temps des crises (1250-1520)* (Paris, 1997). A. Colin and Jean Delumeau, *Les malheurs des temps. Histoire des fléaux et des calamités en France* (Paris: Larousse, 1987).

25. Lucas, "The Great European Famine of 1315-1316," *Speculum 5*, no. 4 (1930), 343-77.

26. Daniel Power, ed., *The Central Middle Ages* (Oxford University Press, 2006), 60.

27. Bois, *La Grande Dépression*, 93-4.

## CHAPTER SEVEN

1. The late medieval social order was constituted by God's Three Estates, in which the Church, nobility, and masses were each to serve one another to the benefit of all. According to historian Barbara Tuchman, "The clergy was to

pray for all men, the knights to fight for them, and the commoner worked that all might eat." This plan derived from the early Christian notion of mankind's fall from an original state of grace.

2.  The concentration of wealth took several centuries to be established and all its effects were not negative. For instance, patronage by the elite gave birth to what became later known as the Renaissance.

3.  From the writings of early church father St. Augustine of Hippo.

4.  The French Philosopher Alexandre Koyré coined the term and definition of "The Scientific Revolution" in 1939, which began in 1543, when Nicolaus Copernicus published his *De revolutionibus orbium coelestium* (On the Revolutions of the Heavenly Spheres), and Andreas Vesalius published his *De humani corporis fabrica* (On the Fabric of the Human body). Some see elements contributing to this shift as early as the Middle Ages. See: Edward Grant, *The Foundations of Modern Science in the Middle Ages: Their Religious, Institutional, and Intellectual Contexts* (Cambridge: Cambridge University Press, 1996).

5.  http://www.nri.org.uk/joseph.html.

6.  http://en.wikipedia.org/wiki/Scientific_revolution.

7.  Both Isaac Newton and Gottfried Wilhelm Leibniz are usually both credited with the invention of calculus. Newton was the first to apply calculus to general physics and Leibniz developed much of the notation used in calculus today. By Newton's time, the fundamental theorem of calculus was known.

8.  Some historians differentiate between the Age of Reason in the 1600s and the Age of Enlightenment in the 1700s. For our purposes, the Age of Enlightenment includes both these intellectual movements.

9.  http://www.riksbank.com; and http://www.bankofengland.co.uk.

10. To be more accurate, while the Charter of the Bank of England dates from 1688, the *monopoly of emission of paper money* was assigned by King William of Orange to that institution only in 1694. See also: http://www.bankofengland.co.uk.

11. See also: http;//www.humanscience.wikia.com/wiki/Social_Development_Theory.

12. Michael D. Bordo, *The Concise Encyclopedia of Economics*. "England adopted a gold standard in 1717 after the master of the mint, Sir Isaac Newton, overvalued the guinea in terms of silver, and formally adopted the gold standard in 1819." http://www.econlib.org/library/Enc/GoldStandard.html.

13. Voltaire, *The Works of Voltaire, Vol. VII, Philosophical Dictionary Part 5* (1764).

14. Personal communication with Alec Tsoucatos (June 15, 2005).

15. See also: David Dugan and Alan Macfarlane , *The Day the World Took Off* (University of Cambridge). http://www.dspace.cam.ac.uk/handle1810/270.

16. Alfred W. Crosby, *The Measure of Reality: Quantification and Western Society 1250-1600* (Cambridge: Cambridge University Press, 1998).
17. This supposition is made because the success of the French experiment with local currencies seemed to have disappeared in the mist of time.
18. The Technocratic Materialistic Mechanistic (TMM) model is a term coined by Anne Wilson Schaef, in *Living in Process: Basic Truths for Living the Path of the Soul* (New York: Ballantine Wellspring, 1999).

## CHAPTER EIGHT

1. Eric Beinhocker, *The Origins of Wealth Complexity, and the Radical Remaking of Economics* (Cambridge, Massachusettes: Harvard Business School Press, 2006). "Many earlier economists, such as Smith (and Bentham) regarded themselves as philosophers rather than scientists, and the mathematics of the Classical periods is generally limited to a few numerical examples and a bit of algebra, but nothing more sophisticated."
2. Ibid., 67.
3. Ibid., 24. A more complete but more cumbersome definition for Traditional Economics is: "the set of concepts and theories articulated in undergraduate and graduate-level textbooks. It also includes the concepts and theories that peer-reviewed surveys claim, or assume, the field generally agrees on."
4. Ibid., 67.
5. Ibid.
6. Ibid., 52-7.
7. Ibid., 33.
8. "GDP only includes goods; GNP does not include goods and services produced by foreign producers, but does include goods and services produced by U.S. firms based abroad. GDP replaced GNP as the primary measure of U.S. production in 1991." http://www.traderslog.com.
9. The U.S. national median salary for a stay at home parent with one pre-school child and another at school is $138,095. http://swz.salary.com/momsalarywizard/.
10. These figures, based on the median salary of the 25th percentile across four different zip codes in the U.S. were calculated using data provided by: http://www.salary.com.
11. Clifford Cobb, Ted Halstead, and Jonathan Rowe, "If the GDP is Up, Why is America Down?" *Atlantic Monthly*, 276 (4), October, 51-8. Cited from Sally Goerner *After the Clockwork Universe: The Emerging Science and Culture of Integral Society* (Edinburgh, Scotland: Floris Publishers, 1999), 331.
12. Ibid. Comments made by Simon Kuznets appear in the first report to the U.S. Congress in 1934, as reported by Measuring Progress: Annex.
13. Ibid. As former World Bank economist Herman Daly puts it, "the current national accounting system treats planet Earth as a business in liquidation." Add pollution to the balance sheet and we appear to be doing even better.

Pollution shows up twice as gain: once when the Chemical factory, say, produces it is a byproduct, then again when the nation spend billions of dollars to clean it up in a toxic Superfund site. It shows up again as medical bills rising as a result of dirty air.

14. Robert Kennedy, Jr., from a lecture at a Friends of the Earth Rally (New York, 13 March 1963).

15. Hazel Henderson, Jon Lickerman, and Patrice Flynn *Calvert_Henderson Quality of Life Indicators* (Calvert Group, 2000). See also, *Ethical Markets* (White River Junction, Vermont: Chelsea Green Publishing, 2006).

16. Cobb, Halstead, and Rowe, "If the GDP is Up, Why is America Down?" 51-8.

17. Ibid.

18. Ibid.

## CHAPTER NINE

1. Paul Krugman, "How Did Economists Get It So Wrong," *New York Times* (2 September, 2009).
http://www.nytimes.com/2009/09/06/magazine/06Economic-t.html.

2. Ibid.

3. "Saving the System, The Panic, The Rescues and a Full Report on the World Economy," *The Economist* (11 October 2008).

4. Paul Krugman, "The Third Depression," *New York Times* (27 June 2010).
http://www.nytimes.com/2010/06/28/opinion/28krugman.html.

5. *The Economist* (11 October 2008).

6. Charles Kindleberger, *Manias, Panics and Crashes* ( New York: Wiley & Sons, 3d ed. 1996), 1.

7. Prior to the Weimar Republic (1919-1933), the German national currency was the "mark." In 1923, the mark was replaced by the "rentenmark" to counter inflation. A year later, when inflation slowed down, the "reichsmark" came into being and remained Germany's national currency throughout WW II. It was demonetized by a new currency law on June 20th 1948 and replaced by the "deutsche mark," which was finally replaced by the euro.

8. Glyn Davies, *A History of Money: From Ancient Times to the Present Day* (Cardiff: University of Wales, 1994), 572-4.

9. In 1929, the "Wära Tauschgesellschaft" was founded by two Gesell followers, Hans Timm and Reinhard Rödiger. Claude Million, Ph.D. dissertation, "Nebenwährungen gegen Absatzstockung und Beschäftigungskrise – Die amerikanischen Versuche mit scrip während der Grossen Depression" (Humboldt Universität zu Berlin, April 1998).

10. Ibid.

11. Ibid. The legislative action taken was the "Brüningsche Notverordnungen," (Brüning's Emergency Regulations), named after Heinrich Brüning, Reichs-chancellor and foreign minister). Letters specific to this case include those

from the Board of the Reichsbank (I 10513) to the Minister of Finance, dated 8/8/1931 (Bundesbank Archiv R 31.01/15345), 145.

12. Margrit Kennedy, *Interest and Inflation Free Money* (Seva International, 1995): "During the Weimar Republic (1924-33), the central bank's president, Hjalmat Schacht, had the desire to create an 'honest' currency in Germany, which—in his understanding—meant a return to the gold standard. Since he could not buy enough gold on the world market adequate to the amount of money in circulation, he began to reduce the latter. The shorter supply of money resulted in rising interest rates, thereby reducing the incentives and possibilities for investment, forcing firms into bankruptcy, and increasing unemployment, which led to the growth of radicalism and finally helped Hitler to gain more and more power."

13. In March 1930, Schacht stepped down from the position of Reichsbank Chairman, but returned to his job after Hitler's rise to power three years later.

14. John Weitz, *Hitler's Banker: Hjalmar Horace Greely Schacht* (London: Warner Books, 1999), 131.

15. Official German unemployment statistics: "Arbeitarktdaten."

16. Max Schwarz, *MdR - Biographisches Handbuch der Reichstage* (Hannover: Verlag für Literatur und Zeitgeschehen, 1965), 810-16.

17. Alex von Murat, *The Wörgl Experiment with Depreciating Money* (1934). Also, see Fritz Schwartz, *Das Experiment von Wörgl* (Bern: Genossenschaft Verlag Freiwirtschaftlicher Schriften, 1951), 14.

18. Ibid.

19. Irving Fisher, *Stamp Scrip* (New York: Adelphi Co., 1933).

20. H.W. Brands, *Traitor to His Class: The Privileged Life and Radical Presidency of Franklin Delano Roosevelt* (New York: Doubleday, 2008). Quoted in *The Economist* (1 November 2008), 83.

21. See: http://en.wikipedia.org/wiki/Currency_Act#Act_of_1764. "The Currency Acts created tension between the colonies and the mother country, and were a contributing factor in the coming of the American Revolution. In all of the colonies except Delaware, the acts were considered to be a 'major grievance.' When the First Continental Congress met in 1774, it issued a Declaration of Rights, which outlined colonial objections to certain acts of Parliament. Congress called on Parliament to repeal the Currency Act of 1764, one of seven acts labeled "subversive of American rights." See also: Jack P. Greene, and Richard M. Jellison, "The Currency Act of 1764 in Imperial-Colonial Relations, 1764–1776," *The William and Mary Quarterly*, Third Series, Vol. 18, No. 4 (October 1961), 517. John Phillip Reid, *Constitutional History of the American Revolution, III: The Authority to Legislate* (Madison: University of Wisconsin Press, 1991) 265.

## CHAPTER TEN

1. John Maynard Keynes, *A Tract on Monetary Reform* (1923).

## ENDNOTES—PART II

### CHAPTER ELEVEN

1.  The National Center for Health Sciences, National Vital Statistics Report 47, no. 28, Table 12. http://www.cdc.gov/nchs.
2.  K. Bruce Newbold, *Six billion plus: world population in the twenty-first century* (Lanham, Maryland: Rowman & Littlefield, 2007), 6.
3.  http://www.worldmapper.org.
4.  Lily Nonomiya, "Japan's Industrial Production Unexpectedly Declines" *Bloomberg News* (28 June 2007).
5.  Heather Landym, Neil Irwin, "Massive Shifts on Wall St. Troubled Investment Bank To File for Bankruptcy," *The Washington Post*, A01 (15 September 2008).
6.  http://www.efluxmedia.com/news_Financial_behemoth_Lehman_Brothers _largest_failure_in_US_24397.html.
7.  Barry Ritholtz, "Bernanke Bombshell: AIG Insurer Exposed to FP," 24 March 2009. http://www.ritholtz.com.
8.  "The salary boost just about matches the profit increase of 11 percent that Wall Street analysts expect for the oil giant's 2008 profit, now pegged at just over $46 billion, according to a survey by FactSet Research." From Steve Gelsi, "Exxon Mobil CEO Tillerson gets 10 percent Raise," MarketWatch, *The Wall Street Journal* (3 December 2008).
9.  "The Bank of England has now cut UK interest rates to an all-time low of 0.5 percent." From Christine Oliver, "Interest Rates through the Ages: From Puritanism to Prudence," *The Guardian* (5 March 2009).
10. Adam Voiland, "2009: Second Warmest Year on Record; End of Warmest Decade," NASA (28 January 2010). http://www.nasa.gov/topics/earth/features/temp-analysis-2009.html.
11. Stephen Dinan, "Obama signs massive stimulus bill," *The Washington Times* (17 February 2009).
12. Sally Goerner, *After the Clockwork Universe: The Emerging Science and Culture of Integral Society.* (Chapel Hill, NC: Triangle Center for Complex Systems, 1999).
13. Duane Elgin and Coleen LeDrew, "Global Paradigm Change: Is a Shift Underway?" (San Francisco, CA: State of the World Forum, 2-6 October 1996).
14. Thomas Griffith, "This Turbulant World: People's Endless Struggles to Change Their Lives," *Time* (5 October 1983). http://www.time.com/time/magazine/article/0,9171,952063,00.html.
15. The concept of Great Change was developed by the authors in collaboration with Dr. Sally Goerner (6 February 2006).
16. Amy Maxmen, "The Gut's 'Friendly' Viruses Revealed," *Nature*, published online, doi:10.1038/news.2010.353 (14 July 2010). "It could be that viruses

are the real drivers of the system because of their ability to modify the bacteria that then modify the human host."

17. Jamshid Garajedaghi, "Systems Methodology: A Holistic Language of Design and Interaction – Seeing through Chaos and Understanding Complexity." http://www.acasa.upenn.edu/JGsystems.pdf.

18. Goerner, *After the Clockwork Universe: The Emerging Science and Culture of Integral Society.*

19. John Langone, "Alternative Therapies Challenging the Mainstream," *Time Special Issue* (Fall 1996), 40.

20. Ibid.

21. John A. Astin, "Why Patients Use Alternative Medicine," *Journal of the American Medical Association,* 279, no. 19 (1998), 1548-1553.

22. James Robbins, "Free market flawed, says survey," *BBC News.* http://news.bbc.co.uk/2/hi/8347409.stm.

23. Paul Ray and Sherry Anderson, *The Cultural Creatives* (New York: Harmony Books, 1999), with updates based on the original survey by Paul Ray, "The Integral Culture Survey: A Study of the Emergence of Transformational Value in America" (Research Monograph sponsored by the Fetzer Institute and the Institute of Noetic Sciences, 1996).

24. Duane Elgin and Coleen LeDrew, *Global Paradigm Change: Is a Shift Underway?* (San Francisco, CA State of the World Forum, 2-6 October 1996).

25. Ibid.

26. Paul Hawken, *Blessed Unrest: How The Largest Movement in the World Came Into Being and Why No One Saw It Coming* (New York: Viking Press, 2007).

27. Goerner, *After the Clockwork Universe: The Emerging Science and Culture of Integral Society.*

28. Astin, "Why Patients Use Alternative Medicine."

## CHAPTER TWELVE

1. Modern energy concepts and flow analyses were formally applied to economics as early as 1951, by Wassili Leontief with his input-output analyses, modeling the flow of goods and value in economic systems. Ecologists then applied these same flow concepts and analyses to ecosystems, only to have economists later reapply these enhanced energy understandings to economics. Odum (1971, 1984), Hannon (1973), and Costanza (1984), for example, have all used thermodynamics and flow-network analysis as the basis for understanding the activities in both economic and ecosystem networks; and Georgescu Roegen (1971) developed an entire thermodynamic foundation for economics. Paul Samuelson stated in 1965, in the Preface to Roegen's *Analytical Economics*, that he considers Roegen as "a scholar's scholar, and an economist's economist." He added: "I

defy any informed economist to remain complacent after meditating over this essay." Nevertheless, complacency is what has greeted that book and its successor, *Entropy Law and the Economic Process.*

2. Predrag Cvitanovič, *Introduction to Universality in Chaos* (Bristol, UK: Adam Hilger), 11.

3. See: Robert Ulanowicz, Sally Goerner, Bernard Lietaer, and Rocio Gomez, "Quantifying Sustainability: Efficiency, Resiliency and the Return of Information Theory," *Journal of Ecological Complexity.* The paper is available for download at: http://www.lietaer.com.

4. R.M. May, "Will a large complex system be stable?" *Nature* 238:413-414 (1972).

5. C.S. Holling, "Resiliency and the stability of ecological systems" Annual Review of Ecology and Systematics, 1973; and Brian H. Walker, John M. Anderies, Ann P. Kinzig and Paul Ryan, "Exploring Resiliency in Social-Ecological Systems: Comparative Studies and Theory Development" in a special issue of *Ecology and Society*, 2006. Guest editors, Walker, Anderies, Kinzig, and Ryan, (Collingwood, Victoria, Australia: CSIRO Publishing). Online version: http://www.ecologyandsociety.org/viewissue.php?sf=22.

6. Graphic was originally published in S. Goerner, R. Dyck, and D. Lagerroos, *The New Science of Sustainability: Building a Foundation for Great Change* (Chapel Hill, NC: Triangle Center for Complex Systems, distributed by Gabriel Island, BC, Canada: New Society Publishers, 2008). Modified graphic in S. Goerner, B. Lietaer, R. Ulanowicz, R. "Quantifying economic sustainability: Implications for free enterprise, theory, policy and practice." *Ecological Economics* 69 (1), 76-81.

7. In the original literature this window is called a "window of vitality" given its biological meaning in natural ecosystems. An ecosystem can support complex life forms only within this range. See R.E. Ulanowicz, *A Third Window: Natural Foundations for Life* (New York: Oxford University Press, 2008); and A.C. Zorach, and R.E. Ulanowicz "Quantifying the complexity of flow networks: How many roles are there?" *Complexity* 8(3): 68-76 (2003).

8. "On Aug. 14, 2003, more than 50 million North Americans find themselves without power in the most widespread blackout in the history of electrical civilization." http://archives.cbc.ca/science_technology/energy_production/clips/13545/.

9. V.V. Gafiychuk, I.A. Lubashevsky, and R.E. Ulanowicz, "Distributed self-regulation in ecological and economic systems," *Complex Systems* 11 (1997), 357-372.

## CHAPTER THIRTEEN

1. See: Robert Ulanowicz, Sally J. Goerner, Bernard Lietaer, and Rocio Gomez, "Quantifying Sustainability: Resilience, efficiency and the return of information theory," *Ecological Complexity*, 6(1), (27 March 2009), 36.

"Since sustainable development requires a balance of efficiency and resilience, Ulanowicz (1980) used configurations of flow pathways and magnitudes in natural ecosystems to develop a measure of network efficiency called the Systemic Efficiency (SE or E), which gauges overall system performance as well as its ability to pull more and more energy into its sway, while reducing extraneous diversity/connectivity." The original paper is also available for download on: http://www.lietaer.com. See also: Ulanowicz, "A hypothesis on the development of natural communities," *Journal of Theoretical Biology.* 85 (1980), 223-245.

2. Ibid. See also: Robert E. Ulanowicz, C. Bondavalli, and M.S. Egnotovich (1996). "Network Analysis of Trophic Dynamics in South Florida Ecosystems, FY 96: The Cypress Wetland Ecosystem," *Annual Report to the United States Geological Service Biological Resources Division* (University of Miami, Coral Gables, FL 33124: 1996).

3. Ibid.

4. E. Goldsmith, J. Mander, *The Case Against the Global Economy and, For a Turn, Towards the Local* (Sierra Club Books, 1997) Cited in S. Goerner, B. Lietaer, R. Ulanowicz, "Quantifying economic sustainability: Implications for free enterprise, theory, policy and practice," *Ecological Economics*, 69 (1), 78.

5. *Walmart: The High Cost of Low Prices* (Brave New Films, 2005).

6. "Civic Economics," Austin Unchained (Austin, October 2003). http://www.civiceconomics.com/Lamar_Retail_Analysis.pdf.

7. "The Economic Impact of Locally Owned Business vs Chains: A Case Study in Mid-coast Maine," New Rules Project, Institute for Local Self-Reliance (ILSR) (Minneapolis, September 2003).

8. Joseph Tainter, *The Collapse of Complex Societies.* (London: Cambridge University Press, 1988).

9. Joseph Stiglitz, *Globalization and its Discontents* (London, New York: Penguin Books, 2002).

10. Robert Pollin, Contours of Descent: U.S. Economic Fractures and the Landscape of Global Austerity. (London, New York: Verso, 2003).

11. John Ralston Saul, "The Collapse of Globalism and the Rebirth of Nationalism," *Harper's Magazine* (March 2004), 33.

12. Caprio and Klingelbiel, "Bank Insolvencies: Cross Country Experience," *Policy Research Working Papers*, no.1620 (Washington, DC: World Bank, Policy and Research Department, 1996).

13. For data on the growing disparity between rich and poor nations and individuals see: Culpeper, Roy, 2005. Approaches to globalization and inequality within the international system. In *Overarching Concerns Programme Paper*, no. 6 (Oct. 2005), United Nations Research Institute for Social Development (UNRISD).

14. Accompanied by "jobless growth," means an increase in GDP growth that is accompanied by a decrease in living-wage jobs. By 1995, for example, almost a third of the world's 2.8-billion person workforce was either jobless or working for such low wages that they faced a life with little chance for advancement. For rates of jobless growth see: Jeremy Rifkin, *The End of Work: The Decline of the Global Labor Force and the Dawn of the Post-Market Era* (New York: Jeremy P. Tarcher, 1995).

15. For details see: N. Klein, *The Shock Doctrine: The Rise of Disaster Capitalism.* (New York: Holt and Company, 2008).

16. Hazel Henderson, *Paradigms in Progress: Life Beyond Economics* (Indianapolis, IN: Knowledge Systems, 1991); *Creating Alternative Futures: the End of Economics* (West Hartford, CT: Kumarian Press 1966); and *Ethical Markets: Growing a Green Economy* (White River Junction, Vermont: Chelsea Green Publishing, 2006).

17. Paul Glover is the initiator of programs such as Ithaca HOURS, the Ithaca Health Alliance, and Citizen Planners. He is author of *Hometown Money: How to Enrich Your Community with Local Currency* (2005), and *Recipe for Successful Local Currency* (2009)

18. Thomas Greco, *New Money for Healthy Communities* (1994) ; *Money: Understanding and Creating Alternatives to Legal Tender* (Chelsee Green, 2001); *The End of Money and the Future of Civilisation* (White River Junction, Vermont: Chelsea Green Publishing, 2009).

19. Edgar S. Cahn, *No More Throw Away People.* (Washington, DC: Essential Books, 2004).

20. Sergio Lub, creator of Friendly Favors. http://www.favors.org/FF/.

21. Susan Witt, was co-founder and Executive Director of the E. F. Schumacher Society, the predecessor of the New Economics Institute, which launched the Berkshares currency and other initiatives.

## CHAPTER FOURTEEN

1. It is particularly difficult to obtain up-to-date estimates of the number of complementary currency systems operational worldwide. Such projects are by nature local, with those engaged in one type of complementary currency system often unaware of other types in operation. Furthermore, a system that stops operating is not easily tracked. For complementary currencies in Japan, see Rui Izumi, "The Development and Future Challenges of the Community-Based Currencies in Japan," *Keizaigaku Ronshu* (2006). For France, see: http://selidaire.org/spip/rubrique.php3?id_rubrique=211.
For Regio systems in Germany see: http://www.regiogeld.de/. For LETS type currencies in Germany, Simone Wagner from the University of Konstanz *simone.wagner@uni-konstanz.de* has the most recently completed study: *Lokale Austauschnetzwerke - Entstehung, Stabilisierung und sozialpolitische Bedeutung* (forthcoming). See also: Susan Wagner,

"Diffusion of a Social Movement: The Example of the German Local Exchange Systems" *ASA Meeting 2007*. See also: http://www.tauschringportal.de/Tauschringportal/index.htmlb. For Austria, see: http://www.tauschkreise.at/. There are also two Regio currencies operational in Austria: the Waldviertler and the Styrion. For Switzerland, see: http://www.tauschnetz.ch/ and http://www.tauschnetz.ch/orgliste.htm. For the Netherlands, see: http://members.home.nl/letsdb/kaart.htm. There exist also a number of sources that are attempting to cover the global complementary currency scene. See: http://www.cyberclass.net/turmel/urlsnat.htm; http://www.lets.org.au/; http://www.lets-linkup.com/; http://www.complementarycurrency.org/;.

2. Michael Linton, interview
3. James Taris, *The LETSaholic Twist* (Camberwell, Australia, 2005).
4. All quotes from personal correspondence with Edgar Cahn, (8 July 2007).
5. http://www.timedollar.org.
6. R. J. Sampson, S. W. Raudenbush; and F. Earls. "Neighborhoods and violent crime: A multilevel study of collective efficacy," *Science* 277 (15 Aug 1997), 918.
7. Robert Wood Johnson Foundation: "Service Credit Banking Project Site Summaries" (University of Maryland Centre of Aging, 1990). This study shows the burn-out rate dropping from 40 percent to 3 percent thanks to the use of a Time Banking complementary currency
8. Time Dollars and Time Banking are gaining support from government officials. At a White House Conference on Aging, Massachusetts and Wisconsin recommended using Time Dollars to work with the elderly. The British Secretary of Health has singled out Time Banking as an effective mechanism to support informal healthcare.
9. Time Banks USA, "Time Bank Models: Youth at Risk," http://www.timedollar.org.
10. Ibid.
11. Ibid.
12. Time Banks USA, "IRS Ruling," (23 February 2006). http://www.timedollar.org.
13. Linton Interview.
14. Double coincidence of wants was coined by economist William Stanley Jevons. See: W.S. Jevons, *Money and the Mechanism of Exchange*, (London: Macmillan, 1875), Chapter 1, paragraphs 5-6.

## CHAPTER FIFTEEN

1. 1.Toshiharu Kato, The New Model of Community Currency from Japan to the World: The Development of Eco-point Succeeding Eco-money, (Aichi, Japan: World Exposition, February 2006).

2. Rui Izumi, "The Development and Future Challenges of the Community-Based Currencies in Japan," Keizaigaku Ronshu (2006).

3. It is generally assumed that the first modern complementary currency system post-World War II is the LETS system started in Canada in 1982. But the Japanese initiatives predate this by over a decade.

4. Mitsui Ichien, Report of Research on Desirable Models of Non-profit Welfare Activities for the Elderly (in Japanese), (Kansai: University of Kansai: Research Institute of Ageless Society, 1991).

5. Yasuyuki (Miguel) Hirota, personal email message to Bernard Lietaer, (summer 2002).

6. Rui Izumi, Associate Professor at the School of Economics, Senshu University in Tokyo personal correspondence (July 2006): Major factors that have contributed to the growth of local currencies: "First, and perhaps surprisingly, was a program on national television in the late 1990's called Michael Ende's Last Message. This broadcast profiled complementary systems from the 1930s in Europe up (to) today's WIR, LETS, and other popular systems. It touched a collective nerve. At that time, Japan was in deflationary depression after The East-Asian Financial Crisis happened in 1997 and a bubble economic collapse in 1991, and these caused many Japanese people to wonder about speculation and money. Second, Toshiharu Kato, a bureaucrat at Department of Trade and Industry, created the term 'Eco-money.' Many people felt an affinity with the term rather than the phrase community or complementary currency, and many books with the title containing the term 'Eco-money' were published."

7. For the developed countries belonging to the OECD, the number of people older than 65 has been growing from one out of 11 in 1965 to one out of seven now. Over the next two decades, it could be as high as one out of four. The same is expected to happen in the developing countries, one or two decades later. Peter G. Petersen, "Gray Dawn: The Global Aging Crisis," Foreign Affairs (January-February 1999).

8. Rui Izumi, personal correspondence

9. As quoted in Makoto Maruyama, "Local Currencies in New Zealand and Australia," in Junji Koizumi, ed., Dynamics of Cultures and Systems in the Pacific Rim (Osaka: 2003), 183.

10. Dr. Gilson Sxhwartz's "Creative Currencies" project dates back to 2003 when the "City of Knowledge" research group, funded by the Presidency of Brazil's Civil House Agency of Information Technology (ITI), developed mobile and complementary currency pilot-projects in Pipa, in a Xavante village in Mato Grosso, and in Pará (Abaetetuba). Research into mobile technologies, innovative digital business models (such as crowdfunding) and cultural trends in the internet society led to the implementation of a second generation roadmap, leading to funding by the Ministry of Science and Technology, the Ministry of Culture and the Brazilian Development Bank

(Portuguese: Banco Nacional de Desenvolvimento Economico e Social, abbreviated: BNDES) with the formal support of the central bank of Brazil.

11. Bernard Lietaer "The Saber: An Education Currency for Brazil," The International Journal for Community Currency Research (27 February 2006). http://www.uea.ac.uk/env/ijccr/abstracts/vol10(3)lietaer.html.

12. http://www.cofc.edu/bellsandwhistles/research/retentionmodel.html. See also: http://www.know.org/.

13. F. Taddei, "Training creative and collaborative Knowledge Builders: a major challenge for 21st century education" (Paris: OECD, 2009). http://q.liberation.fr/pdf/20090414/10901_telechargez-le-rapport.pdf.

14. Bernard Lietaer, "Proposal for a Brazilian Education Complementary Currency," *International Journal for Community Currency Research*, Vol. 10, 18-23; http://www.uea.ac.uk/env/ijccr/pdfs /IJCCR%20vol%2010%20(2006)%203%20Lietaer.pdf.

15. Thom Hartmann, *Beyond ADD* (Nevada City, California, Underwood Books, 1996).

16. See: H. Gardner, *Frames of Mind: The Theory of Multiple Intelligences* (Tufts University Press, 1993). See also: Thomas Armstrong, *Seven kinds of Smarts: Identifying and Developing your Multiple Intelligences* (Plume Books, 1999).

17. Jeffrey Freed and Laurie Parsons Cantillo, *Right-Brained Children in a Let-Brained World, Unlocking the Potential Of Your ADD Child* (New York: Simon and Schuster, 1997).

18. See: http://visualspatial.org.

19. As reported to Stephen Belgin by Jeffrey Freed (20 March 2011).

20. See: http://visualspatial.org.

21. Marusa Vasconcelos Freire, "Social Economy and Central Banks: Legal and Regulatory Issues On Social Currencies (Social Money) As A Public Policy Instrument Consistent With Monetary Policy," *International Journal Of Community Currency Research* Vol 13 (2009) p. 76-94

## CHAPTER SIXTEEN

1. Webflyer Press Room edited by Randy Peterson. http://www.webflyer.com.

2. *Bureau of Labor Statistics press release* (11 March 2011). http://www.bls.gov/news.release/pdf/empsit.pdf.

3. Jeannine Aversa, "Poll Finds Debt-Dogged Americans Stressed Out," (30 May 2010). http://abcnews.go.com/Business/wireStory?id=10782052.

4. AP-GfK Poll, "Politics and Economy Topline" (9 March 2010). http://www.ap-gfkpoll.com/pdf/AP-GfK%20Poll%20March%202010%20Topline%20Release2%203.9.10.pdf.

5. James Stodder, "Complementary Credit Networks and Macro-Economic Stability: Switzerland's Wirtschaftsring," *Journal of Economic Behavior & Organization,* 72 (October 2009), 79–95; and , "Reciprocal Exchange

Networks: Implications for Macroeconomic Stability," paper presented at the International Electronic and Electrical Engineering (IEEE) Engineering Management Society (EMS) (Albuquerque, NM, August 2000), 3.

6.  Tobias Studer, "Le Système WIR dans l'optique d'un chercheur Américan" *WirPlus* (October 2000). http://www.wir.ch.
7.  The system was credited with saving many of the businesses involved.
8.  WIR annual report 2006. See more details at: http://www.wir.ch.

**CHAPTER SEVENTEEN**

1.  For those interested in a deeper understanding, please consult the White Paper available for download at: http://www.lietaer.com/2010/01/terra/.
2.  Such portfolio rebalancing can also be achieved through use of the futures markets in the relevant commodities, including the possibility to take delivery of the commodity itself at maturity.
3.  Shared by Paul Volcker with Bernard Lietaer personally.
4.  The overall discount rate to be applied to a project involves three components: the interest rate on the currency, the risk of the project, and the cost of equity capital. The demurrage fee is similar to a negative interest rate. Therefore, particularly for low risk projects, the overall discount rate could be negative, making future cash flows more valuable than those in the immediate future.
5.  "In the year 1717, master of the Royal Mint Sir Isaac Newton established a new mint ratio between silver and gold that had the effect of driving silver out of circulation and putting Britain on a gold standard. However, it was in 1821, following the introduction of the gold sovereign coin by the new Royal Mint at Tower Hill in the year 1816, that the United Kingdom formally put on a gold specie standard. Canada followed in 1853, Newfoundland in 1865, and the USA and Germany *de jure* in 1873. The USA used the Eagle as their unit, and Germany introduced the new gold mark, while Canada adopted a dual system based on both the American Gold Eagle and the British Gold Sovereign." See: http://en.wikipedia.org/wiki/Gold_standard.

**CHAPTER EIGHTEEN**

1.  Paul Hawken, *"Commencement Address to the Class of 2009"* (University of Portland, 3 May, 2009). http://www.commondreams.org/view/2009/05/23-2.
2.  http:data.worldbank.ort/indicator/FS.AST.PRVT.GD.ZS /countries /1W-US?display=graph.
3.  "Betting the balance-sheet, Why managers loaded their companies with debt," A special report on debt by *The Economist* (24 June, 2010). http://www.economist.com/node/16397174.
4.  Ibid.
5.  Adam Smith, *Wealth of Nations*, (1776), 929-30.

6. Ludwig von Mises, *Human Action, A Treatise on Economics* (1949) 1st and 4th editions. http://mises.org/resources/3250.

7. "Betting the balance-sheet, Why managers loaded their companies with debt," *The Economist* (24 June 2010). http://www.economist.com/node/16397174.

8. The full list involves in alphabetical order: Abertis, Allen & Overy LLP, Barclays Capital, Carlyle Infrastructure Partners, Chadbourne & Parke LLP, Citi Infrastructure Investors (CII), Credit Suisse, Debevoise & Plimpton, Freshfields Bruckhaus Deringer, Fulbright & Jaworski, Mayer Brown, McKenna Long & Aldridge LLP, Merrill Lynch, Morgan Stanley, RBC Capital Markets, Scotia Capital, and UBS. The document "Benefits of private investment in infrastructure,"was made public in January 2009.

9. *Euromoney* (April 2010), 85.

10. Nick Lord, "The Road to Wiping Out the US Deficit," *Euromoney* (April 2010), 84-9.

11. Ibid., 88

12. This includes several islands in the Venice lagoon, an ancient royal palace in Palermo, and the Etruscan museum at Villa Giulia in Rome. John Follain, "Hard-up Italy sells islands and palaces" *Sunday Times* (7 March 2010), 24.

13. President Barack Obama, Presentation of the U.S. budget for 2010, (1 February 2010).

## ENDNOTES—PART III

### CHAPTERS NINETEEN

1. Gareth Cook, "A Fish, a Gene, and a Source of Skin Color," *The Boston Globe* (19 December 2005).

2. The ancient Greeks considered the psyche to be the self, or soul, housed within each individual, which is responsible for behavior. Psychologist James Hillman, offers a more complex theory, by which the soul is not a substance or entity that is located inside the brain or head of a person. Rather, it is "a perspective, a viewpoint towards things… [it is] reflective; it mediates events and makes differences…" (1975). Hillman sees human beings as in psyche. The world, in turn, is the *anima mundi*, or the world ensouled. Hillman often quotes a phrase coined by the Romantic poet John Keats: "Call the world the vale of soul-making." http://en.wikipedia.org/wiki/Archetypal_psychology.

3. Jacob Needleman, *Money and the Meaning of Life* (New York: Currency Doubleday, 1991).

4. The field of Archetypal Psychology was initiated by Carl Gustav Jung and further developed by scholars such as Erich Neumann, Jolande Jacobi, Edward F. Edinger, Christine Downing, and Jean Shinoda Bolen. James Hillman formally founded a school of Archetypal Psychology.

5. Jung elaborates on this laconic statement: "To the extent that the archetypes intervene in the shaping of the conscious contents by regulating, modifying, and motivating them, they act like instincts." Carl Gustav Jung, "On the Nature of the Psyche," *Collected Works Volume 8: The Structure and Dynamics of the Psyche* (Princeton: Princeton University Press, 1969), 408.
6. Bernice Hill, *Money and the Spiritual Warrior* (Boulder: Five Centuries Foundation, 2004), 17.
7. Joseph Campbell, *Myths to Live By,* 13.
8. Eric Robertson Dodds, *The Greeks and the Irrational* (Berkeley: University of California Press, 1951), 104.
9. Carl Gustav Jung et al., *Man and His Symbols* (London: Picador, 1978), 101.
10. Carl Gustav Jung, "The Structure of the Psyche," (1927) in *Collected Works Volume 8,* 342.
11. Ibid.
12. Moore and Gillette developed their Quaternion map in five books, one for each archetype, and one presenting a synthesis of their approach. They are: *King, Warrior, Magician, Lover* (San Francisco: Harper Collins, 1991); *The King Within* (New York: William Morrow, 1991); *The Warrior Within* (New York: William Morrow, 1992); *The Lover Within* (New York: Avon Books, 1993); and *The Magician Within* (New York: Avon Books, 1993). A number of modifications have been made to make these archetypes more gender balanced and relevant to our purpose. For instance, the Sovereign (Queen + King) is used instead of the King.

**CHAPTER TWENTY**

1. Craig S. Barnes, "The Great Goddess Debate," *The Salt Journal: Reconstructing Meaning* 2, no. 3 (March-April 2000), 6.
2. Marilyn Yalom, *A History of the Breast* (New York: Alfred Knopf, 1997), 9.
3. Starhawk, *The Spiral Dance: A Rebirth of the Ancient Religion of the Goddess* (San Francisco: Harper and Row, 1979).
4. Marija Gimbutas, *The Language of the Goddess: Unearthing the Hidden Symbols of Western Civilization* (San Francisco: Harper & Row, 1989), 321.
5. This title is borrowed from the section on cattle currency in Glyn Davies, *A History of Money from Ancient Times to the Present Day* (Cardiff: University of Wales Press, 1994).
6. Negley Farson, *Behind God's Back* (London: Harcourt, Brace and Company, 1941), 264.
7. From the same origin as the term "capital punishment," referring to execution by severing the head.
8. Georges Ifrah, *Histoire Universelle des Chiffres* (Paris: Robert Laffont, 1995), 180.
9. Thorkild Jacobsen, *The Treasures of Darkness: A History of Mesopotamian Religion* (New Haven: Yale University Press, 1976), 138.

10. Demetra George, *Mysteries of the Dark Moon* (San Francisco: Harper Collins, 1992), 162.
11. Davies, *A History of Money*, 35.
12. Ibid.
13. Abbé Breuil quoted in Jean Servier, *L'homme et l'invisible* (Paris, 1964), 37-8.
14. Jean Chevalier and Alain Gheerbrant, *Dictionnaire des Symboles* (Paris: Robert Laffont, 1982), 283.
15. "All her idols will be broken to pieces; all her temple gifts will be burned with fire; I will destroy all her images. Since she gathered her gifts from the wages of prostitutes, as the wages of prostitutes they will again be used." *Holy Bible, Micah* 6:8 NIV (Colorado Springs: International Bible Society, 1984).
16. Patricia Monaghan, *The Book of Goddesses and Heroines* (St. Paul, MN: Llewellyn Publications, 1990), 185.
17. Ibid.

## CHAPTER TWENTY ONE

1. James DeMeo, *Saharasia: The 4000 BCE Origins of Child Abuse, Sex-repression, Warfare and Social Violence in the Deserts of the Old World* (Greensprings, OR: Orgone Biophysical Research Lab, 1998).
2. Philip Van Doren Stern, Prehistoric *Europe, From Stone Age Men to the Early Greeks* (New York: W.W. Norton, 1969), 230, 302.
3. For an architectural and archeological analysis of this process, see Vincent Scully, *The Earth, the Temple and the Gods: Greek Sacred Architecture* (New Haven: Yale University Press, 1979).
4. Richard Tarnas, *The Passions of the Western Mind: Understanding the Ideas that Have Shaped Our World View* (New York: Ballantine Books, 1991), 21.
5. Aristotle, "De Generatione Animalium II" 3 (737a, 26-31) in *The Works of Aristotle*, J.A. Smith and W.D. Ross, trans. (Oxford: Clarendon Press, 1912).
6. Aristotle, *Politics*, 1254b, 6-14.
7. Sigmund Freud, "Some Physical Consequences of the Anatomical Distinction Between the Sexes" (1925) in James Strachey, trans. and ed., *The Standard Edition of the Complete Psychological Works of Sigmund Freud* (London: Hogarth Press, 1953-1974).
8. Matthew 5:44-45 NIV.
9. Jutta Voss, *Frauenrequiem: Totenmesse für alle Frauen die als 'Hexen' ermordet wurden* (Stuttgart: Kreuz, 1989); Matilda Joslyn Gage, *Women, Church, and State* (Watertown, MA: Persephone Press, 1980); Susan Griffin, *Woman and Nature* (New York: Harper and Row, 1980), 17-8; Barbara Ehrenreich and Deirdre English, *Witches, Midwives and Nurses* (New York: Feminist Press, 1973), 6-14; Gordon Rattray Taylor, *Sex in History* (London: Thames & Hudson, 1953).
10. In 1468, the Pope defined witchcraft as crimen exceptum, thereby eliminating any limits to the level of torture that could be inflicted. The Dominican Order,

initially created to combat the Cathar heresy, was now redirected to preach specifically against witches. The Malleus Malleficiarum (Hammer to Kill Evils) was the official manual that prescribed the questions and correct answers, as well as the tortures to be applied to obtain those answers. Armed with this document, Pope Innocent VIII officially started a holy war on witches in 1488. This manual went through 29 editions over the next 300 years.

**CHAPTER TWENTY TWO**

1. Carl Gustav Jung, et. al., *Man and his Symbols* (London: Picador, 1978), 83.
2. Another definition of a shadow: "A negative ego-personality that includes all those qualities that we find painful or regrettable," from Carl Jung, *Collected Works Vol. 12: Psychology and Alchemy* (Princeton: Princeton University Press, 1980), 177 in footnote 178. Erich Neumann defines the shadow as "the unknown side of the personality…in the form of a dark, uncanny figure of evil to confront whom is always a fateful experience for the individual." Erich Neumann, *Depth Psychology and a New Ethic* (New York: G.P. Putnam and Sons, 1969), 137. Today's clinical definition of shadow is an autonomous complex, often resulting from a childhood trauma, of an aspect of ourselves that we do not accept.
3. Translation of *The Gospel of St. Thomas* by Thomas O. Lambdin, B.P. Grenfell, and A.S. Hunt, trans. http://www.sacred-texts.com.

**CHAPTER TWENTY THREE**

1. Jung developed this idea as the necessary integration of the *animus* (masculine energy, which is conscious in men and unconscious in women) and *anima* (feminine energy, which is conscious in women and unconscious in men). Human individuation is defined as the full integration of both the animus and anima.
2. Carl Gustav Jung, *Collected Works Vol. 3,* R.F.C. Hull, trans., (Princeton: Princeton University Press, 1960), 203.
3. Bernard Lietaer and Stephen Brunhubber, *Money and Sustainability—The Missing Link: A report to the Club of Rome* (2010).
4. Lao-Tzu translated by Stephen Mitchell, *Tao Te Ching* (New York, Harper Perennial, 1992).
5. Humberto R. Maturana, "The Organization of the Living: A Theory of the Living Organization," *Journal of Man-Machine Studies 7* (1975), 313-32 as quoted in Riane Eisler, *The Chalice and the Blade* (New York: Harper Collins, 1987), 82.

**CHAPTER TWENTY FOUR**

1. James Hillman, "Little Acorns: A Radical New Psychology," *The Sun Magazine* (March 1998).
2. Matthew wrote in his gospel that the *love* of money is the root of all evil.

3. Bono, Live Aid Concert (July 1985).
4. Olusegun Obasanjo, comment on the G8 meeting (2000), http://www.jubileeresearch.org.
5. Soren Ambrose, "Multilateral Debt: The Unbearable Burden" (November 2001). http://www.irc-online.org.
6. Merriam-Webster, ed., *Webster's Third New International Dictionary of the English Language, Unabridged* (Springfield, MA: Merriam-Webster, 1993).
7. Gustave Le Bon, *The Crowd, A Study in the Popular Mind* (London: T.F. Unwin, 1896, reprint 1921), 29.
8. Wesley C. Mitchell, "Analysis of Economic Theory," *American Economic Review,* no. 15 (March 1925), 1-12.
9. Ondine Norman, "Healing the Empty Self: Narcissism and the Cultural Shift from Dominance to Mutuality" unpublished thesis (Pacifica Graduate Institute, 1997), 8, 15.
10. Ibid., 38.
11. Christopher Lasch, *The Culture of Narcissism: American Life in an Age of Diminishing Expectations* (New York: Warner Books, 1979), 91.
12. Mario Jacoby, *Individuation and Narcissism: The Psychology of Self in Jung and Kohut* (New York: Routledge, 1990), 84.
13. Stephen Donadio and Susan Davidson, eds., *The New York Public Library Book of Twentieth-Century American Quotations* (New York: Warner Books, Inc., 1992).
14. Jacoby, *Individuation and Narcissism,* 174.
15. Susan Faludi, *Stiffed: The Betrayal of the American Man* (New York: William Morrow, 1999), 9.
16. Ibid., 13.
17. Bernice H. Hill, *Money and the Spiritual Warrior* (Boulder, CO: Five Centuries Foundation, 2004), 56-9.
18. Jacob Needleman, *Money and the Meaning of Life* (New York: Doubleday Currency, 1994), 239.

## ENDNOTES—PART IV

### CHAPTER TWENTY FIVE

1. Erika Uitz, *The Legend of Good Women: The Liberation of Women in Medieval Cities* (London, Wakefield: Myer Bell, 1994), 9.
2. Joan Kelly-Gadol, "Did Women Have a Renaissance?" in Renate Bridenthal, Susan Mosher Stuard, and Merry E. Wiesner (eds.), *Becoming Visible: Women in European History* (Boston: Houghton Mifflin, 1977). This formally refutes Jacob Burckhardt's classic assessment of women's progress in *The Civilization of the Renaissance in Italy,* Book Five, Chapter Five (New York: Harper, 1929).

3. Uitz, *The Legend of Good Women*, 10.
4. Régine Pernoud, *La Femme au Temps des Cathédrales* (Paris: Stock, 1980), 84.
5. Robert Lacey and Danny Danziger, *The Year 1000: What Life was like at the Turn of the First Millennium* (London: Little Brown & Co, 1999), 164.
6. Christine Fell, *Women in Anglo-Saxon England* (London: British Museum, 1984), 109.
7. Claude Marks, Pilgrims, *Heretics and Lovers* (New York: Macmillan, 1975).
8. Pernoud, *La Femme au Temps des Cathédrales*, title of Chapter 7, 134.
9. C.S. Lewis, *The Allegory of Love* (Cambridge: Cambridge University Press, 1965), 101.
10. Meg Bogin, *The Women Troubadours* (New York, London: Norton & Co, 1980), 12.
11. Ibid.
12. Denis de Rougemont, *L'Amour et l'Occident* (Paris: Union Générale d'Editions, 1971).
13. Ean Begg has identified by name more than 500 such statues, but this inventory is incomplete given the large number of these statues that were lost in fires, wars, or upheavals such as the French Revolution. See Ean Begg, *The Cult of the Black Virgin* (London: Routledge, 1985). See also Pierre Gordon, *Essais sur les Vierges Noires* (Neuilly sur Seine: Arma Artis, 1983).
14. Petra von Cronenburg, *Schwarze Madonnen: Das Mysterium einer Kultfigur* (München: Hugendubel Verlag, 1999), 172.
15. Ibid., 154.
16. Pierre A. Riffard, *L'Ésotérisme: Anthologie de l'Ésotérisme Occidental* (Paris: Robert Laffont, 1990).
17. See among others: Manuela Dunn Mascetti, *Christian Mysticism* (New York: Hyperion, 1998).
18. Malek Chebel, *Dictionnaire des Symboles Musulmans: Rites, Mystique et Civilization* (Paris: Perrin, 1995); keywords: Sufisme, Nuit, Marie.
19. Jacques Bonvin, *Vierges Noires: La Réponse vient de la Terre* (Paris: Dervy Livres, 1988), 75.
20. Begg, *The Cult of the Black Virgin*, 25-6.
21. Louis Charpentier notes the surprise of the priest Vacandard on discovering, between 1108 and 1115, a whole team of Hebraic scholars active in Citeaux, directly under the supervision of Abbot Etienne Harding. See Louis Charpentier, *Les Mystères Templiers* (Paris: Laffont, 1967), 15.
22. Jacques Huynen, *L'énigme des Vierges Noires* (Paris: Robert Laffont, 1972), 116-7.
23. At their height, it is estimated that 500,000 people traveled the pilgrimage routes every year. See Claude Marks, *Pilgrims, Heretics and Lovers* (New York: Macmillan, 1975), 111.

24. Hans C. Binswanger, *Geld und Magie: Deutung und Kritik der Modernen Wirtschaft an hand von Goethe's "Faust"* (Stuttgart: Weinbrecht Verlag, 1985), 20-1.

25. de Rougemont, *L'Amour et l'Occident.*

26. The Kabbalah is reputed to have begun in Southern France and then spread to Spain, where it flourished. See the article, "Kabbale" in André Vauchez, *Dictionnaire Encylcopédique du Moyen Age*, Vol. 1 (Paris: Editions du Cerf, 1997), 8.

27. Huynen, *L'énigme des Vierges Noires*, 145-9.

28. For instance, one of the classical dictionaries specializing in alchemy was written by Don Pernety, a Benedictine monk from the abbey of Saint Maur, near Paris. See Antoine-Joseph Pernety, *Dictionnaire Alchimique* and *Les Fables Egyptiennes et Grecques Dévoilées et Réduites au même Principe* (Paris: Delalain l'Ainé, 1706).

29. Carl Gustav Jung, *Psychology and Alchemy*, Bollingen Series, Volume XX (Princeton: Princeton University Press, 1968).

30. Carl Gustav Jung, *Collected Works*, Vol. XIV, Mysterium Conjunctionis (Princeton: Princeton University Press, 1956), 44, note 72.

31. See, for instance: Dürer's famous engraving entitled "Melancholia." The Greek word melas means black.

32. Jung, *Psychology and Alchemy*, Bollingen Series, Volume XX .

33. *Aurfontina Chymica* (London: 1680), http://www.levity.com.

34. Robert Graves, *Mammon and the Great Goddess* (London: Cassells, 1964), 126.

35. "Until the last third of the 11th century, one should really speak of 'Christian Churches' in the plural, rather than the singular. The Church of Rome tried to present itself as a coordinator for Christianity, but before the 12th century the practice was completely different." Giuseppe Sergi, *L'Idée du Moyan Age: Entre Sens Commun et Pratique Historique* (Paris: Flammarion, 1999), 75-6.

36. Robert Moore, *La Persécution sa Formation en Europe, 950-1250* (Paris: Les Belles-Lettres, 1991) and "A la Naissance de la Société Persécutrice: les Clercs, les Cathares et la Formation en Europe," in *La Persécution du Catharisme, XII-XIVe siècle. Actes de la 6ieme Session d'Histoire Médiévale* (Carcassonne: Centre d'Etudes Cathares, 1996), 11-37.

37. Anne Brenon, "La Catharisme Méridional: Questions et Problèmes," in Jacques Berlioz, *Le Pays Cathare: Les Religions Médiévales et Leurs Expressions Méridionales* (Paris: Editions du Seuil, 2000), 87.

38. Until 1246, the king of France had no authority over any part of the southern half of France or any access to the Mediterranean area. The Crusade against the Albigensians would give him both.

39. The detailed texts of the Inquisitor Jacques Fournier have been preserved for the period 1318 to 1325. The analysis by Jacques Berlioz reveals that the Inquisitor's ultimate purpose was not really about doctrinal issues, but aimed

at crushing any local powers that might oppose the centralizing power of either the king or the Pope, or the payment of papal tax (la dime). "Jacques Fournier was in fact working at the elimination of any local forces who might limit the King's power." See Berlioz, *Le Pays Cathare*, 62.

40. Jacques Berlioz, *Tuez-les Tous. Dieu Reconnaîtra les Siens. Le Massacre de Bézier at la Croisade des Albigeois vus par Césaire de Heisterbach* (Portet-sur-Garonne: Loubatières, 1994).
41. von Cronenburg, *Schwarze Madonnen: Das Mysterium einer Kultfigur*, 143-7.
42. Ibid., 149.
43. Jacques Turgot, *ncient Guild Statutes of France* (1776).

## CHAPTER TWENTY SIX

1. The dates are calculated from ancient lists, especially the Turin royal papyrus, and from various other sources. The margin of error is from a decade or so in the 3$^{rd}$ Intermediate Period and New Kingdom to perhaps 150 years for the 1$^{st}$ Dynasty; dates for the 3$^{rd}$ Millennium are given for whole dynasties and are rounded, as are numerous later dates. From the 12$^{th}$ Dynasty on, possible sequences of dates can be calculated from astronomy; currently accepted sequences are used here. Dates from 664 BCE on are precise to within a year, http://www.bbc.co.uk. A more extensive study of the Egyptian dual currency system andd its effects on society is available in Chapter Six of Bernard Lietaer *Mysterium Geld: Emotionale Bedeutung und Wirkungsweise eines Tabus* (Munich: Riemann Verlag, 2001)
2. Moses I. Finley, *The Ancient Economy, Sather Classical Lectures* 43 (Berkeley: University of California Press, 1985), 138
3. Joyce Tyldesley, *The Daughters of Isis: Women in Ancient Egypt* (London: Penguin Books, 1995), 104.
4. Ibid., 106-7.
5. Finley, *The Ancient Economy,* 166.
6. Moses I. Finley, *The Ancient Economy, Sather Classical Lectures* 43 (Berkeley: University of California Press, 1985), 112.
7. Ibid., 155.
8. Ibid., 138.
9. Brian Handwerk, "Pyramid Builders' Village Found in Egypt," *National Geographic News* (Updated 18 September 2002), http://news.nationalgeographic.com/news/2002/08/0805_020805_giza.html. There are several possibilities for the ill health of the workers, including that they were from a low caste of Egyptian society and trying to start a new life in challenging, arid conditions. Additionally, there could have been sabotage of the project given that Akhenaten broke away from the priests and the doctrine of the time.

10. Alaa Shahine, "Study shows life was tough for ancient Egyptians," *Reuters, U.K. Edition* (30 March 2008), http://uk.reuters.com /article/2008/03/30/us-egypt-archaeology-study-idUKL2886575820080330.

11. Pharaoh Akhenaten, who abandoned most of Egypt's old gods in favor of the Aten sun disk, built and lived in Tell el-Amarna in central Egypt for 17 years. The city was largely abandoned shortly after his death and the ascendance of the famous boy king Tutankhamen to the throne.

12. Friedrich Preisigke, *Girowesen im Griechischen Ägypten enthalted Korngiro, Geldgiro, Girobanknotariat mit Einschluß des Archivwesens* (Strasbourg: Verlag von Schlesier and Schweikhardt, 1910; reprint, Hildesheim and New York: Georg Olms, (1971), 13.

13. Hugo Godschalk, "Wurden die ägyptischen Pyramiden mit einer Demurrage-Währung gebaut?" *Zeitschrift für Sozialökonomie*, no.149 (June 2006). The idea that demurrage currencies were first initiated during the Ptolemaic period on the basis of Preisigke's work would be similar to assuming on the basis of a book entitled "19th Century Dutch Paintings" that there were no paintings in Holland during the 16th, 17th, or 18th century.

14. Finley, *The Ancient Economy*, 166.

15. Friedrich Preisigke, *Girowesen im Griechischen Ägypten enthalted Korngiro, Geldgiro, Girobanknotariat mit Einschluß des Archivwesens* (Strasbourg: Verlag von Schlesier and Schweikhardt, 1910; reprint, Hildesheim and New York: Georg Olms, (1971).

16. No fewer that 1.6 million ostraka have been gathered in the dynastic village of Medinet, currently in the Egyptian desert. Almost all remain untranslated to this day.

17. Medinet was believed to be where the Ogdoad—the four pairs of first primeval gods—were buried, and was also one of the earliest places within the Theban region to be associated with the worship of Amun.

18. Preisigke, Girowesen im Griechischen Ägypten, 13.

19. Ibid., 75.

20. Ibid., 101.

## CHAPTER TWENTY SEVEN

1. Anne Baring and Jules Cashford, *The Myth of the Goddess: Evolution of an Image* (London: Penguin Books, Arkana, 1993), 250.

2. "Isis was originally the throne personified. The throne made manifest a divine power that changed every one of several princes into a king fit to rule." This all-important throne symbolism of Isis was incorporated in the medieval Black Madonna as the cathedra, one of her unique identifying characteristics. Henri Frankfort, *Ancient Egyptian Religion* (New York: Harper and Row, Torch Books, 1961), 17.

3. These "precautions" were both precise and exacting. They included that the dead remember a series of elaborate passwords at different stages of the

journey in the underworld (hence the *Egyptian Book of the Dead* which accompanied each burial, and which provided a textbook reminder of those stages and the relevant magical passwords for each) as well as the appropriate physical supports for the afterlife. The Egyptians believed that what we call the human "soul" was made of three components, respectively the *Ka*, the *Ba,* and what we might call the individual consciousness. The Ka was destined to remain close to the corpse; the Ba was represented as a human-headed bird that could leave the tomb but sometimes needed to return; and finally, the consciousness would experience the journey into the afterlife. All three needed to be taken care of, hence the need to preserve the body forever through mummification, and the elaborate food, furniture, and other amulets that would be necessary for a successful journey toward and life in the realm of Osiris. If the transition failed for whatever reason, there would be a second and final death. Therefore, the "first" physical death was inevitable but not necessarily final. Hence the importance of taking all the right precautions to ensure a pleasant afterlife, since, according to the Egyptians, you really had a chance to "take it all with you."

4. Erich Neumann, *The Great Mother, Bollington Series XLVII* (Princeton: Princeton University Press, 1955), 223.

5. Myrionymos (whose names are innumerable) is significantly different from polynomos (whose names are numerous). Several gods and goddesses were referred to as having many names (e.g., Aphrodite, Apollo, Helios, Hermes, Artemis). Reginald Eldred Witt, *Isis in the Ancient World* (Baltimore, London: The Johns Hopkins University Press, 1971), 121: "Isis, however, was the only divinity whose epiclesis marked that the number of her names was not merely large but infinite. It was in this endless diversity that her uniqueness rested. It was the source of her strength, and her weakness. She alone claimed an infinity of divine titles and became all things to all men. She could be 'chaste' and yet raise the phallus. She could banish life's storms by her calm and yet become the Roman goddess of war." And: "To many critics the picture may seem riddled with contradictions. But the evidence that Isis is mutilated by the removal of any of these elements is irrefutable," 138. In the archetypal yin-yang framework, she embodies the yin "capacity to hold ambivalence."

6. Georges Posener, *Dictionnaire de la Civilisation Egypytienne* (Paris, 1959), 140.

7. Witt, *Isis in the Ancient World,* 137.

8. Robert R. Briffault, *The Mothers,* Vol. 1 (New York: Charles Scribner's Sons, 1924), 384.

9. Janet H. Johnson, "The Legal Status of Women in Ancient Egypt," in Anne K. Capel and Glenn E. Markoe, eds., *Mistress of the House, Mistress of the Heavens: Women in Ancient Egypt* (New York: Hudson Hills Press, 1996), 175.

10. Ibid., 183. The marriage contract acted like "annuity contracts" since they were concerned predominately with financial matters.

11. Joyce Tyldesley, *The Daughters of Isis: Women in Ancient Egypt,* (London: Penguin Books, 1995), 48.

12. Ibid., 58.

13. Witt, *Isis in the Ancient World,* 41. Original quote from Diodorus Siculus in *Geography of Strabo Book I* (Boston: Loeb Classical Library, Harvard University Press), 27.

14. Gerda Lerner, *The Creation of Patriarchy* (Oxford: Oxford University Press, 1986), 114.

15. Louis M. Epstein, *Sex Laws and Customs in Judaism* (New York, 1948), 194.

16. Gay Robins, *Women in Ancient Egypt* (London: British Museum Press, 1993).

17. When no other references are provided, the data from this section refers to Catherine H. Roehrig, "Women's Work: Some Occupations of Non-Royal Women as Depicted in Ancient Egyptian Art," in Capel and Markoe, eds., *Mistress of the House, Mistress of the Heavens,* 13-24.

18. Herbert E. Winlock, *Excavations at Deir el-Bahri 1911-1931* (New York: 1942), 226.

19. Henry Fischer, "Administrative Titles of Women in the Old and Middle Kingdom," in *Egyptian Studies*; William Ward, "Non-Royal Women and their Occupations in the Middle Kingdom," in Lesko, ed., *Women's Earliest Records;* Gay Robins, *Women in Ancient Egypt,* 114-7.

20. Four women ascended to the Egyptian throne: Nitokret (Dynasty 6), Sobeknefru (Dynasty 12), Hatshepsut (Dynasty 18) and Tauseret (Dynasty 19).

21. Quoted by Sir Alan Gardiner, *Egypt of the Pharaohs* (Oxford: Oxford University Press, 1961), 431.

22. Lerner, *The Creation of Patriarchy,* 115-6.

23. Peter B. Ellis, *Celtic Women* (Grand Rapids: William Eerdmans Publishing Co., 1995), 99

24. "On Men and Women" from *Oikonomikos* (ca. 370 BCE).

25. "The third class was known as the Hetaerae, which were akin to the Geisha's of China. Hetaerae women were given an education in reading, writing, and music, and were allowed into the Agora and other structures, which were off limits to citizen and slave women. Most sources about the Hetaerae indicate however, that their standing was at best at the level of prostitutes, and the level of power they attained was only slightly significant." From: "The Women of Athens," *Ancient Greek Civilizations* (Minnesota State University).

26. Tyldesley, *The Daughters of Isis: Women in Ancient Egypt,* back cover page.

27. Witt, *Isis in the Ancient World,* 110.

28. Moses I. Finley, *The Ancient Economy, Sather Classical Lectures* 43, (Berkeley: University of California Press, 1985), 99.

29. Jean Chevalier and Alain Gheerbrant, *Dictionnaire des Symbols,* (Paris: Laffont, 1983), 524.

30. Fred Gustafson, *The Black Madonna,* (Boston: Sigo Press, 1990), 90.

31. Witt, *Isis in the Ancient World*, 193-4.

32. Black Madonna statues, like others, were burned during the French Revolution of 1793. In Chartres it was done under the cries *"A bas l'Egyptienne,"* literally "Down with the Egyptian one!"

33. H. W. Müller, in *Münchener Jahrhundert Bild Kunst* (1963), 35, cites the original passage documenting this episode from *Histoire Généalogique de la Maison des Briçonnet* (1620). Witt also mentions this same episode in Witt, *Isis in the Ancient World*, 274. Dr. Witt conjectures that this Isis statue was also a Black Madonna.

34. Faujas de Saint-Fons' study entitled, "Recherches sue les Volcans Éteints du Vivarais et du Velay," is primarily a geological report, but it also contains the notes of his investigations on the Black Madonna of Le Puy. See also: Bonvin, *Vierges Noires: La Réponse vient de la Terre,* 205-12, and von Cronenburg, *Schwarze Madonnen,* 35-8.

35. The engraved "Table of Isis" (Mensa Isaica), dating back to the first century CE, was discovered in 1720 and exhibited in 1775 in the Royal Archives at the Egyptian Museum of Turin. Faujas de Saint-Fons, in referring to this piece, may, thus, have based his findings not only on published records, but also on first-hand exposure to these hieroglyphs, making his testimony more valid.

36. The subtitle of his book makes this explicit: Guy Bois, *La Grande Dépression Médiévale du XIVe et XVe Siècles: Le Précédent d'une Crise Systémique* (Paris: PUF, 2000).

**CHAPTER TWENTY EIGHT**

1. Tyra de Kleen, "Bali: Its Dances and Customs," *Sluyter's Monthly* 2 (1921), 129.

2. Michel Picard, *Bali: Cultural Tourism and Touristic Culture* (Singapore: Archipelago Press, 1996), 138.

3. Clifford Geertz and Hildred Geertz, *Kinship in Bali* (Chicago: University of Chicago Press, 1987) and Carol Warren, *Adat and Dinas: Balinese Communities in the Indonesian State* (Kuala Lumpur: Oxford University Press, 1993).

4. Agung and Purwita, *Pemantapan Adat Dalam Menunjang Usaha-Usaha Pembangunan* (Denpasar: Majelis Pembina Lembaga Ada, 1983), 18.

5. Fred B. Eiseman, *Bali Sekala and Niskala: Essays on Society, Tradition and Craft,* Volume II (Berkeley: Periplus Editions, Inc., 1989), 74.

6. Geertz and Geertz, *Kinship in Bali.*

7. Pak Ketut Suartana, personal interview, Klian Banjar Sambahan, North Ubud Banjar, Ubud Kaja (30 July 2002).

8. Pak Wayan Suecha, personal interview, Klian Banjar Kelod–Ubud (6 August 2002).

9. The study of the Balinese dual-currency system was part of a four-month research project performed by Bernard Lietaer and Stephen Demeulenaere in 2002 on the economics of Banjars in the area of Ubud, the "cultural capital" of Bali. Any quotations without specific references in this chapter come from field notes from interviews during this research. For published results see: Bernard Lietaer and Stephen Demeulenaere, "Sustaining Cultural Vitality in a Globalizing World: the Balinese Example," *International Journal for Social Economics* (September 2003).

10. In most cases, enough people can be found to contribute the time needed to complete an activity. Therefore, such contributions do not even have to be recorded. In those Banjars, however, whose members have less time available, or if complaints are logged about the lack of contribution by others, time contributions are recorded by the Klian Banjar. Those who cannot contribute their share of time are asked to send a substitute person, to whom they then "owe" a similar service. If neither option is possible, they must pay a charge of between 5,000 and 10,000 Rupiah for each time block missed. Nevertheless, substitutions in Rupiah can only be partial and conditional. They are not acceptable as a systematic way to avoid service to and personal participation in the Banjar.

11. Geertz and Geertz, *Kinship in Bali.*

12. Kepeng is etymologically related to the word chip or fragment. This is likely a reference to the traditional square hole in the middle of each Uang Kepeng coin. See: S. Hassan and J. Echols, *Kamus Indonesia-Inggris* (PT Gramedia, Jakarta, Indonesia, 2004).

13. Ida Bagus Sidemen, "Nilai Historis Uang Kepeng" (Historical Value of Uang Kepeng), (Denpasar, Bali: Larasan-Sejarah, 2002). The oldest Uang Kepeng coins found in Bali were minted by the Chinese Tang Dynasty (618-909 CE). Other types of trading coins and brass gongs have been discovered in Bali, some of which originate from the Dong Son culture of Vietnam in the 4th century CE.

14. Ibid.

15. Ibid.

16. De Kat Angelino, Arnold Dirk Adriaan. (1930) Staatkundig beleid en bestuurszorg in Nederlandsch-Indie. Gravenhage: Nijhoff.

17. M.Covarrubias, *Island of Bali*, (First edition: New York: Knopff 1937), (republished: Singapore: Periplus, 1998).

18. Personal communication between Stephen DeMeulenaere and the authors (May 2007).

19. Technically, the Uang Kepeng is still a yang currency, given that it was not created by the Balinese themselves but imported into Bali from abroad (i.e. the Chinese merchants). But it can be considered as a "weak yang" currency compared to conventional national moneys such as the Rupiah, because of its lack of or weak enforcement of the interest feature. Therefore, strictly speaking, what has happened since the 1950s in Bali is the gradual

replacement of the dual currency system of Uang Kepeng and the Banjar time currency (a dual currency system consisting of a weak yang complementing a strong yin) to a Rupiah and Banjar time currency (a dual currency system consisting of a strong yang complementing strong yin). However, such a shift seems to have had a sufficient effect to contribute to some changes in the social behavior patterns among the Balinese. Obviously, we do not claim that the shift towards a more yang currency by itself is the *only* cause for the gradual degradation of the yin-yang balance in Balinese society. Other factors mentioned in the text, and changes such as the introduction of commercial television in the local language, also play contributing roles. As with all social changes, we are dealing with complex mutually reinforcing processes, in which even subtle monetary changes can play a non-negligible role.

20. With Nyoman Bahuha, Klian Banjar of Banjar Kaja in Ubud (2 August 2002).

21. Francine Brinkgreve and David Stuart-Fox, *Offerings: The Ritual Art of Bali* (Singapore: Select Books, 1992), 199-219.

22. *Bali: A Traveller's Companion* (Singapore: Editions Didier Millet Pte Ltd., 1995), 57.

23. Miguel Covarrubias, *Island of Bali* (New York: Alfred Knopf, 1946), p. 359.

24. Ibid., 361.

25. Bernard Lietaer, "A World in Balance," *Reflections: Journal of the Organizational Learning Society* (Summer 2003).

26. Viebeke L. Asana, "Now We Move Forward!" See: http://www.foothill.net.

27. On 8 November 2008 three Islamist militants were sentenced to death and executed in an Indonesian prison for their involvement in the 2002 bombing. http://www.bbc.co.uk/news.

28. "Berfungsi Religius: Uang Kepeng Perlu Diproduksi Kembali" (Religious Function: Uang Kepeng Needs to be Produced Again), *The Bali Post* (23 December 2003), http://www.balipost.co.id/balipostcetak/2003/12/23/b4.htm. Also "Keberadaan 'Pis Bolong' di Bali: Dulu Uang Kartal, Sekarang Sarana Budaya" (The History of Pis Bolong [Uang Kepeng] in Bali, Formerly a medium of Exchange, Today a Medium of Culture) *The Bali Post* 10 January 2004. http://www.balipost.co.id/balipostcetak/2004/1/10/topik.html.

# INDEX

height of Londoners   53
Henry II   253
Henry VIII   38
Hera   210
Herodotus   289
Hill, Bernice   195, 244, 304
Hillman, James   191, 195
Hiranuma, Takeo   143
*A History of the Breast*   202
Hitler, Adolph   82, 86
Homer   205
Horus   284, 292
Hotta, Tsutomu   142
hyperinflation   59, 80-1
Hyperrationalist archetype *see* Magician archetype, shadows of

# I

identity   194, 240, 244, 304
ILO (International Labour Organization)   21
Imanishi, Kinji   43
IMF (International Monetary Fund)   94, 168, 188, 236
Impotent archetype *see* Lover archetype, shadows of
Inanna   205, 208-9
income   22, 47, 165, 294
Indonesian rupiah   296-301
Industrial Age
  mindset of   75-6
  objectives of   12, 37, 61-2, 152
  values of   44, 48, 92
Industrial Revolution   12, 32, 65
inflation   37, 39-40, 59, 137, 155, 176, 311
Innocent III   263
Inquisition   218, 264, 266-7
insured invoices   163-4
integral science   107
interconnectivity   113, 115, 117
interest   36, 38-9, 93-4, 177, 236, 299
  behavioral effects of   40
  charging   38, 40
  concentrating wealth   46
  encouraging competition   41-2
  fueling economic growth   45
  reason for   40
interest rates   39-40, 45, 141, 177, 236

CPSIA information can be obtained at www.ICGtesting.com
Printed in the USA
BVOW010622150113

310553BV00004B/5/P